Quality and Safety in Medical Imaging

THE ESSENTIALS

Quality and Safety in Medical Imaging

THE ESSENTIALS

Jeffrey P. Kanne, MD

Professor and Chief of Thoracic Imaging
Vice Chair of Quality and Safety
Department of Radiology
University of Wisconsin School of Medicine and Public Health
Madison, Wisconsin

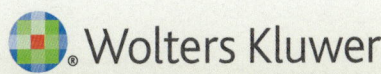

Wolters Kluwer

Philadelphia • Baltimore • New York • London
Buenos Aires • Hong Kong • Sydney • Tokyo

Acquisitions Editor: Ryan Shaw
Product Development Editor: Lauren Pecarich
Production Project Manager: David Saltzberg
Design Coordinator: Joan Wendt
Manufacturing Coordinator: Beth Welsh
Marketing Manager: Dan Dressler
Prepress Vendor: S4Carlisle Publishing Services

Copyright © 2017 Wolters Kluwer

All rights reserved. This book is protected by copyright. No part of this book may be reproduced or transmitted in any form or by any means, including as photocopies or scanned-in or other electronic copies, or utilized by any information storage and retrieval system without written permission from the copyright owner, except for brief quotations embodied in critical articles and reviews. Materials appearing in this book prepared by individuals as part of their official duties as US government employees are not covered by the above-mentioned copyright. To request permission, please contact Wolters Kluwer at Two Commerce Square, 2001 Market Street, Philadelphia, PA 19103, via email at permissions@lww.com, or via our website at lww.com (products and services).

9 8 7 6 5 4 3 2 1

Printed in China

Library of Congress Cataloging-in-Publication Data
Names: Kanne, Jeffrey P., author.
Title: Quality and safety in medical imaging : the essentials / Jeffrey P. Kanne.
Description: Philadelphia: Wolters Kluwer Health, [2017] | Includes bibliographical references and index.
Identifiers: LCCN 2016034590 | ISBN 9781451186864
Subjects: | MESH: American College of Radiology. | Diagnostic Imaging—standards | Quality Control | Safety Management
Classification: LCC RC78.7.D53 | NLM WN 180 | DDC 616.07/54— dc23 LC record available at https://lccn.loc.gov/2016034590

This work is provided "as is," and the publisher disclaims any and all warranties, express or implied, including any warranties as to the accuracy, comprehensiveness, or currency of the content of this work.

This work is no substitute for individual patient assessment based upon health-care professionals' examination of each patient and consideration of, among other things, age, weight, gender, current or prior medical conditions, medication history, laboratory data, and other factors unique to the patient. The publisher does not provide medical advice or guidance, and this work is merely a reference tool. Health-care professionals, and not the publisher, are solely responsible for the use of this work including all medical judgments, and for any resulting diagnosis and treatments.

Given continuous, rapid advances in medical science and health information, independent professional verification of medical diagnoses, indications, appropriate pharmaceutical selections and dosages, and treatment options should be made and health-care professionals should consult a variety of sources. When prescribing medication, health-care professionals are advised to consult the product information sheet (the manufacturer's package insert) accompanying each drug to verify, among other things, conditions of use, warnings, and side effects and identify any changes in dosage schedule or contraindications, particularly if the medication to be administered is new, infrequently used, or has a narrow therapeutic range. To the maximum extent permitted under applicable law, no responsibility is assumed by the publisher for any injury and/or damage to persons or property, as a matter of products liability, negligence law, or otherwise, or from any reference to or use by any person of this work.

LWW.com

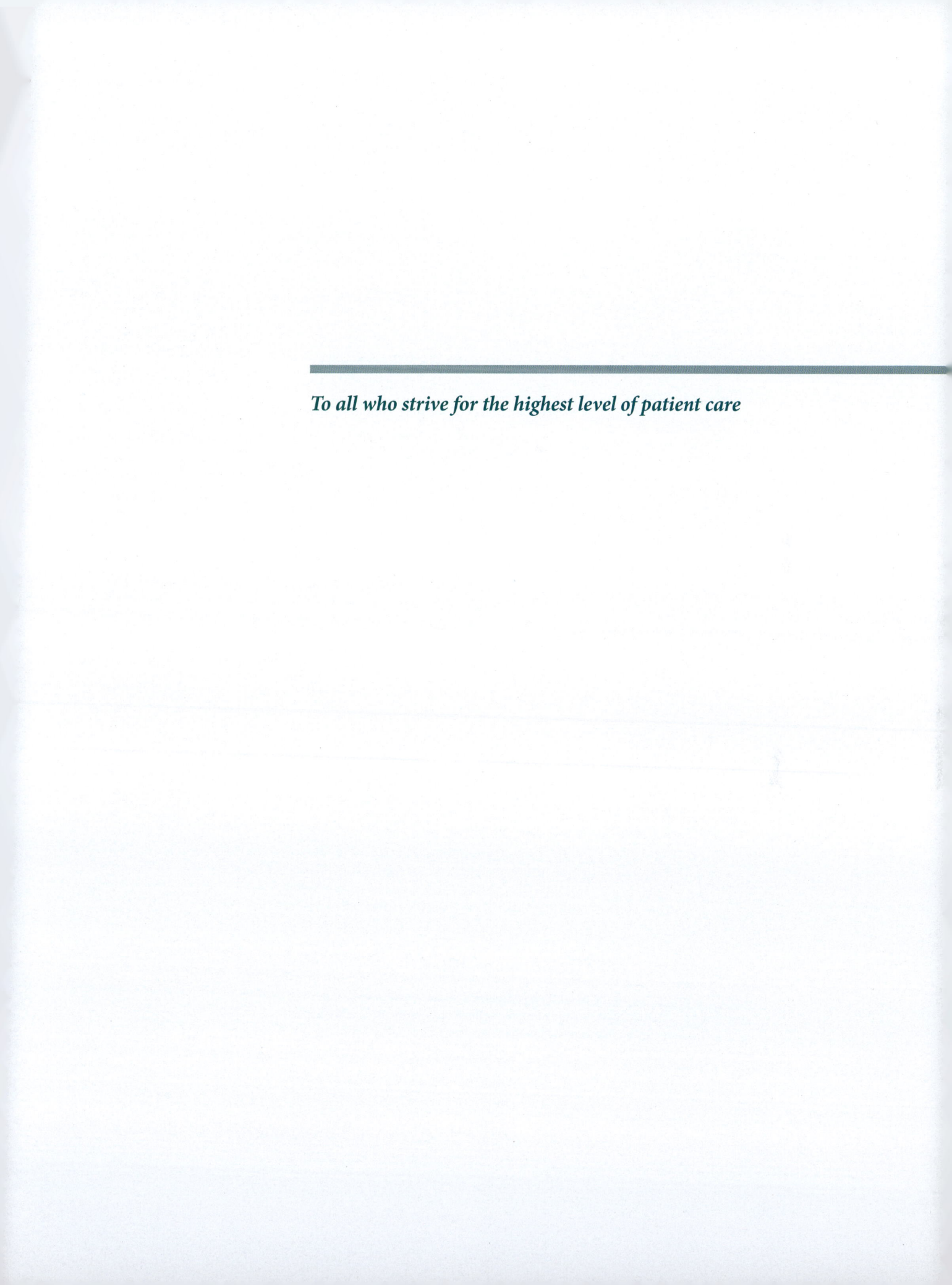

To all who strive for the highest level of patient care

SERIES FOREWORD

The *Essentials* series is a collection of radiology textbooks following a standardized format. Each book in the *Essentials* series is a practical tool for those wanting to quickly acquire a broad base of knowledge in a specialty area. The content is limited to the essentials of that specialty so as not to overwhelm the novice, yet provides enough detail that it can serve as a quick review for residents or practicing radiologists, a guide for those who teach the specialty, and a reference for specialty physicians and other health-care professionals whose patients are referred for imaging in that specialty area. What sets *Essentials* texts apart from other similar texts is that they (a) are compact and of practical size for a resident to read during an initial 4-week rotational experience, (b) include learning objectives at the beginning of each chapter, and (c) provide an exercise for self-assessment. Each book includes citations from the most recent literature that are called out in the text.

Self-assessment is a key component of the *Essentials* texts. Multiple-choice items are included at the end of every chapter, and a self-assessment examination is included at the end of each text. This should be of particular benefit to those who are preparing for the new image-rich computer-based examinations that are a component of professional certification and maintenance of certification.

The series includes texts related to not only clinical specialties that are rich with radiologic images and illustrations but also to noninterpretive subjects such as radiologic physics and quality and safety in medical imaging. The goal of the *Essentials* series is to provide a collection of practical references to accompany a well-rounded education in diagnostic imaging and imaging-guided therapy.

JANNETTE COLLINS

PREFACE

Advances in science and technology have contributed to the rapid growth of diagnostic medical imaging and image-guided treatments, giving radiologists and other medical imaging professionals a central role in the care of many patients. With this growth comes the need to deliver care that is consistent, appropriate, safe, and effective.

Quality management, once confined to the realm of industrial engineering, has become a key component of running an effective health-care organization. Forces driving this focus on quality and safety include the public, independent regulatory organizations, government, and medical professionals themselves. Thus, all members of the health-care team need to understand the basic principles of quality and safety to meaningfully contribute to the success of any health-care organization.

The aim of this book is to familiarize the reader with the principles of quality and safety and how they apply to the practice of radiology, focusing on the essential elements. Although this book is by no means a comprehensive text on quality and safety management, the reader will gain knowledge about important facets related to quality management in radiology including regulatory agencies and requirements, patient safety including radiation exposure, and key features of quality committees and quality officers. The self-assessment questions aim to ensure that content is understood and to guide additional readings or investigation.

As health care continues to focus more energy and resources on quality and safety, opportunities and resources will be in constant evolution. However, the guiding principles of quality-driven care will continue to serve as the foundation for these new opportunities and resources, and the informed practitioner will be well positioned to use them to optimize patient care.

JEFFREY P. KANNE

CONTRIBUTORS

Bryan P. Bednarz, PhD
Assistant Professor
Department of Medical Physics
Wisconsin Institutes for Medical Research
University of Wisconsin-Madison
Madison, Wisconsin

Mai A. Elezaby, MD
Assistant Professor of Radiology
Department of Radiology
University of Wisconsin School of Medicine and Public Health
Madison, Wisconsin

Jeffrey P. Kanne, MD
Professor and Chief of Thoracic Imaging
Vice Chair of Quality & Safety
Department of Radiology
University of Wisconsin School of Medicine and Public Health
Madison, Wisconsin

Saima Muzahir, MD
Clinical Assistant Professor
University of Tennessee at Chattanooga
Tennessee Interventional and Imaging Associates
Chattanooga, Tennessee

John R. Vetter, PhD
Associate Professor
Department of Medical Physics
University of Wisconsin School of Medicine and Public Health
Madison, Wisconsin

CONTENTS

Series Foreword vii

Preface ix

Contributors xi

Chapter 1	ACR Quality and Safety Programs	1
Chapter 2	Quality and Safety in Medical Imaging	13
Chapter 3	Patient Satisfaction	26
Chapter 4	Report Turn-Around Time	28
Chapter 5	Image Quality Assurance Programs	34
Chapter 6	Monitoring and Reporting of Complications	41
Chapter 7	Agencies and Programs	45
Chapter 8	Quality and Safety in Breast Imaging	50
Chapter 9	Quality and Safety in Nuclear Medicine	70
Chapter 10	Evidence-Based Radiology	79
Chapter 11	Peer Review	84
Chapter 12	Credentialing and Certification of Programs and Individuals	92
Chapter 13	Quality Dashboards	97
Chapter 14	Departmental and Institutional Quality Committees	105

Self-Assessment Exam 111

Index 119

ACR Quality and Safety Programs

Jeffrey P. Kanne

LEARNING OBJECTIVES

1. Describe the quality programs offered by the American College of Radiology (ACR)
2. Understand the purpose behind ACR registries and how participants can improve their respective practices through registry participation

The American College of Radiology (ACR) is a not-for-profit organization that aims "to serve patients and society by maximizing the value of radiology, radiation oncology, interventional radiology, nuclear medicine and medical physics by advancing the science of radiology, improving the quality of patient care, positively influencing the socioeconomics of the practice of radiology, providing continuing education for radiology and allied health professions and conducting research for the future of radiology."[1] ACR has developed various programs to support quality improvement and safety core elements of its mission, many in response to requirements of accrediting bodies and government mandates. These programs include accreditation and other designations, radiology data registries, and peer review.

ACCREDITATION

The Medicare Improvements for Patients and Providers Act (MIPPA) and Mammography Quality Standards Act (MQSA) mandate accreditation of certain imaging modalities. MIPPA requires all private outpatient facilities that offer computed tomography (CT), magnetic resonance imaging (MRI), breast MRI, nuclear medicine, and positron emission tomography (PET) be accredited to bill for technical components of examinations under Part B of the Medicare Physician Fee Schedule. The requirements focus on personnel qualifications (nonphysician medical staff, medical directors, and supervising physicians), image quality, equipment performance, safety standards for both staff and patients, and quality control and quality assurance. MQSA mandates that all facilities providing mammography be accredited.[2]

ACR offers accreditation programs in various imaging modalities (Table 1.1) and also provides accreditation for radiation oncology through the Radiation Oncology Practice Accreditation Program (ROPA). Other accrediting bodies include The Joint Commission (TJC) and the Intersocietal Accreditation Commission (IAC). After initial accreditation with ACR, facilities must engage in ongoing quality assurance and maintain records of personnel qualifications, as well as apply for renewal to maintain accreditation. To preserve the integrity of accreditation programs, ACR may make unannounced site visits to ensure that facilities continue to meet accreditation requirements after accreditation is granted.

Personnel qualifications for physicians include training, board certification, ongoing experience with interpretation and reporting, and continuing medical education. Radiologic technologists must meet appropriate licensure and continuing education requirements. Medical physicists must meet training or board certification requirements and must document continuing experience with specific equipment surveys and continuing education.

NATIONAL RADIOLOGY DATA REGISTRY

The National Radiology Data Registry (NRDR) is an ACR program that consists of several registries (Table 1.2) and allows participating

Table 1.1 **CURRENTLY AVAILABLE ACR ACCREDITATIONS.**

Imaging Modality	Requirement
Breast MRI	MIPPA
Breast ultrasound	None
Computed tomography	MIPPA
Mammography	MQSA
MRI	MIPPA
Nuclear medicine and PET	MIPPA
Radiation oncology	ROPA
Stereotactic breast biopsy	None
Ultrasound	None

MIPPA, Medicare Improvements for Patients and Providers Act; MQSA, Mammography Quality Standards Act; ROPA, Radiation Oncology Practice Accreditation Program; PET, positron emission tomography; and MRI, magnetic resonance imaging.

2 QUALITY AND SAFETY IN MEDICAL IMAGING

> **Table 1.2 REGISTRIES AND DATABASES CURRENTLY PART OF THE NATIONAL RADIOLOGY DATA REGISTRY.**
>
> CT Colonography Registry
> Dose Index Registry
> General Radiology Improvement Database
> IV Contrast Extravasation
> National Mammography Database

facilities to compare their own benchmarks with regional and national peers. Currently, the NRDR consists of the National Oncology PET Registry (NOPR), the CT Colonography Registry, the General Radiology Improvement Database (GRID), the National Mammography Database (NMD), IV Contrast Extravasation Registry (ICE), and the Dose Index Registry (DIR).[3] In 2014, the NRDR was designated a Qualified Clinical Data Registry (QCDR) for the Centers for Medicare & Medicaid Services' (CMS) Physician Quality Reporting System (PQRS).

The DIR enables facilities to compare their CT dose indices with aggregate data from other participating facilities, itemized by body part and exam type (Fig. 1.1). DIR data can be used for the practice quality improvement (PQI) component of the American Board of Radiology (ABR) Maintenance of Certification (MOC) program.[4]

The CT Colonography Registry tracks both process measures and outcome measures for CT colonography (CTC) (Fig. 1.2). Process measures include optimal bowel cleansing and distention, rate of adequacy of diagnostic CTC exam, and rate of adequacy of screening CTC examination. Outcome measures tracked include rate of colonic perforation, true positive rate, and extracolonic findings.[5]

GRID consists of multiple measures related to MRI, patient safety, process, and outcomes (Table 1.3). Current process measures include patient wait time, time from order to exam, reacquisition rate, and report turnaround time. Outcome measures include rates of nondiagnostic liver and lung biopsies, rate of lung biopsies resulting in pneumothorax that require tube drainage, rates of contrast extravasation, and rate of nonconcordant stereotactic breast biopsies.[6] Each participating site is provided with a feedback report showing performance and comparison with other GRID sites (Fig. 1.3).

ICE enables facilities to track their own rates of intravenous contrast extravasation and review treatments and outcomes. Furthermore, participating sites can compare their respective data with those of other institutions, and a PQI project involving ICE is available to participating radiologists.[7]

SSDE Per Scan (mGy) Executive Summary: Facility 999999

RPID Shortname	1: Site 999999 (25th-Med-75th)	2: All DIR sites (25th-Med-75th)	3: Sites in location Metropolitan (25th-Med-75th)	4: Sites in division South Atlantic (25th-Med-75th)	5: Sites of type Community hospital (25th-Med-75th)
CT ABDOMEN	(14/20/25)	(13/19/24)	(10/13/18)	(21/24/30)	(16/22/27)
CT ABDOMEN PELVIS		(11/16/22)	(11/16/22)	(15/21/25)	(13/19/26)
CT ABDOMEN PELVIS KIDNEY CALC WO IVCON	(12/14/18)	(10/15/20)	(9/14/19)	(12/16/20)	(10/15/20)
CT ABDOMEN PELVIS W IVCON	(12/15/22)	(12/16/21)	(12/16/21)	(12/16/22)	(12/16/22)
CT ABDOMEN PELVIS WO IVCON	(12/16/20)	(13/17/22)	(13/17/22)	(13/17/22)	(13/17/22)
CT ABDOMEN PELVIS WO THEN W IVCON	(14/23/31)	(13/18/24)	(13/17/24)	(15/20/27)	(14/20/26)
CT ABDOMEN W IVCON	(11/16/25)	(13/17/22)	(13/18/22)	(16/19/22)	(13/16/22)
CT C SPINE W IVCON	NA	NA	NA	NA	NA
CT C SPINE WO IVCON	NA	NA	NA	NA	NA
CT CHEST	(9/13/20)	(10/15/21)	(10/15/21)	(9/13/20)	(11/17/23)
CT CHEST ABDOMEN PELVIS W IVCON	(10/17/22)	(12/16/21)	(12/16/21)	(12/17/20)	(12/17/22)
CT CHEST ANGIO W IVCON	(18/28/40)	(14/18/26)	(14/18/25)	(14/19/28)	(14/19/26)
CT CHEST ANGIO WO THEN W IVCON	(16/18/23)	(15/19/29)	(15/20/30)	(16/19/26)	(15/19/28)
CT CHEST PULMONARY ARTERIES W IVCON	(12/19/33)	(11/17/23)	(11/17/24)	(14/20/31)	(13/18/24)
CT CHEST W IVCON	(11/17/23)	(9/14/20)	(9/13/20)	(9/14/21)	(10/14/20)
CT CHEST WO IVCON	(8/13/18)	(8/12/17)	(7/11/16)	(8/13/18)	(9/13/18)
CT HEAD		NA	NA	NA	NA
CT HEAD BRAIN WO IVCON	NA	NA	NA	NA	NA
CT HEAD MAXILLOFACIAL WO IVCON	NA	NA	NA	NA	NA
CT HEAD PARANASAL SINUSES WO IVCON	NA	NA	NA	NA	NA

A

FIG. 1.1 • **A-C:** Selected pages from a sample report of ACR's Dose Index Registry.

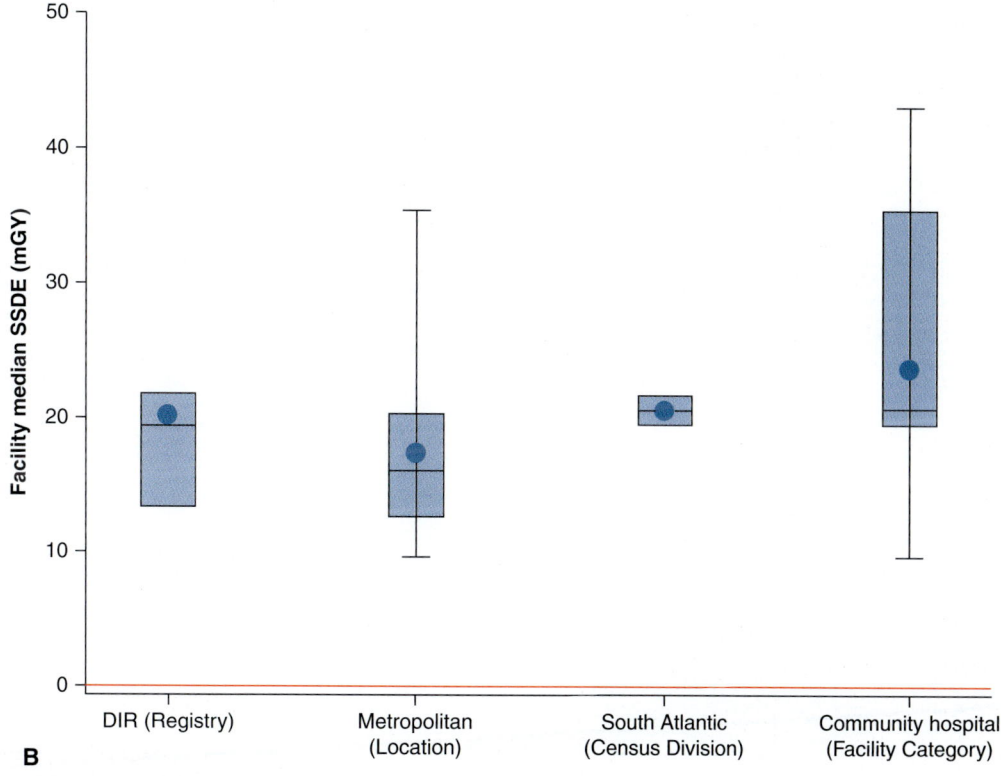

FIG. 1.1 • **A-C:** (continued)

NMD allows participating facilities to compare mammographic data with other facilities and with national benchmark data provided by the National Cancer Institute–funded Breast Cancer Surveillance Consortium (Fig. 1.4). Data collected for NMD mirror those mandated by MQSA, and several third-party software packages used in mammography reporting can transmit these data to the NMD. Four outcome measures are currently part of the NMD: diagnostic mammography positive predictive value, screening mammography positive predictive value, cancer detection rate, and abnormal interpretation rate (recall rate).[8]

ACR DIAGNOSTIC IMAGING CENTER OF EXCELLENCE

ACR offers designation as a Diagnostic Imaging Center of Excellence[9] to facilities that meet program requirements, which include ACR accreditation in all modalities employed for which ACR accreditation is offered, DIR and GRID participation, Image Gently and Image Wisely pledges, and a comprehensive site survey. The site survey assesses governance, personnel, facility organization and management, physical environment, equipment and information technology infrastructure, radiation and general safety, quality management, policies and procedures, patient rights, and medical records.

ACR-DESIGNATED LUNG CANCER SCREENING CENTER

In response to anticipated growth of CT lung cancer screening and recently published practice guidelines for performing and reporting CT lung cancer screening, ACR also offers facilities the opportunity to apply to be an ACR-designated Lung Cancer Screening Center. In addition to ACR CT-accreditation requirements, this program specifically addresses appropriateness, radiologist expertise, and appropriate CT screening acquisition protocol.[10]

RADPEER

RADPEER is a retrospective peer-review program developed by ACR in 2001.[11] This web-based program allows radiology practices and individual radiologists to report and review their own peer-review summary

4 QUALITY AND SAFETY IN MEDICAL IMAGING

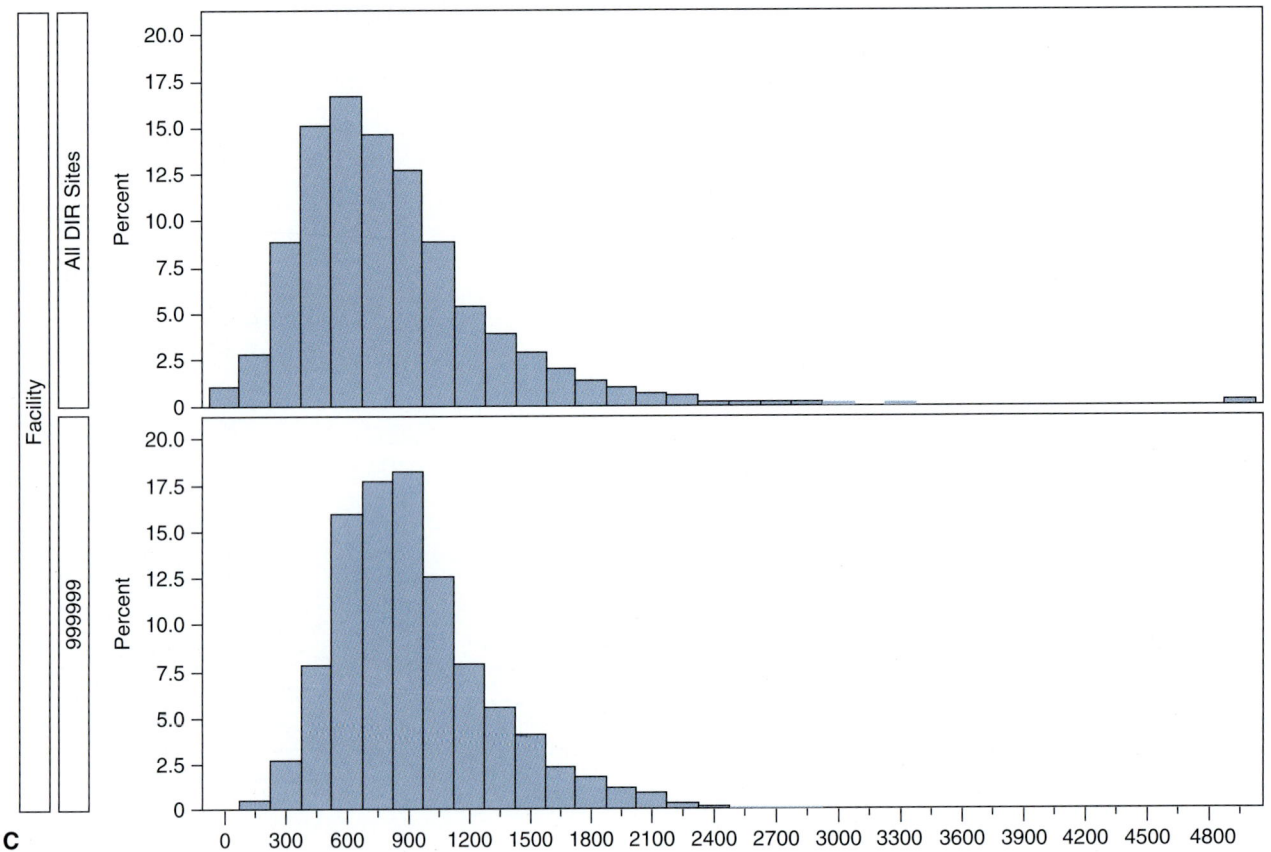

FIG. 1.1 • **A-C:** (continued)

CT Colonography Registry
July 2013 - December 2013
Summary Report of N = 584 Total Cases
Summary Table - Sample facility

	Your facility: 999999			Other facilities			Registry		
	Num	Den	%	Num	Den	%	Num	Den	%
Adequate Bowel Cleansing and Distention	118	125	94.4	403	443	91.0	521	568	91.7
Adequacy of Screening CTC Exam	47	49	95.9	128	133	96.2	175	182	96.2
Adequacy of Diagnostic CTC Exam	38	38	100.0	149	154	96.8	187	192	97.4
Colonic Perforations	0	74	0.0	1	261	0.4	1	335	0.3
True Positives	0	1	0.0	6	8	75.0	6	9	66.7
Clinically Significant Extracolonic Findings	16	127	12.6	44	457	9.6	60	584	10.3

A

FIG. 1.2 • **A-D:** Selected pages from a sample report of ACR's CT Colonography Registry.

ACR Quality and Safety Programs 5

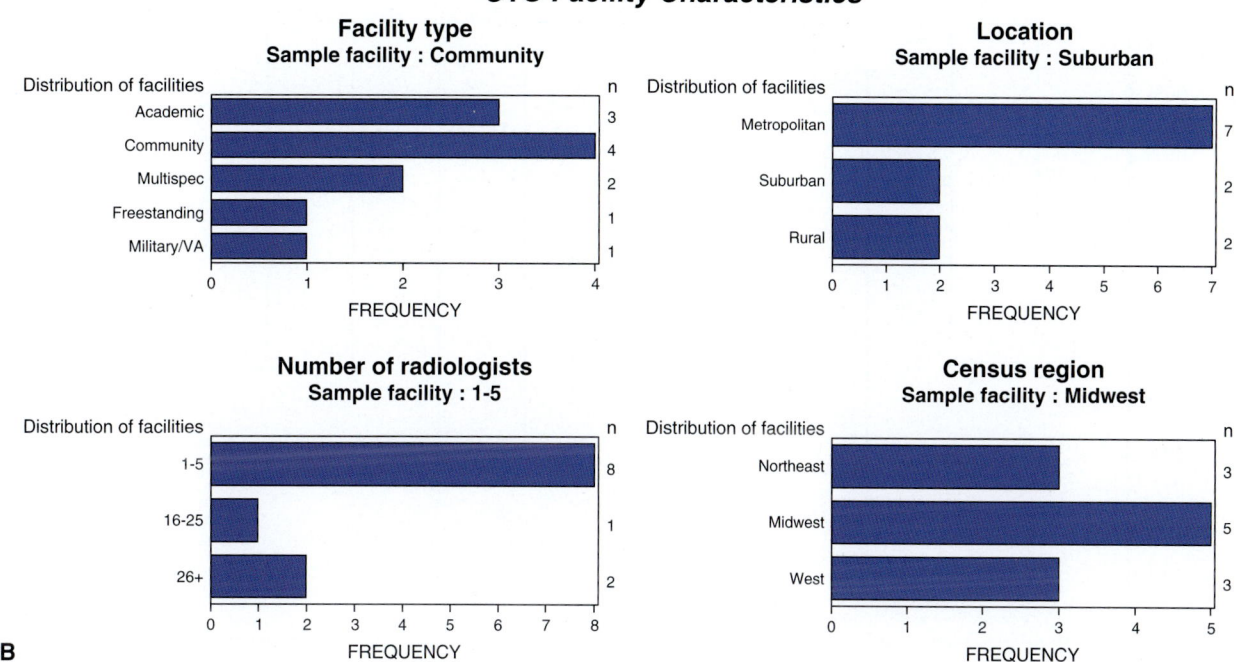

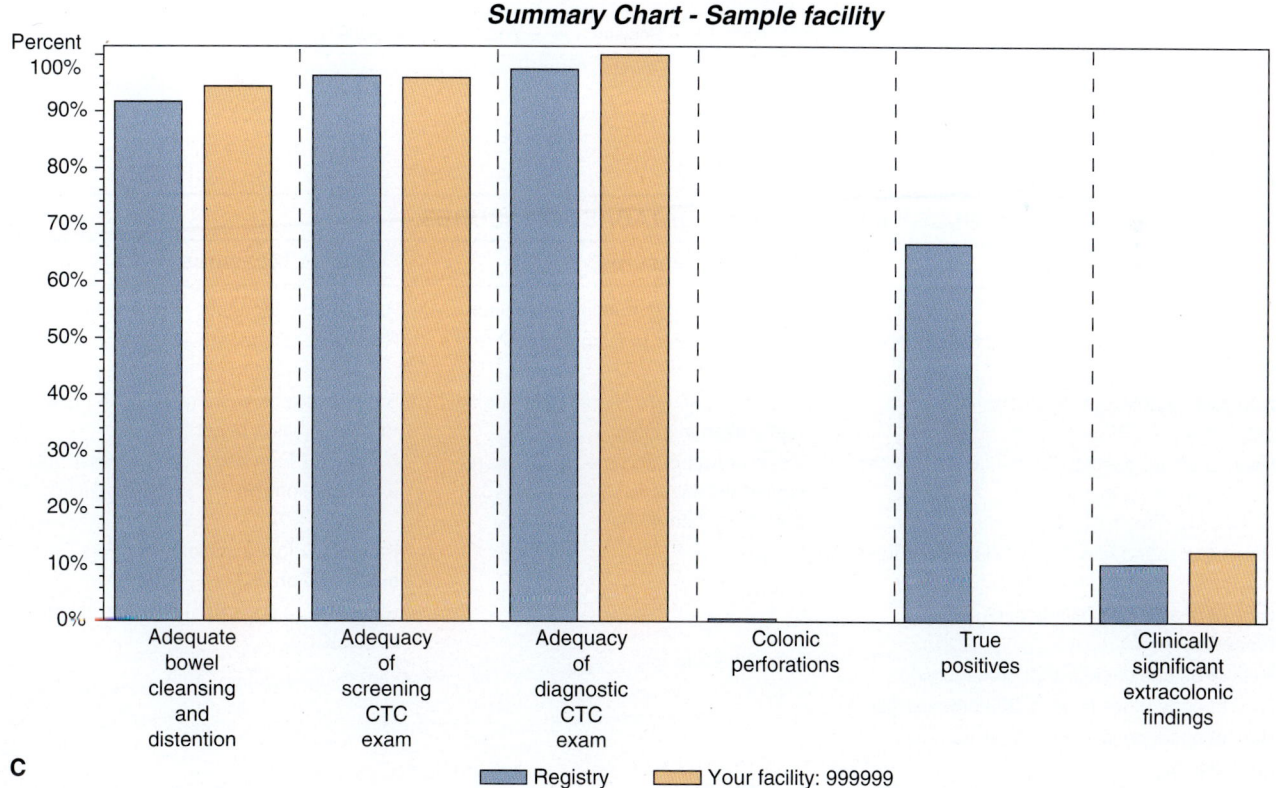

FIG. 1.2 • **A-D:** (continued)

6 QUALITY AND SAFETY IN MEDICAL IMAGING

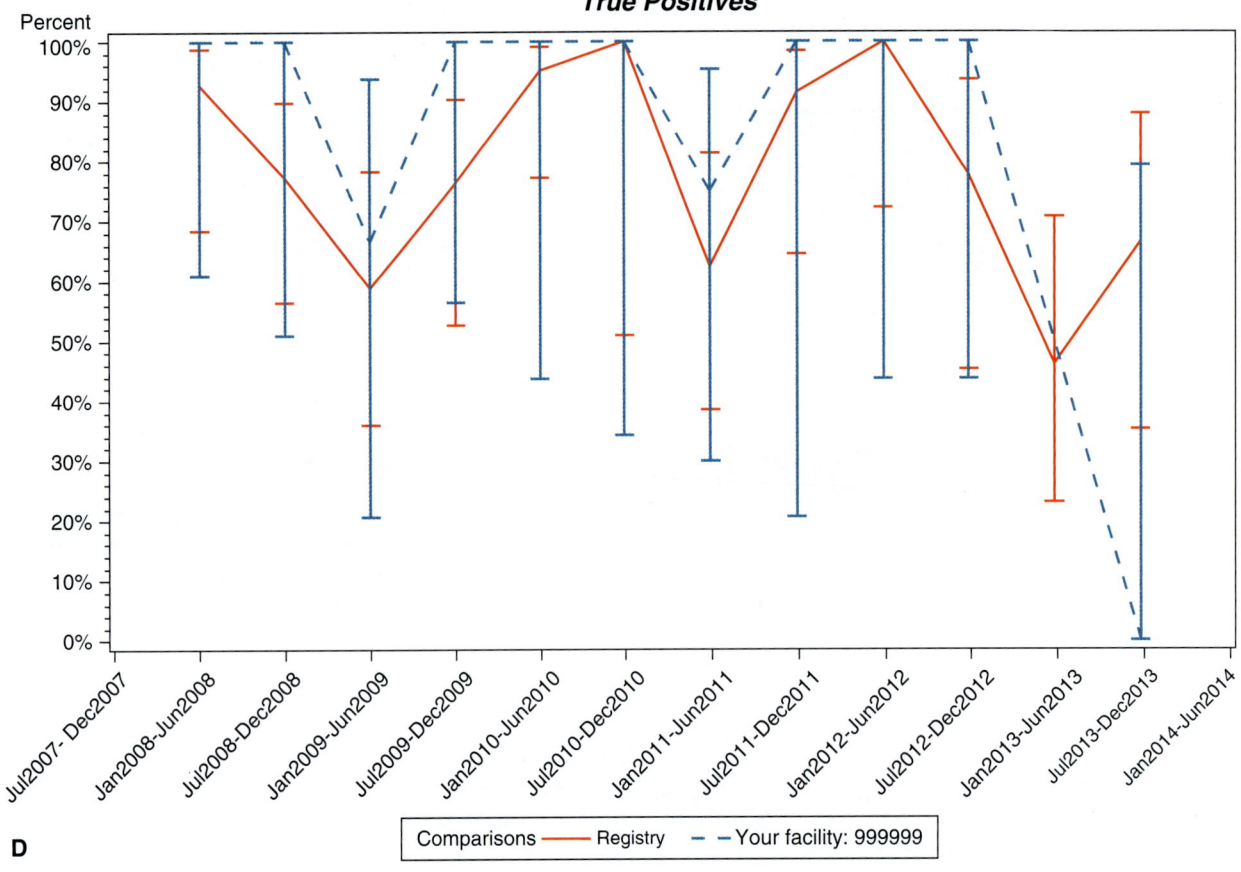

FIG. 1.2 • **A-D:** (continued)

Table 1.3 **GENERAL RADIOLOGY IMPROVEMENT DATABASE MEASURES.**

Annual Measures	Process Measures	Outcome Measures
Magnet incidents	Patient wait time (median and mean)	Rate of nondiagnostic liver biopsies (%)
Cases of nephrogenic systemic fibrosis (NSF)	Time from order to exam (median and mean)	Rate of nondiagnostic lung biopsies (%)
Non-NSF gadolinium reactions	Reacquisition rate (% of digital radiography examinations)	Rate of lung biopsies resulting in pneumothorax requiring chest tube (%)
Reactions for patients with implanted devices	Report turnaround time (% of reports signed within 12 h, 12–24 h, 24–48 h, and more than 48 h)	Rate of CT high osmolality contrast extravasation (%)
Rate of attended falls (# per 1,000 procedures)		Rate of CT low osmolality contrast extravasation (%)
Rate of unattended falls (# per 1,000 procedures)		Rate of nonconcordant stereotactic breast biopsies (%)
Rate of deaths (# per 1,000 procedures)		
Rate of code blues (# per 1,000 procedures)		
Rate of nosocomial infections (# per 1,000 procedures)		
Rate of wrong exams (# per 1,000 procedures)		
Rate of exams on wrong patients (# per 1,000 procedures)		
Rate of exams on wrong site (# per 1,000 procedures)		

GRID Process Measures Summary
Fall 2013
Sample Facility - Facility 999999

Measure	Site 999999	Sites with volume 150,000 and more	Sites in the Midwest	Sites of type Community hospital-based	All GRID sites
Mean radiography wait time(minutes)	19.7	10.7	14.8	22.2	18.5
Median radiography wait time(minutes)	16.9	7.3	10.8	15.6	13.0
Mean ultrasound wait time(minutes)	43.6	20.3	17.3	36.5	26.7
Median ultrasound wait time(minutes)	36.1	12.6	10.3	28.5	16.7
Mean MRI wait time(minutes)	57.3	39.8	45.3	50.5	48.0
Median MRI wait time(minutes)	51.6	33.2	20.2	33.1	36.3
Mean CT wait time(minutes)	33.6	23.3	26.5	42.5	35.7
Median CT wait time(minutes)	34.4	14.3	13.8	24.9	21.7
Mean PET wait time(minutes)	141.6	51.7	12.3	16.7	43.0
Median PET wait time(minutes)	85.2	53.3	7.8	8.2	37.8
Mean wait time for inpatient stat CT(minutes)	85.5	84.5	61.3	78.7	86.2
Median wait time for inpatient stat CT(minutes)	44.5	48.8	39.2	52.3	58.8
Mean wait time for inpatient routine CT(minutes)	581.8	418.9	443.7	334.3	390.2
Median wait time for inpatient routine CT(minutes)	95.9	179.6	198.0	192.2	229.9
Digital radiography repeat rate (Percent)	3.9	4.7	5.0	6.3	4.7
Mean TAT - Radiography (Hours)	1.7	4.7	3.5	5.7	5.3
Mean TAT - Ultrasound (Hours)	7.6	5.3	3.7	6.3	5.0
Mean TAT - MRI (Hours)	5.9	12.4	9.3	7.5	11.3

A

FIG. 1.3 • A-E: Selected pages from a sample report of ACR's General Radiology Improvement Database.

data by modality and compare performance among all RADPEER participants.[12] Refer to Chapter 11 for more details on peer review.

PRACTICE GUIDELINES AND TECHNICAL STANDARDS

ACR publishes practice guidelines and technical standards for radiologic practice to "help advanced the science of radiology and to improve the quality of service to patients throughout the United States."[13] These practice guidelines and technical standards are reviewed or renewed at least once every 5 years and earlier if necessary. Technical standards and practice parameters cover a range of topics from general modality standards to specific body-part imaging. Radiation oncology practice guidelines are also published in conjunction with the American Society for Radiation Oncology (ASTRO). In addition, ACR maintains practice guidelines for continuing medical education and communication.

ACR APPROPRIATENESS CRITERIA

ACR Appropriateness Criteria (ACR AC) are designed to assist physicians and other health-care providers in selecting the most appropriate imaging or therapeutic procedure for a specific clinical scenario (Fig. 1.5).[14] The ACR AC are developed by a multidisciplinary panel of experts using published data and, when needed, expert opinion. Physicians from other medical specialties are included on expert panels so as to provide appropriate clinical perspectives. ACR AC are developed following the guidelines issued by the Agency for Healthcare Research and Quality as designed by the Institute of Medicine. As of summer 2014, more than 200 ACR AC have been published, covering nearly 1,000 variants. ACR AC are readily available for scientific, research, and informational purposes. Additionally, ACR licenses the ACR AC for commercial use such as in an electronic health record or decision support system.

GRID Outcome Measures and Incident Rates Summary
Fall 2013
Sample Facility - Facility 999999
FOR GOLD LEVEL PARTICIPANTS ONLY

Measure	Site 999999	Sites with volume 150,000 and more	Sites in the Midwest	Sites of type Community hospital-based	All GRID sites
Non-diagnostic liver biopsy (Percent)	0.0	0.0	0.0	0.0	0.0
Non-diagnostic lung biopsy (Percent)	4.7	0.0	4.2	3.8	0.5
Lung biopsies resulting in pneumothorax requiring chest tube (Percent)	0.0	4.5	2.1	3.3	3.3
Extravasations - HOCM (percent)	.	.	.	.	.
Extravasations - LOCM (percent)	0.2	0.3	0.2	0.2	0.2
Non-concordant findings - stereotactic breast biopsy (Percent)*	0.0	1.2	0.0	0.0	0.4
Magnet incidents per 100,000 exams	0.0	0.0	0.0	0.0	0.0
Cases of NSF per 100,000 exams	0.0	0.0	0.0	0.0	0.0
Reactions for patients with implanted devices per 100,000 exams	0.0	0.0	0.0	0.0	0.0
Attended falls in radiology department per 100,000 exams	3.1	1.7	2.1	2.9	1.1
Unattended falls in radiology department per 100,000 exams	3.6	1.1	0.4	0.9	0.0
Deaths in the radiology department per 100,000 exams	0.0	0.0	0.0	0.0	0.0
Code blues in radiology department per 100,000 exams	0.6	0.9	0.6	0.6	0.5
Nosocomial infections in radiology department per 100,000 exams	0.0	0.0	0.0	0.0	0.0
Wrong exams per 100,000 exams	4.2	1.5	0.0	1.0	1.0
Exams on wrong patients per 100,000 exams	0.7	0.9	0.9	0.7	0.0
Exams on wrong sites per 100,000 exams	0.8	0.5	0.0	0.3	0.0

B

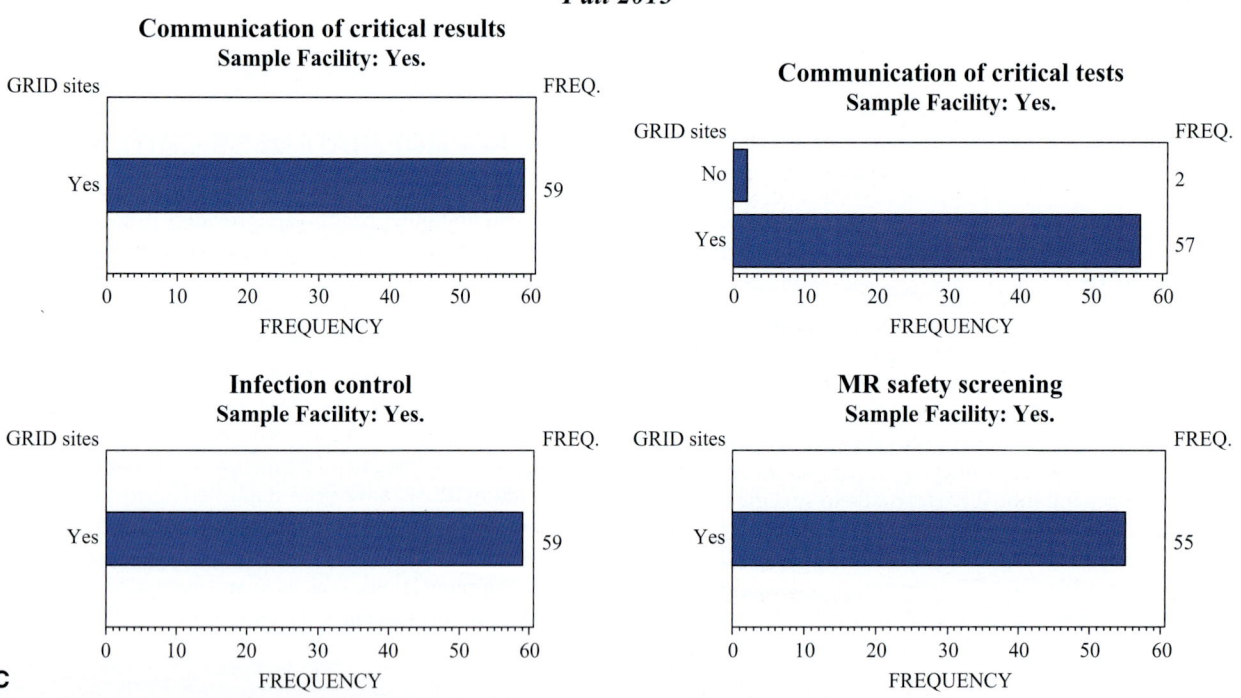

C

FIG. 1.3 • **A-E:** (*continued*)

ACR Quality and Safety Programs

GRID Process Measure Variation
MRI wait time (minutes)

Variation across sites in current average reported Mean	Site 999999	Sites with volume 150,000 and more	Sites in the Midwest	Sites of type Community hospital-based	All GRID sites
N	1	12	12	17	49
Site Rank (Ascending)	.	11	11	12	32
Mean	57.34	46.96	43.68	198.80	188.27
Standard deviation	.	37.70	30.57	272.24	294.30
Min	57.34	10.17	10.00	18.00	10.00
25th percentile	57.34	25.00	17.75	31.83	30.25
Median	57.34	39.75	45.25	50.50	48.00
75th percentile	57.34	55.50	55.58	342.33	116.67
Max	57.34	151.50	116.67	790.83	970.33

Variation across sites in current average reported Median	Site 999999	Sites with volume 150,000 and more	Sites in the Midwest	Sites of type Community hospital-based	All GRID sites
N	1	11	11	16	47
Site Rank (Ascending)	.	10	11	11	32
Mean	51.65	39.06	24.12	90.90	96.84
Standard deviation	.	33.38	17.41	108.49	147.08
Min	51.65	4.67	4.67	10.33	4.67
25th percentile	51.65	10.33	10.00	18.33	19.50
Median	51.65	33.17	20.17	33.08	36.33
75th percentile	51.65	47.83	37.33	143.58	83.67
Max	51.65	125.33	62.00	338.17	647.33

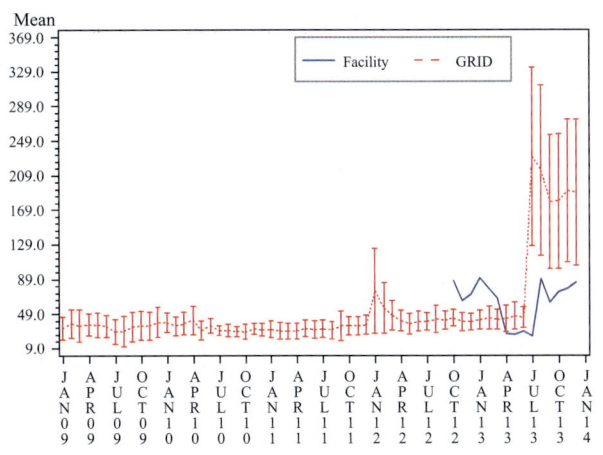

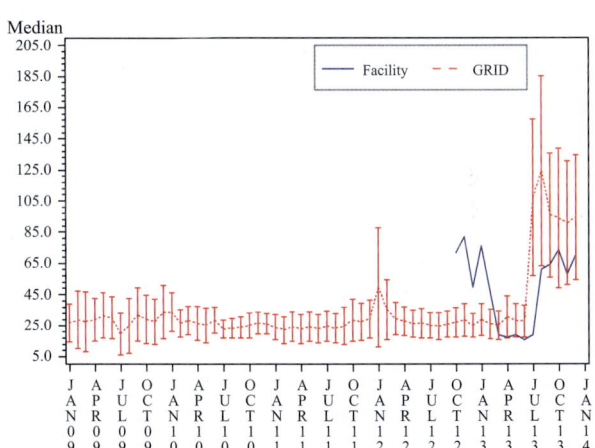

D

GRID Process Measure Variation
Radiography turnaround time (hours)

Variation across sites in current average reported Mean	Site 999999	Sites with volume 150,000 and more	Sites in the Midwest	Sites of type Community hospital-based	All GRID sites
N	1	14	13	21	56
Site Rank (Ascending)	.	2	5	2	6
Mean	1.73	6.85	5.31	13.18	8.22
Standard deviation	.	8.93	4.59	18.25	12.00
Min	1.73	1.00	1.00	1.00	1.00
25th percentile	1.73	2.33	1.00	3.67	2.75
Median	1.73	4.67	3.50	5.67	5.33
75th percentile	1.73	6.33	8.80	11.40	8.48
Max	1.73	36.17	12.50	77.17	77.17

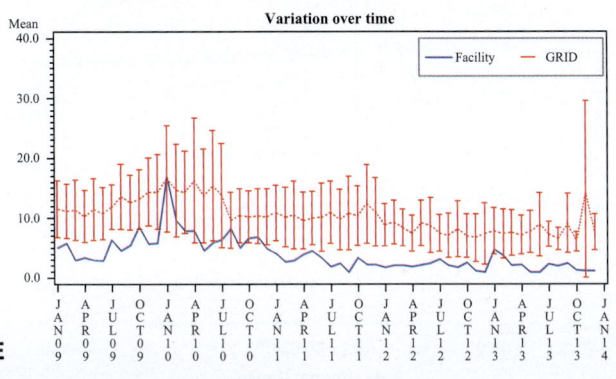

E

FIG. 1.3 • **A–E:** (*continued*)

RADIOLOGYINFO.ORG

RadiologyInfo.org is a patient-centered resource published jointly by ACR and the Radiologic Society of North America (RSNA).[15] This website provides information in both English and Spanish for patients regarding diagnostic imaging, radiologic procedures, and radiation therapy. For each topic, an explanation is provided of what the test or procedure is, reasons for performing the test or procedure, a description of equipment used, how the test or procedure works, what the patient will experience during and after, risks and benefits, and limitations. Pediatric-specific content is flagged with an icon, and links to additional resources are provided. Information on other topics such as airport scanners, contrast safety, pregnancy, and radiation exposure is also included.

10 QUALITY AND SAFETY IN MEDICAL IMAGING

Abnormal Interpretations and Cancers for Screening Mammography
Physician 1000000991: January 2012 - December 2012

Measure	Value	1000000991 Rate	(Num-Den)	Facility 999999 Rate	(Num-Den)	All NMD facilities (N=101) Rate	(Num-Den)	BCSC benchmark Rate	(Num-Den)
All exams			182		707		1,098,102		2,410,932
Recall rate		10.44%	(19/182)	8.20%	(58/707)	9.84%	(108,102/1,098,102)	10.95%	(263,905/2,410,932)
Biopsy recommended		2.75%	(5/182)	1.98%	(14/707)	2.38%	(26,150/1,098,102)	1.38%	(33,239/2,410,932)
Cancers and PPV2		40.00%	(2/5)	33.33%	(4/12)	16.54%	(4,015/24,269)	22.90%	(7,613/33,239)
Biopsy		2.75%	(5/182)	1.70%	(12/707)	1.80%	(19,788/1,098,102)	0.99%	(23,786/2,410,932)
Biopsy results	Negative	60.00%	(3/5)	63.64%	(7/11)	70.26%	(10,777/15,338)	71.79%	(17,076/23,786)
	Positive	40.00%	(2/5)	36.36%	(4/11)	29.30%	(4,494/15,338)	28.21%	(6,710/23,786)
Cancers and CDR per 1000		10.99	(2/182)	5.66	(4/707)	3.66	(4,015/1,098,102)	4.18	(10,072/2,410,932)
DCIS		0.00%	(0/2)	25.00%	(1/4)	25.38%	(1,019/4,015)	23.58%	(2,375/10,072)
Invasive cancer		100.00%	(2/2)	75.00%	(3/4)	74.69%	(2,999/4,015)	76.42%	(7,697/10,072)
Minimal cancer		50.00%	(1/2)	50.00%	(2/4)	64.43%	(1,703/2,643)	52.40%	(4,980/9,504)
Nodal status	Negative	100.00%	(2/2)	100.00%	(3/3)	86.22%	(1,082/1,255)	75.95%	(5,629/7,411)
	Positive	0.00%	(0/2)	0.00%	(0/3)	13.78%	(173/1,255)	24.05%	(1,782/7,411)
Tumor size	1-5mm	0.00%	(0/1)	0.00%	(0/2)	12.03%	(201/1,671)		
	6-10mm	0.00%	(0/1)	0.00%	(0/2)	29.20%	(488/1,671)		
	11-15mm	100.00%	(1/1)	100.00%	(2/2)	28.37%	(474/1,671)		
	16-20mm	0.00%	(0/1)	0.00%	(0/2)	11.61%	(194/1,671)		
	> 20mm	0.00%	(0/1)	0.00%	(0/2)	18.79%	(314/1,671)		
Tumor stage	0	0.00%	(0/1)	33.33%	(1/3)	23.37%	(233/997)		
	I	100.00%	(1/1)	66.67%	(2/3)	53.76%	(536/997)		
	II	0.00%	(0/1)	0.00%	(0/3)	20.66%	(206/997)		

A

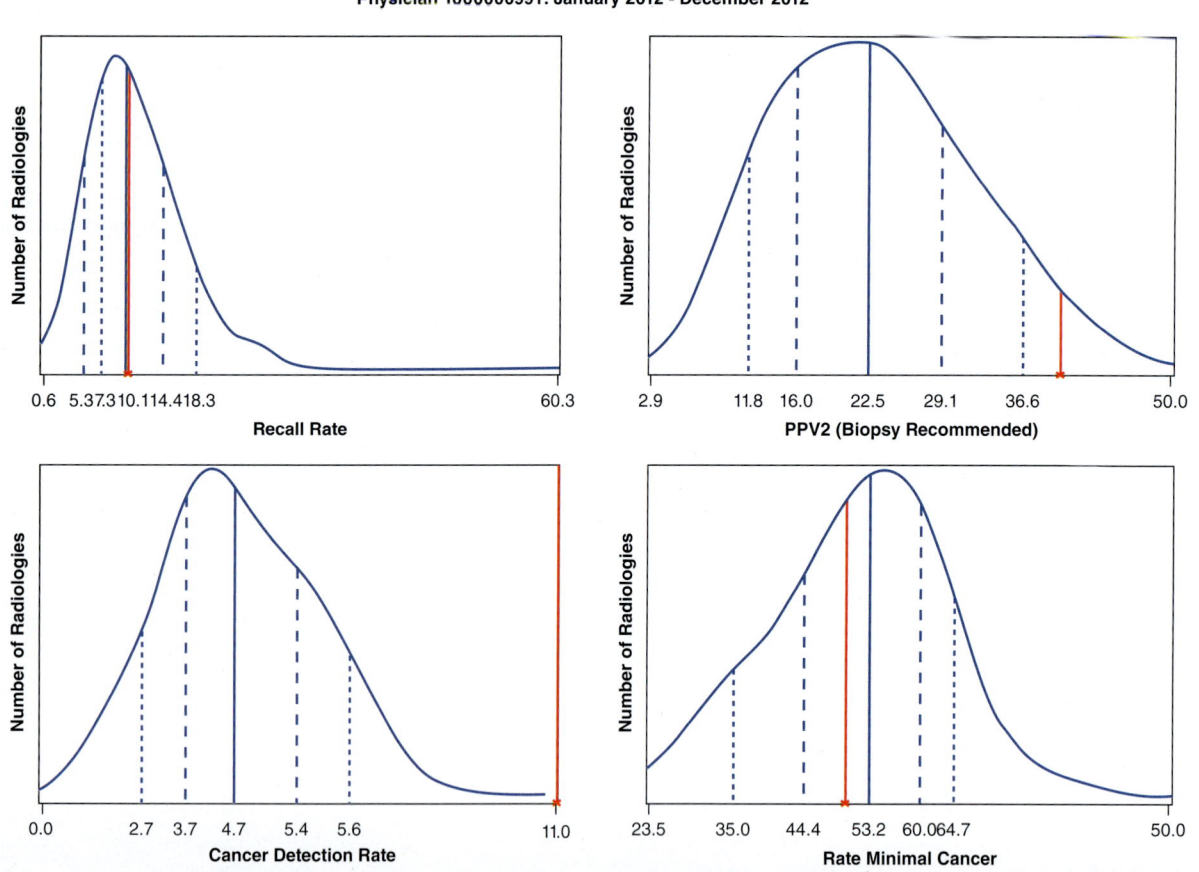

B

FIG. 1.4 • **A-C:** *(continued)*

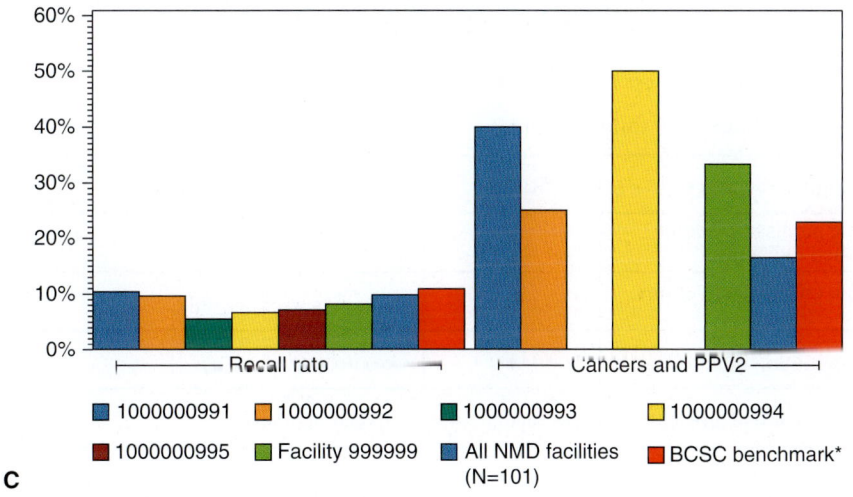

FIG. 1.4 • A-C: (continued)

References

1. American College of Radiology. About Us. http://www.acr.org/About-Us. Accessed May 30, 2016.
2. American College of Radiology. Accreditation. http://www.acr.org/Quality-Safety/Accreditation. Accessed May 30, 2016.
3. American College of Radiology. National Radiology Data Registry. http://www.acr.org/Quality-Safety/National-Radiology-Data-Registry. Accessed May 30, 2016.
4. American College of Radiology. Dose Index Registry. http://www.acr.org/Quality-Safety/National-Radiology-Data-Registry/Dose-Index-Registry. Accessed May 30, 2016.
5. American College of Radiology. CT Colonography Registry. http://www.acr.org/Quality-Safety/National-Radiology-Data-Registry/CT-Colonography-Registry. Accessed May 30, 2016.
6. American College of Radiology. General Radiology Improvement Database. http://www.acr.org/Quality-Safety/National-Radiology-Data-Registry/General-Radiology-Improvement-DB. Accessed May 30, 2016.
7. American College of Radiology. IV Contrast Extravasation. http://www.acr.org/Quality-Safety/National-Radiology-Data-Registry/IV-Contrast-Extravasation. Accessed May 30, 2016.
8. American College of Radiology. National Mammography Database. http://www.acr.org/Quality-Safety/National-Radiology-Data-Registry/National-Mammography-DB. Accessed May 30, 2016.
9. American College of Radiology. Diagnostic Imaging Center of Excellence. http://www.acr.org/Quality-Safety/DICOE. Accessed May 30, 2016.
10. American College of Radiology. ACR Lung Cancer Screening Center. http://www.acr.org/Quality-Safety/Lung-Cancer-Screening-Center. Accessed May 30, 2016.
11. Jackson VP, Cushing T, Abujudeh HH, et al. RADPEER scoring white paper. *J Am Coll Radiol.* 2009;6:21–25.
12. American College of Radiology. RADPEER. http://www.acr.org/Quality-Safety/RADPEER. Accessed May 30, 2016.
13. American College of Radiology. Practice parameters and technical standards. http://www.acr.org/Quality-Safety/Standards-Guidelines. Accessed May 30, 2016.
14. Cascade PN. The American College of Radiology. ACR Appropriateness Criteria project. *Radiology.* 2000;214(suppl):3–46.
15. American College of Radiology, Radiologic Society of North America. http://www.radiologyinfo.org/. Accessed May 30, 2016.

SELF-ASSESSMENT QUESTIONS

1. Which of the following requirements for physicians constitutes a part of the American College of Radiology's imaging modality accreditation program?

   A. Continuing medical education in the accredited modality
   B. Membership in the American College of Radiology
   C. Subspecialty fellowship training
   D. Peer-reviewed publication in the accredited modality

2. Which of the following is *not* part of the National Radiology Data Registry (NRDR)?

   A. CT Colonography Registry
   B. General Radiology Improvement Database
   C. National Mammography Database
   D. Neuroradiology Database

Answers to Chapter Self-Assessment Questions

1. A. The American College of Radiology's modality accreditation requirements for physician qualifications include training, board certification, ongoing experience with interpretation and reporting, and continuing medical education.

2. D. Currently, a neuroradiology-specific database is not part of the National Radiology Data Registry (NRDR). The NRDR currently comprises the CT Colonography Registry, Dose Index Registry, General Radiology Improvement Database, IV Contrast Extravasation, and National Mammography Database. The Interventional Radiology Registry and Lung Cancer Screening Registries are being added in 2015. The IV Contrast Extravasation Registry is scheduled to be discontinued at the end of 2016.

Date of origin: 1995
Last review date: 2011

American College of Radiology
ACR Appropriateness Criteria®

Clinical Condition: Routine Chest Radiographs in ICU Patients

Variant 1: Monitoring stable patient.

Radiologic Procedure	Rating	Comments	RRL*
X-ray chest portable admission and/or transfer with specified indication	9		☢
X-ray chest portable clinical indications only	9	Clinical worsening only.	☢
X-ray chest portable routine monitoring	1		☢

Rating Scale: 1,2,3 Usually not appropriate; 4,5,6 May be appropriate; 7,8,9 Usually appropriate

*Relative Radiation Level

Variant 2: Respiratory failure. Patient receiving mechanical ventilation.

Radiologic Procedure	Rating	Comments	RRL*
X-ray chest portable clinical indications only	9		☢
X-ray chest portable routine daily	3	Some subgroups may benefit from a daily chest radiograph.	☢

Rating Scale: 1,2,3 Usually not appropriate; 4,5,6 May be appropriate; 7,8,9 Usually appropriate

*Relative Radiation Level

Variant 3: Compromised respiratory function. Patient with endotracheal tubes.

Radiologic Procedure	Rating	Comments	RRL*
X-ray chest portable after catheter/tube insertion	9		☢
X-ray chest portable clinical indications only	9		☢
X-ray chest portable follow-up	1		☢

Rating Scale: 1,2,3 Usually not appropriate; 4,5,6 May be appropriate; 7,8,9 Usually appropriate

*Relative Radiation Level

Variant 4: Central venous pressure catheter (CVP) insertion.

Radiologic Procedure	Rating	Comments	RRL*
X-ray chest portable after catheter/tube insertion	9		☢
X-ray chest portable clinical indications only	9		☢
X-ray chest portable follow-up	1		☢

Rating Scale: 1,2,3 Usually not appropriate; 4,5,6 May be appropriate; 7,8,9 Usually appropriate

*Relative Radiation Level

FIG. 1.5 • Selected page from ACR Appropriateness Criteria for routine chest radiographs in ICU patients. (From American College of Radiology. ACR Appropriateness Criteria for routine chest radiographs in ICU patients.2011. https://acsearch.acr.org/docs/69452/Narrative/. Accessed May 30, 2016.)

Quality and Safety in Medical Imaging

Bryan P. Bednarz and John R. Vetter

LEARNING OBJECTIVES

1. Discuss common radiation quantities used in medical imaging quality and safety
2. Overview possible biologic effects caused by medical imaging
3. List effective doses resulting from various medical imaging examinations
4. Discuss the guiding tenets of patient and personnel radiation safety
5. Give examples of the use of time, distance, and shielding to reduce radiation dose to patients and personnel

Ionizing radiation has been used in medicine for various diagnostic and therapeutic purposes since its discovery over a century ago. It is universally accepted that noninvasive or minimally invasive diagnostic imaging is a crucial component of health care and the benefits from such procedures greatly outweigh any associated risks. Modern imaging technology is replacing the need for more invasive procedures, which in turn is making the practice of medicine more precise, safe, and cost-effective. However, it is well known that ionizing radiation can be viewed as a "double-edged sword"; despite all of its beneficial uses, overexposure to ionizing radiation can be detrimental to human health. As a result, strict radiation safety practices to patients and medical personnel have been paramount to the success of modern diagnostic imaging. As the use of diagnostic imaging involving ionizing radiation continues to rapidly increase, there has been an even greater emphasis on radiation safety, particularly as patients and medical personnel are living longer than ever before, leaving more time for negative health effects from ionizing radiation to manifest.

This chapter is meant to provide an overview of radiation safety principles and practices in diagnostic imaging. First, a brief overview of the history of radiation safety in diagnostic imaging is covered. Next, several definitions of important terms used in radiation safety are presented, which will be followed by a section covering the biologic effects of radiation damage in humans and a section overviewing the current usage and amount of radiation dose received from several types of diagnostic radiology scans. Finally, the remaining sections of the chapter are devoted to issues related to patient and occupational radiation safety.

HISTORICAL OVERVIEW

It became clear since the early usage of diagnostic imaging that ionizing radiation could impose serious, if not fatal, health effects when not used safely. One of the first documented cases of radiation damage to humans occurred in early 1896 when two scientists named Daniel[1] and Dudley at Vanderbilt University observed skin changes and epilation following an experimental radiograph of Dudley's head. Not surprisingly, documented health effects due to early diagnostic examinations, like those inflicted on Dudley, were almost entirely related to skin damage considering the low energy and intensity of the sources being used for diagnostic imaging. For example, in 1897, Scott[2] of Cleveland reported on 69 cases of skin damage, and in 1902, Codman[3] of Boston reported on 170 cases of skin damage both due to X-ray examinations. Despite these reports, the use of X-rays for diagnostic purposes continued to rise in the early part of the 20th century, and several physicians and scientists began to investigate the root causes of radiation damage. Some hypothesized that indirect effects caused the damage, as did famed inventor Nikola Tesla[4] in 1897, who proposed that the radiation near the X-ray tube produced both ozone and nitrous oxide, which subsequently led to skin damage. However, in the same year, Thomson[5] correctly attributed the effects directly to damage caused by the X-rays themselves on human tissue.

It was also around this time that radiation protection practices were being implemented into clinical practice. In 1896, Fuchs[6] was the first to provide recommendations on radiation exposure, advising operators to make the exposure as short as possible, to stand at least a foot from the X-ray tube, and coat the skin with petroleum jelly and leave an extra layer on the most exposed area. This in fact covered the three basic tenets of radiation protection (i.e., time, distance, and shielding) all within a year of the discovery of the X-ray. In 1897, Walsh[7] described the reduction of acute effects in radiation workers using lead aprons. Pfahler[8] in 1901 introduced a shielding apparatus during radiographic examinations placing a thin ring-shaped sheet of aluminum around the cathode tube, and as a result introduced the concept of collimation. Several years later, Pfahler[9] again was the first to recommend the use of film for personnel monitoring.

Although the first decade of use of X-rays for diagnostic examinations led to a better understanding of early effects such as skin damage caused by X-rays and important safety improvements in these procedures, much less was known about late effects that could be caused by radiation exposure. In fact, it was not until 10 to 30 years after exposure to individuals that late effects, most notably second cancers, were being diagnosed particularly in radiologists. While multiple reports in the early part of the 20th century on radiation-induced cancer in animals were published, it was not until 1902 when Frieben[10] reported on a cancer in a patient that was believed to be developed following chronic ulceration. In 1911, Hesse[11] collected histories of 94 cases of tumors induced in individuals by radiation, where 54 of these cases were among physicians or technicians. The same year, Krausse[12] reported on the death of 54 radiologists from occupational exposure and further described 126 cases in 1930. Three years later, Feygin[13] tabulated 104 cases of cancer caused by irradiation, and in 1922, Ledoux-Lebard[14] estimated that 100 radiologist had died from chronic radiation exposure.

By the early 1920s, it was clear that guidelines and standards needed to be established that aimed to protect patients and hospital staff from unsafe levels of radiation exposure. This effort was spearheaded by a group of medical professionals in England who established the X-ray and Radium Protection Committee and released the first recommendations on radiation safety practices in 1921.[15] A similar safety committee was established in 1920 by the American Roentgen Ray Society in the United States, whose recommendations published in 1923 were closely modeled after those produced in England.[15]

Because of the infancy of the field, early radiation safety recommendations were heuristic in nature, but these committees recognized that a standard unit of measurement for radiation was needed. In fact, the first International Congress of Radiology in London in 1925 was almost entirely devoted to discussions of international units and standards for X-ray work.[15] At this meeting, the International X-ray Unit Committee was established with the primary objective to propose a unit for radiation measurements as applied to medicine. This committee eventually evolved into the International Commission on Radiation Units and Measurements (ICRU). Motivated by the excitement on standards at the International Congress of Radiology, the Radiological Society of North America (RSNA) established the Standardization Committee to investigate and propose a standard unit of measurement for X-rays.[16] The Committee published their first series of recommendations in March of 1926. Concurrently, the Standardization Committee also sent multiple influential letters to scientists and politicians that highlighted the need for the establishment of an X-ray unit within the National Bureau of Standards (NBS) to develop a standard unit for X-ray measurements.[16] This effort led to the formation of the X-ray Measurement and Protection Unit within the NBS in 1927.[16] Note the NBS is now known as the National Institute of Standards and Technology (NIST). By the second International Congress of Radiology in Stockholm in 1928, the X-ray Measurement and Protection Unit officially proposed the adoption of the roentgen unit as a measurement of electrostatic charge formed in air by X-rays.[16]

International efforts on the establishment of a radiation protection committee were also underway. Although interest in the formation of an international radiation protection committee was discussed at the first ICRU, a formal committee was not formed until the second International Congress of Radiology and was called the International X-ray and Radium Protection Committee, which eventually became the International Commission on Radiological Protection (ICRP).[15] The International X-ray and Radium Protection Committee also recommended that each represented country develop a coordinated program of radiation protection, which led to the formation of the U.S. Advisory Committee on X-ray and Radium Protection. This committee is now known as the National Council on Radiation Protection and Measurements (NCRP). Along with the ICRP, the NCRP develops guidelines to protect individuals and the public from excessive radiation exposure. These two bodies alongside several national and international professional organizations have maintained a commitment to ensure the safe use of radiation in medicine in the United States and abroad.

RADIATION QUANTITIES AND UNITS

There are two important nonstochastic quantities that are used to describe the impact of radiation on a medium. These quantities are (1) the exposure (X) and (2) the absorbed dose (D). The exposure is the amount of ionization that is produced in air from photons whereas dose represents the energy imparted to a medium by all kinds of radiation, but ultimately delivered by charged particles. The exposure is defined as

$$X = \frac{dq}{dm} \quad (1)$$

where dq is the total charge of one sign produced in air when all electrons liberated by photons in air of mass dm deposit all of their energy in the air. The classical unit of exposure is the Roentgen (R), which is equivalent to the production of $2.58 \times 10^{-4}\,\mathrm{C\,kg^{-1}}$ in dry air.

From a radiation safety standpoint, it is most convenient to focus on absorbed dose. By definition, the absorbed dose is equal to

$$D = \frac{d\varepsilon}{dm} \quad (2)$$

where ε is the expectation value of the energy imparted in a finite volume V at a point P. The expectation value is appropriate, given that energy imparted by charged particles is fundamentally a stochastic process governed by laws of probability and subject to statistical uncertainty. A reasonable estimate of the mean of this process is only realized once enough events accumulate in V. The SI unit for dose is the Gray (Gy), where

$$1\,\mathrm{J/kg} = 1\,\mathrm{Gy} \quad (3)$$

Another quantity that accounts for the differences in radiation quality is known as the equivalent dose. Since only photons are used in diagnostic imaging, which has a radiation weighting factor of unity, it can be assumed that the absorbed dose is equal to the equivalent dose, which has units of sievert (Sv). Given that equivalent dose corresponds to the energy deposited in tissue, it is often the preferred quantity over exposure in diagnostic radiology.

Each tissue or organ in the human body responds differently to ionizing radiation. For the same absorbed dose, the probability of inducing a stochastic effect in one organ will be different from that in another. To account for these differences, tissue-weighting factors have been developed by the ICRP and NCRP. The product of the equivalent dose and the tissue-weighting factor gives a quantity that correlates to the overall detriment to the body from damage to the organ or tissue being irradiated. The detriment includes both mortality and morbidity risks associated with cancer and severe genetic effects. The sum of the tissue-weighting factors equals unity. The total risk for all stochastic effects in an irradiated individual is known as the effective dose, which is defined as

$$E = \sum_T w_T H_T \quad (4)$$

The unit of effective dose is the sievert (Sv). It is important to remember that the concept of effective dose was designed for radiation protection purposes. It reflects the total radiation detriment from an exposure averaged over all ages and both sexes. Effective dose is calculated in a reference computational phantom that is not representative of a single patient given that the phantom is androgynous and of an age representing the average age of a working adult. It should be noted that recent recommendations have called for a modified effective dose calculation procedure that uses sex-specific phantoms. Effective dose should never be used to predict risk to an individual patient, but only to compare potential risk between different exposures to ionizing radiation, such as computed tomography (CT) examinations. For example, effective dose can be used to compare relative risks, averaged over the population from different proposed CT protocols or scanners.

Given the large volume of CT scans performed each year and associated concerns about absorbed dose to the patient, various metrics have been developed to characterize dose from CT scans. The most fundamental radiation dose metric used for CT imaging is the Computed Tomography Dose Index (CTDI).[17,18] The $CTDI_{vol}$ parameter is most commonly displayed on CTDI scanners. The $CTDI_{vol}$ is derived from measurements of the $CTDI_{100}$, which is defined as

$$CTDI_{100} = \frac{1}{nT} \int_{z=-50mm}^{+50mm} D(z)dz \quad (5)$$

where n is the number of slices acquired during the scan, T is the width of each slice, and $D(z)$ is the dose profile resulting from single axial rotation measured from a 10-cm-long ionization chamber. The chamber is placed either at the center or at the periphery of a polymethyl methacrylate dose phantom. Typically, the measurements are made in units of air kerma (K), where K (mGy) = 8.73 × X (R). There are two standard dose phantoms used to acquire the $CTDI_{100}$: one has a 16-cm diameter and the other has a 32-cm diameter. Both of these phantoms have a length of 15 cm. Such measurements may be used to provide an indication of the average dose delivered over a single slice. The $CTDI_{vol}$ value is given as

$$CTDI_{vol} = \frac{CTDI_w}{Pitch} \quad (6)$$

where the pitch is defined as the ratio of the table feed (in mm) per 360° gantry rotation to the nominal beam width (nT), and $CTDI_w$ is given by

$$CTDI_w = \frac{1}{3} CTDI_{100}^{center} + \frac{2}{3} CTDI_{100}^{periphery} \quad (7)$$

Several variables impact $CTDI_{vol}$, including tube voltage, tube current, gantry rotation time, and pitch.

Another parameter that is often used to characterize dose from a CT scan is called the dose length product (DLP). The DLP is simply defined as

$$DLP = CTDI_{vol} \times Scan\ Length \quad (8)$$

where the scan length is the product of the total number of scans and the scan width. Given that the intention of the DLP is to provide information about the total exposure over the entire volume of the scan, an approximation of the effective dose from the scan can be made using a DLP to effective dose conversion factor. The effective dose is given as

$$E = k \times DLP \quad (9)$$

where k is the conversion factor (typically in units of mSv × mGy^{-1} × cm^{-1}) that varies depending on the region of the body being scanned. The conversion factor k is derived from Monte Carlo calculations in a computation anthropomorphic phantom.

BIOLOGIC EFFECTS OF RADIATION

Biologic effects from ionizing radiation are generally classified as being stochastic or deterministic. Stochastic effects are injuries that manifest from the damage of one or only a few cells. Stochastic effects include hereditary effects and cancer. Deterministic effects result from damage to a large collection of cells, leading to damage to tissue or entire organs and systems in the body. Therefore, incidence and severity increase as a function of dose once a certain threshold for the effect to occur has been reached. Tissue reactions that are classified as deterministic effects include skin burns, hair loss, loss of thyroid function, and cataracts.

Cancer

The most studied radiation-induced stochastic effect is cancer. Most of the data on radiation-induced cancer risks come from Japanese atomic bomb survivors through the Life Span Study (LSS), although other exposed populations have been studied as well, including patients receiving medical treatments, occupationally exposed groups, and environmentally exposed groups. Given these data, a clear linear relationship has been established between cancer induction and absorbed dose at high doses. Exceptions to this relationship have been found for leukemia and nonmelanoma skin cancer in atomic bomb survivor data and bone cancer in radium dial painters. It is also well known that the damage to a single cell or small number of cells can result in the induction of cancer even at very low doses. However, the exact relationship between the absorbed dose and the induction of a cancer in humans at low doses associated with diagnostic imaging procedures has been the subject of intense debate. For radiation protection purposes, it is generally assumed that a linear no-threshold (LNT) relationship exists between dose and effect, although evidence for a variety of other dose–effect relationships exists as illustrated in Figure 2.1. If the LNT holds for low doses, then a general rule of thumb for

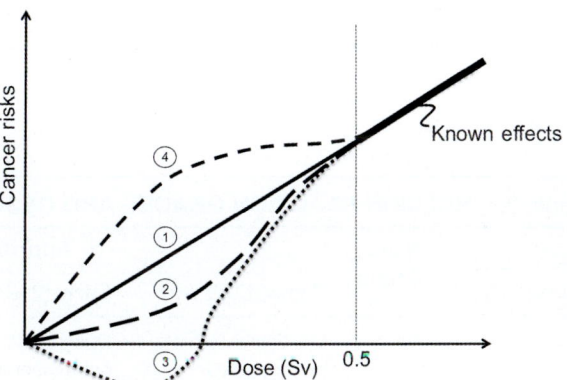

FIG. 2.1 • Illustration of different cancer risks versus dose relationships at low doses that have been derived from human and animal studies.[19] Curve 1 is known as the linear no-threshold (LNT) model. In this model, it is assumed that the risk of cancer formation is directly proportional to the dose. Most recommending bodies related to radiation safety recommend the LNT model for solid cancer formation induced by low doses of ionizing radiation. Curve 2 is the linear-quadratic (LQ) model. There is significant evidence to support that the LQ model best represents radiation-induced leukemia risk. Several investigations in humans and animals have also demonstrated a hormesis effect as shown in curve 3, where below some dose threshold radiation exposures to humans have produced a positive benefit. Finally, supralinear responses as shown in curve 4 where hypersensitivity of risk is expected at low doses have also been documented.

fatal cancer risk of 5% per sievert effective dose for a working adult has been proposed. For more detailed risk calculation methods, one should refer to the Biological Effects of Ionizing Radiation (BEIR) Report VII.[20]

Skin Burns

Skin reactions from ionizing radiation have been well documented, particularly from external beam radiation therapy. Factors that impact the severity of the skin reaction include total dose, time interval between incremental exposures (known as dose fractionation), and size of the irradiated area on the patient. The most sensitive site on the patient is the anterior portion of the neck followed by the flexor portion of the extremities, the trunk, the back, the extensor surfaces of the extremities, the back of the neck, the scalp, and the palms of the hands and soles of the feet, in that order.[21] Skin reactions include damage to the epidermis, dermis, and subcutaneous tissue. Skin reaction from diagnostic imaging can be classified by severity following the NCI Skin Reaction Grade, as shown in Table 2.1.[21] This classification also considers the approximate time of onset of the effects. Prompt reactions occur within 2 weeks following exposure, early reactions occur 2 to 8 weeks after exposure, midterm reactions occur 6 to 52 weeks after exposure, and long-term reactions occur more than 40 weeks after exposure.

Cataracts

Severe adverse effects to the eye from radiation were reported within years after the discovery of X-rays,[22] and cataract formation was one of the earliest effects observed among atomic bomb survivors.[23,24] It is now well known that the subcapsular lens epithelium, particularly where it differentiates to lens fibers, is susceptible to radiation damage. The development of radiation-induced cataracts is dependent on radiation dose, dose rate, and age of the lens[25] and is a known late effect from radiation exposure.[26–29] While the current guidelines for the threshold dose of cataract formation ranges from 2 to 5 Gy, recent studies indicate that the dose could be less than 0.5 Gy on the basis of evidence from various exposure situations.[30,31] There is also strong evidence that cataract risk is better described by an LNT model.[30] While limited data are available on cataract formation resulting from diagnostic exposures, studies have indicated that very low doses can lead to cataract formation 25 years or more after exposure.[32]

Pacemakers

Although not a direct biologic effect in patients, radiation damage to pacemakers can lead to serious health implications. It is well known that pacemakers are sensitive to ionizing radiation. Most pacemakers use small electronic circuits known as complementary-metal-oxide semiconductor (CMOS) circuits to detect, using leads connected to the heart muscle, the electrical activity of the heart. If a deficient signal is detected, then the pacemaker will automatically stimulate heart pumping to return the heart to normal function. The electronic component responsible for detecting the electrical activity of the heart is the CMOS. Given a similar effect is induced in a CMOS by free electrons produced from X-ray interactions, the radiation dose deposited in a CMOS circuit can induce spurious signals that adversely affect pacemaker operation. It was once generally believed that the radiation doses received from diagnostic imaging were not high enough to induce deleterious effects in pacemakers, unlike in external beam radiation therapy where pacemaker dose is a significant concern.[33] However, recent investigations found that adverse events in pacemaker operation can be experienced during CT imaging.[34]

PATIENT SAFETY

Diagnostic imaging continues to make a significant impact on the quality and effectiveness of health care in the United States and worldwide. As more physicians exploit diagnostic imaging for medical procedures and as patient access to advanced diagnostic imaging equipment has improved, the utilization of diagnostic imaging and, in particular, imaging that uses ionizing radiation, has dramatically increased in recent years. In fact, as of 2006, more than 48% of the annual amount of radiation exposure to an average member of the general public in the United States has been due to medical procedures.[35] In contrast, only 15% of the annual exposure was due to medical procedures in the early 1980s.[35] Figure 2.2 compares

Table 2.1 **NCI SKIN REACTION GRADES AND DESCRIPTIONS [21].**

Skin Dose Range (Gy)[a]	NCI Grade	Approximate Time to Onset of Skin Effects			
		Prompt (<2 wk)	Early (2–8 wk)	Midterm (6–52 wk)	Long Term (>40 wk)
0–2	NA	Observable effects not expected	Observable effects not expected	Observable effects not expected	Observable effects not expected
2–5	1	Transient erythema	Epilation	Observable effects not expected	Observable effects not expected
5–10	1–2	Transient erythema	Erythema, epilation	Prolonged erythema, permanent partial epilation	Possible dermal atrophy or induration
10–15	2–3	Transient erythema	Erythema, epilation, possible dry or moist desquamation	Prolonged erythema, permanent epilation	Telangiectasia, dermal atrophy or induration
>15	3–4	Transient erythema; possible edema and acute ulceration		Dermal atrophy, secondary ulceration due to failure of moist desquamation to heal, dermal necrosis	Telangiectasia, dermal atrophy or induration, possible late skin breakdown, wound progression into deeper lesion

[a]Acute dose to single site.

Quality and Safety in Medical Imaging   17

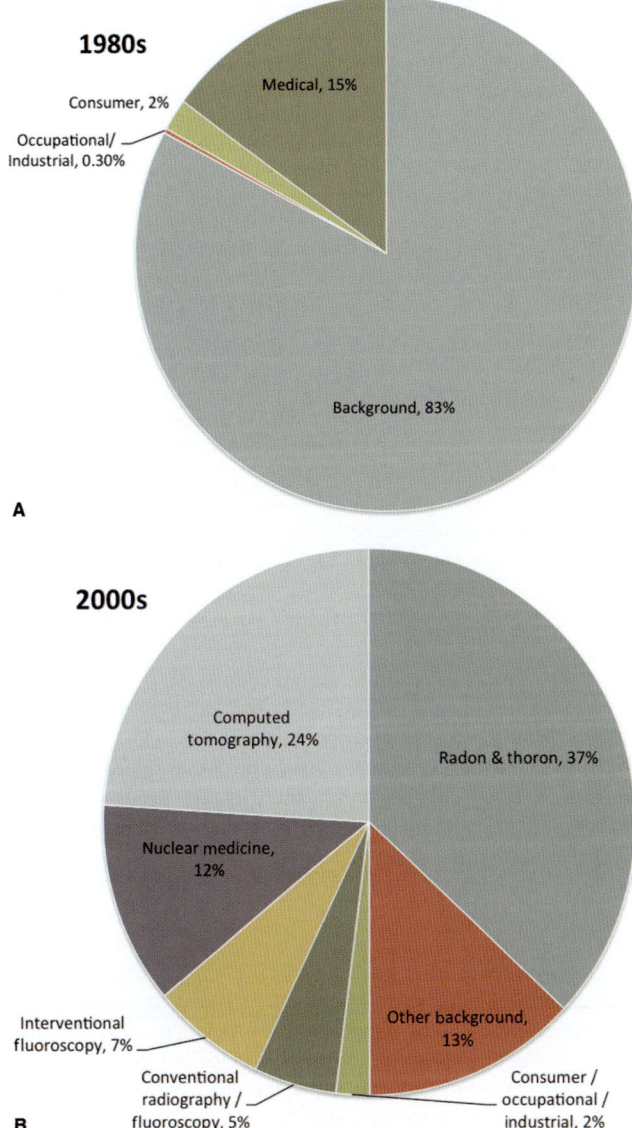

FIG. 2.2 • Percentage contribution of various sources of exposure to the average individual in the United States in the **(A)** 1980s and **(B)** 2000s. (Data extracted from NCRP. *Ionizing Radiation Exposure of the Population of the United States* (Report No. 160). Bethesda, MD; 2009.)

the various types and amounts of annual exposures to the average member of the general public in the United States between the early 1980s and 2006. Primarily due to the rapid rise in medical imaging use, the average annual effective dose to the U.S. population is now roughly 6.2 mSv, and probably higher, which is nearly double the average effective dose reported only two decades earlier.[35]

Conventional Radiographic Examinations

Conventional radiography comprises the largest number of X-ray examinations of patients in the United States. Nearly 300 million conventional scans are performed each year.[35] However, the effective dose from conventional scans is substantially lower than other types of scans and as such conventional scans make up only a small percentage of the average annual effective dose to the population from diagnostic procedures. Typical conventional radiographic units include screen-film imaging receptors, computed radiography, digital radiography, direct x-ray film exposure, and any other type of X-ray imaging system that produces two-dimensional images. Figure 2.3 provides the average effective dose received from different conventional radiography scans.

Except in extremely rare instances, two-dimensional radiographic imaging delivers radiation doses that are far below the thresholds for inducing deterministic effects. Therefore, the main patient safety concern in conventional radiography is to limit the probability of inducing stochastic effects, most notably radiation-induced cancers. Because conventional radiography is the most common form of X-ray examination involving a large number of patients exposed, there is at least a potential for producing a number of stochastic effects in these patients even though individual radiation doses are low. Fortunately, chest radiographs are both the most common and lowest dose X-ray examinations, with about 130 million examinations at an average effective dose of approximately 0.1 mSv. Chest radiographs are a good example of a screening procedure that is low dose, inexpensive, and effective. One of the keys to limiting the number of adverse stochastic effects caused by screening procedures such as this is to ensure that each X-ray examination that is ordered has a clear medical benefit. This can be as simple as checking for previous images that may have recently been taken. Electronic medical records with shared access by different medical providers help to alleviate much of the wasted radiation exposure that has occurred in the past by unnecessarily repeated examinations.

Another way to limit the potential for stochastic effects from radiation exposure is to use the lowest possible dose for each image. Film-screen radiography has largely given way to digital methods, which have the potential to reduce patient dose for a number of reasons. Most digital image receptors have higher absorption efficiency for detecting ionizing radiation, so for the same image quality, fewer X-ray photons and thus a lower radiation dose can be used. In addition, film-screen systems produce good image quality over only a narrow range of radiation dose, which can lead to retakes simply caused by films that are too light or too dark. This does, however, force relatively tight control over the amount of dose that is used. In digital images, on the other hand, the brightness and contrast are freely selectable after the exposure independently of dose, eliminating one important cause of extra radiation dose associated with repeating exposures. Underexposure in a digital image results in increased noise whereas overexposure results in an image with less noise. Because changes in the level of noise are not nearly as apparent as the changes in image brightness and contrast, it is possible to produce images that are diagnostic with much more latitude in the amount of radiation used.

To avoid images that look too noisy, there is a tendency to use a higher-than-necessary radiation dose resulting in "exposure creep" over time.[36] For preventing this, an exposure index is provided with the digital image that indicates the radiation dose to the image receptor. A systematic quality control program that monitors the exposure indices of images and incorporates feedback from the radiologists can be used to produce images with an acceptable level of noise for the diagnostic requirements of the imaging task while using a reasonably low radiation dose.

Computed Tomography

The data presented in Figure 2.1 represent a dramatic shift in the distribution of exposures due to the increased use of diagnostic imaging in medicine. Evidently, the largest contributor to this shift was the surge of CT procedures in the past couple of decades. The

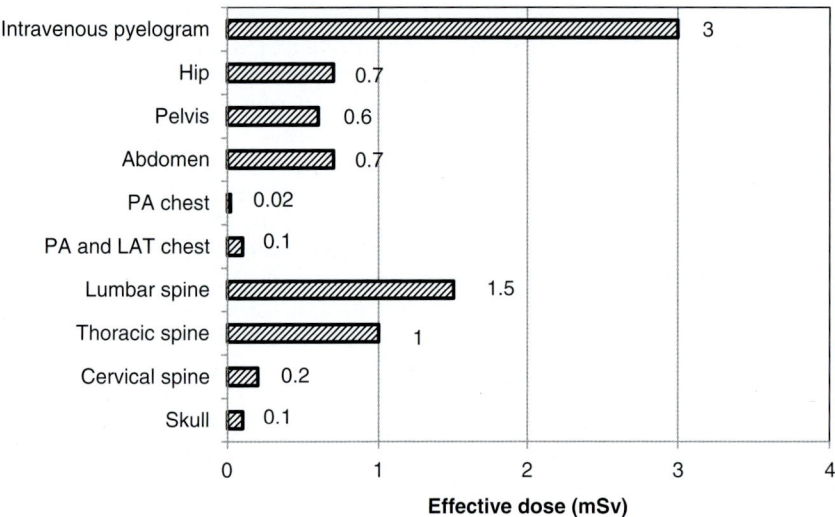

FIG. 2.3 • The average effective dose from various conventional radiography scans. (Data extracted from NCRP. *Ionizing Radiation Exposure of the Population of the United States* (Report 160). Bethesda, MD; 2009.)

annual number of CT procedures in the United States increased from 18.3 million in 1993 to 60 million in 2006, during which the average increase in CT use was greater than 10% per year.[35] This surge has been attributed to the advent of helical CT and multidetector CT scanners (MDCT) that have enabled rapid image acquisitions and a larger volume of patients to be scanned.[35] With these technologies, it is now possible to scan the entire body of a patient in less than 30 s.

Given the large number of CT scans performed each year, a great deal of attention has been afforded to understating the factors that influence radiation dose from CT scans and developing ways to reduce this dose. CT scans require a higher dose than projection radiographs because many more images are produced during each procedure, thus providing much more information about the structures within the patient. A fundamental principle of all X-ray imaging is that more photons are required to produce images with more information whether it involves higher spatial resolution or better contrast resolution. The resolution of projection images is limited to only two dimensions, whereas CT images provide anatomical detail in all three dimensions. This greatly improves the visibility of low-contrast features by eliminating overlap in the images of structures that lie over one another, but does require more radiation dose.

The amount of dose a patient receives from a CT procedure typically depends on both scanner design factors and clinical protocol factors. The dose efficiency of a scanner is defined as the fraction of primary X-rays exiting the patient that contribute to the image.[37] Obtaining maximum sensitivity from a scan for a given dose requires collecting as many primary photons that exit the patient as possible. The dose efficiency is a combination of the geometric and absorption efficiency of the detection system. The geometric efficiency is the fraction of exiting photons interacting with the active volumes of the detector. Loss in geometric efficiency is caused by absorption in the collimation and detector housing. As a result, there is a loss of geometric efficiency when going from a single slice scanner to a multislice scanner as a result of an increase in "dead space" between detectors in these systems. In addition, the beam penumbra in multislice CT scanners is removed to avoid field nonuniformities in the detectors. The absorption efficiency is the fraction of those photons that are collected in the active volume of the detectors. The detector material can influence the absorption efficiency. Therefore, dose reduction can be achieved with improvements in scanner design factors.

Like other digital modalities, increased radiation dose increases the quality of CT images, and so a conscientious effort is needed to ensure that excess dose is not used above that required for diagnostic accuracy. This is accomplished through the development and refinement of clinical scanning protocols, and much effort is now focused on this activity. Current protocols are quite complex because of the advanced capabilities and flexibility of modern CT scanners, the wide variety of examinations performed, and the need to tailor the techniques for different patient sizes. Protocol development requires a team approach involving technologists, medical physicists, and radiologists who each have unique skills and perspectives on the many aspects of the imaging process. Because this is difficult to achieve at each scanning facility, efforts are being made by academic institutions in collaboration with CT manufacturers to develop better protocols to provide with the scanners.

Various clinical protocol factors influence the absorbed dose from a CT, including tube current, slice scan time, tube voltage, slice thickness, and pitch.[37-42] The absorbed dose is directly proportional to the product of the tube current and slice scan time (i.e., doubling the mAs will double the absorbed dose). Increasing the tube voltage can reduce the patient dose because the resulting higher energy X-rays are more penetrating. For higher energy X-rays, the number of photons transmitted through the patient and reaching the detector is greater for a given amount of energy absorbed in the patient. However, higher energy X-rays undergo less photoelectric absorption within the patient, which is the source of contrast in the image. Thus, the contrast is reduced at a high tube voltage. Therefore, there is a clear tradeoff between the image quality and dose when choosing the tube voltage. Variations in patient size and the imaging task can be used to determine the optimal tube voltage for a given CT scan. In addition, on multislice scanners, the absorbed dose is inversely proportional to the pitch of the scan if all other factors remain constant. Recent technological advances have been introduced with the aim of improving image quality while reducing radiation dose. These include automatic exposure control and iterative reconstruction techniques, as well as improved detectors with very high absorption and geometric efficiency.

The amount of absorbed dose delivered during CT imaging, though higher than conventional radiography, is still in the dose range where limiting the probability for stochastic effects is the primary radiation protection concern. Using the LNT model for radiation effects at low doses, some investigators have concluded that CT scans may actually cause a significant number of radiation-induced cancers given the large number of examinations performed each year and the higher radiation dose per examination. A particular concern for pediatric patients was expressed when surveys revealed that many facilities scanned them using protocols designed for adults resulting in higher radiation doses because of the reduced attenuation of their smaller bodies. Pediatric patients are more susceptible to radiation-induced cancers given that there is more time for these cancers to manifest over their lifetime. Considering the high incidence of cancer from many different causes, it is not possible to prove or disprove the hypothesis of radiation-induced cancer at doses used in CT, so the conservative approach is to limit the number of CT examinations performed and the amount of dose per examination.

Deterministic effects are a concern only in patients that undergo numerous CT scans over their lifetime, resulting in significant cumulative radiation exposures. In some cases, it is possible that patients receive doses to the lenses of their eyes that reach the threshold for radiation-induced cataracts. To account for this, many centers use head scanning protocols designed to avoid having the lenses in the direct radiation beam. This is possible in most cases and eliminates this potential adverse effect.

Skin effects can also occur when inappropriate techniques and procedures are used. With the need for a larger radiation dose, and to keep exposure times short to reduce the effects of patient motion, much more powerful X-ray tubes are used in CT than in conventional radiography. This creates the potential for over exposure to radiation with doses that can reach a threshold to produce other deterministic effects, including hair loss and skin reddening. Well-known instances of this occurred when perfusion scanning was done using techniques appropriate for anatomical imaging intended for scans sweeping over the patient, rather than for the repeated images in one location necessary to measure perfusion over time. Because there is a time delay between radiation exposure and the appearance of skin effects, this error was not discovered until a number of patients at several facilities were affected. To prevent this from happening again, CT manufacturers are now required to provide calculated dose information before any scan being taken with warnings and explicit preapprovals required when the dose reaches certain threshold values.

As illustrated in Figure 2.4, the amount of dose a patient has received from a CT scan depends on the area of interest of the patient that is being scanned.[35] This is primarily due to the range of scanning volumes involved in each type of scan. For example, much less mAs is needed to adequately scan the head of a patient, which is one reason why the average effective dose from this procedure is much smaller than other procedures performed in the chest and abdomen.

Screening Procedures

The use of diagnostic imaging for screening has also increased over the last several years. Together with chest radiographs, the most common screening examination performed is mammography for the detection of early stage breast cancers. A woman living in the United States has a one in eight lifetime risk of being diagnosed with breast cancer. Survival rates are 89% at 5 years after diagnosis, 83% after 10 years, and 78% after 15 years. Survival is lower among women with a more advanced stage at diagnosis with a 5-year relative survival at 99% for localized diseases, 85% for regional diseases, and 26% for distant-stage diseases. Larger tumor size at diagnosis is also associated with decreased survival.[43] Although there are known risk factors for breast cancer, most women who develop the disease have only average risk factors, so a universal screening program to detect breast cancer at an early, highly treatable stage with effective therapy is currently the most practical method for controlling breast cancer mortality. Mammography has the ability to detect early breast cancer before it is palpable and is well suited to screening with nearly 9,000 facilities currently performing approximately 39 million mammography examinations annually in the United States.[44]

Mammography examinations involve the use of low energy X-rays (less than 50 keV) to detect lesions within compressed breast tissue. Full-field digital mammography (FFDM) is replacing screen-film

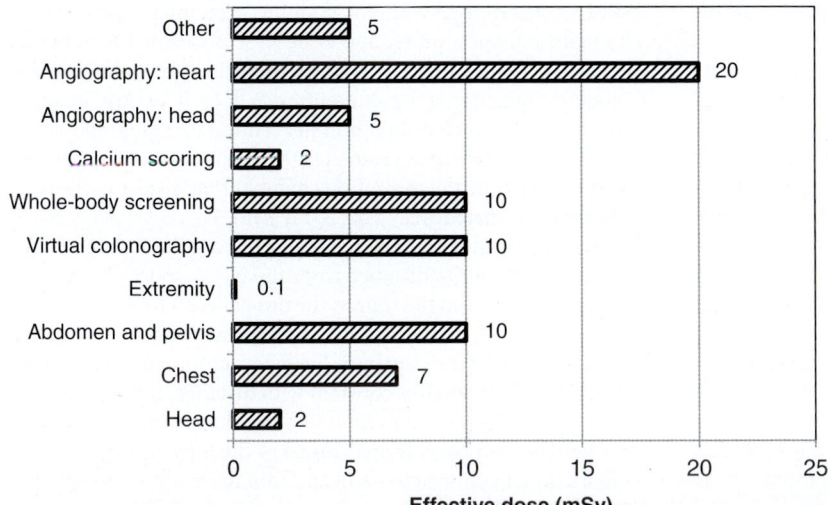

FIG. 2.4 • The average effective dose from several types of CT scans. (Data extracted from NCRP. *Ionizing Radiation Exposure of the Population of the United States* (Report No. 160). Bethesda, MD; 2009.)

mammography where this current technique offers a 20% dose reduction on average compared to its older counterpart.[45] Both scan types typically acquire two primary views per breast. The typical effective dose from a mammography examination is 0.42 mSv.[35]

Given the radiation exposure levels used in mammography, the main radiation protection consideration is the potential for radiation-induced cancer from the large number of examinations performed over a large population. A roughly one in eight lifetime risk for breast cancer implies that in a universal screening program, seven out of eight women undergoing screening examinations are expected to never develop breast cancer. Because of the large number of asymptomatic patients receiving radiation exposures and the fact that breast tissue has a known sensitivity to radiation-induced cancer, it is especially important to maintain radiation dose at a reasonably low level. However, if one calculates the benefit to risk ratio based on the apparent benefits for early detection, it is very high.

It is generally assumed that radiation-induced breast cancers arise in the glandular tissue, and so the quantity of interest in mammographic imaging is usually the average glandular dose and not the effective dose. The average glandular dose is not a quantity that can be measured directly but can be calculated using mathematical models assuming various glandular/fatty tissue compositions and glandular tissue distributions. In practice, breast entrance exposure is measured, and tabulated conversion factors are used to derive the average glandular dose. Current production mammography units display average glandular dose for each view that is taken.

Primarily as a result of concerns about consistency in the quality of mammographic imaging, the Mammography Quality Standards Act (MQSA) was created, which puts into place standards for imaging equipment, quality control practices, and personnel qualifications required for facilities offering mammography screening.[46] A provision of MQSA is to limit the radiation dose that can be given to an average size and composition breast for a single view of a mammography screening examination. The dose limit is 3.0 mGy for a 4.2-cm compressed breast thickness with a 50% glandular/50% fatty breast composition. The national average value is between 1.5 and 1.8 mGy. It has been reduced somewhat with the replacement of nearly all film/screen systems with digital systems. Actual patient doses are a strong function of the thickness and glandular density of the breast because of the low energy X-rays used, so individual patient doses may be considerably different from the average. A standard practice in the United States is to take two views of each breast for a normal screening examination, resulting in a dose approximately two times that of a single view.

Advanced imaging techniques, particularly tomosynthesis imaging, are also being increasingly used for screening mammography. The most commonly used tomosynthesis unit uses the same radiation dose used for a tomosynthesis series as it does for a single-view projection image. On this unit, the tomosynthesis series and projection view together fall just under the regulatory limit of 3.0 mGy per view.

Virtual colonoscopy (also known as virtual colonography) is a CT intervention for the screening of cancer in the colon. Virtual colonoscopy is an accurate and reproducible method for detecting colonic polyps larger than 5 mm in diameter.[47-54] It is currently recommended that screening virtual colonoscopy should be repeated every 5 years according to the joint guidelines of the American Cancer Society, the U.S. Multi-Society Task Force, and the American College of Radiology.[55] A major drawback of virtual colonoscopy is the exposure of the patient to ionizing radiation. Reported effective dose values from virtual colonoscopy range from 1 to 10 mSv.[56,57]

Several investigators have attempted to reduce patient dose from virtual colonoscopy. A significant amount of dose reduction can be achieved by lowering the CT tube voltage and tube current for virtual colonoscopy procedures, especially with the use of MDCT.[58-60] For example, in a large nationwide trial on virtual colonoscopy ran by the American College of Radiology Network (ACRIN), patients were scanned using a protocol consisting of 50 mA and 120 kV, which led to lower doses to the patients compared to older techniques, but with clinically acceptable sensitivities and specificities.[51] Also, improved iterative image reconstruction techniques have also been shown to reduce dose from virtual colonoscopy.[61]

Fluoroscopy-Guided Interventions

Many procedures have been developed using various tools that are inserted through catheters to provide fluoroscopically guided minimally invasive interventions. Some of these procedures are highly complex, requiring a substantial amount of live X-ray imaging time with high resolution, low noise, and in some cases high frame rates. In most cases, the fluoroscope geometry is either a single plane or biplane system mounted on one or two multirotational c-arms. The area of interest in the patient is placed near the center of rotation (isocenter) of the c-arm so that it can be easily viewed from different angles as needed during the procedure. It is not uncommon for an interventional procedure to use more than an hour of live fluoroscopy time with additional recorded images. Figure 2.5 provides the average effective dose from various interventional fluoroscopy examinations. As will be discussed in the next section, the major patient safety concern for interventional fluoroscopy is skin reactions.

The X-ray tubes used in dedicated interventional fluoroscopes are similar to those used in CT scanners, so with the protracted exposure times, especially with large patients, skin doses can be very high. The pictures in Figure 2.6 depict the time course in an extreme case where the dose is estimated to have been very much higher than is normally seen.[62] They do illustrate, however, the fact that the most severe reactions, if they do occur, are delayed for a number of weeks following the procedure.

Because there are relatively few of these procedures performed compared with other X-ray examinations, and they are performed on patients who benefit greatly from the result of the intervention and the minimally invasive nature of the procedure, the small risk of a stochastic effect that may occur many years later is much less of a concern than with, for example, screening examinations. The main radiation protection issue in this case is the potential for causing deterministic effects in the skin. Thus, the relevant dosimetric quantity is the skin entrance dose. The dose quantity that is actually measured on an interventional angiography unit, however, is the dose area product (DAP). The X-ray tube collimator contains a thin, flat ionization chamber that measures the dose within the collimated area of the X-ray field. This is proportional to the dose at a point within the field multiplied by its area. The DAP is independent of the distance from the X-ray source because as one moves away from the source, the dose falls off by a factor equal to the inverse square of the distance whereas the area of the field increases with distance squared. The two factors cancel each other out, and the DAP remains constant with distance. If the area of the X-ray field on the patient's skin is known, along with the DAP, one can calculate the skin entrance dose. For dosimetric purposes, the patient's skin is assumed to be 15 cm from the isocenter toward the X-ray source. This is termed the interventional reference point. The DAP is divided by the field size at this point to obtain an estimate

Quality and Safety in Medical Imaging 21

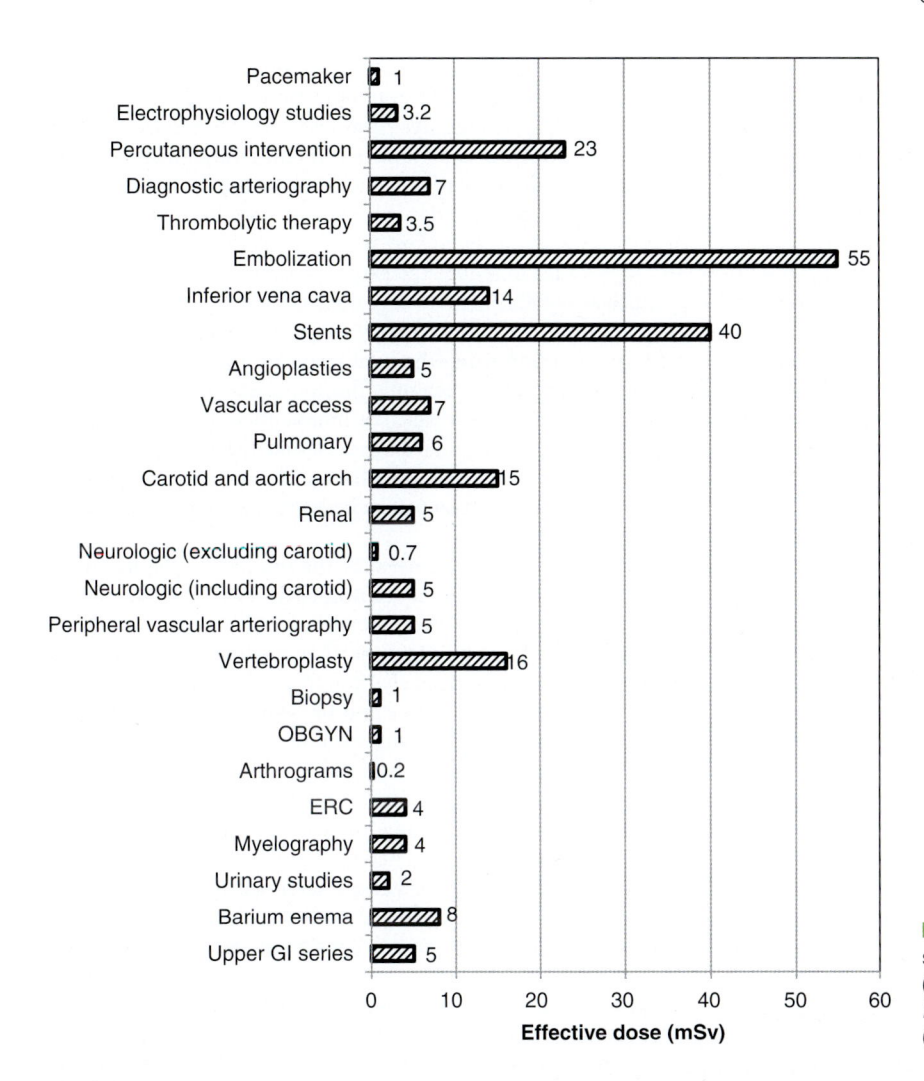

Procedure	Effective dose (mSv)
Pacemaker	1
Electrophysiology studies	3.2
Percutaneous intervention	23
Diagnostic arteriography	7
Thrombolytic therapy	3.5
Embolization	55
Inferior vena cava	14
Stents	40
Angioplasties	5
Vascular access	7
Pulmonary	6
Carotid and aortic arch	15
Renal	5
Neurologic (excluding carotid)	0.7
Neurologic (including carotid)	5
Peripheral vascular arteriography	5
Vertebroplasty	16
Biopsy	1
OBGYN	1
Arthrograms	0.2
ERC	4
Myelography	4
Urinary studies	2
Barium enema	8
Upper GI series	5

FIG. 2.5 • The average effective dose from several interventional fluoroscopy procedures. (Data extracted from NCRP. *Ionizing Radiation Exposure of the Population of the United States* (Report No. 160). Bethesda, MD; 2009.)

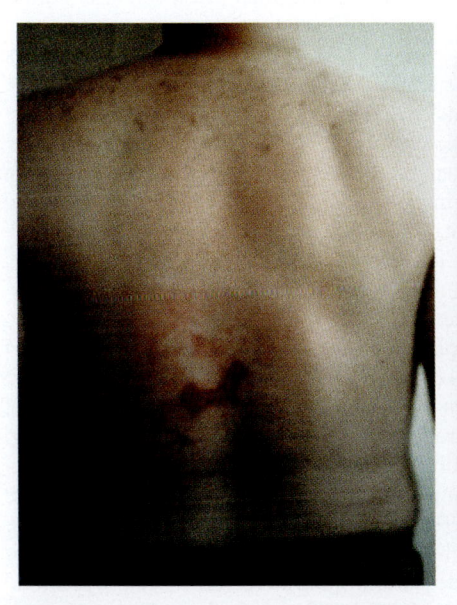

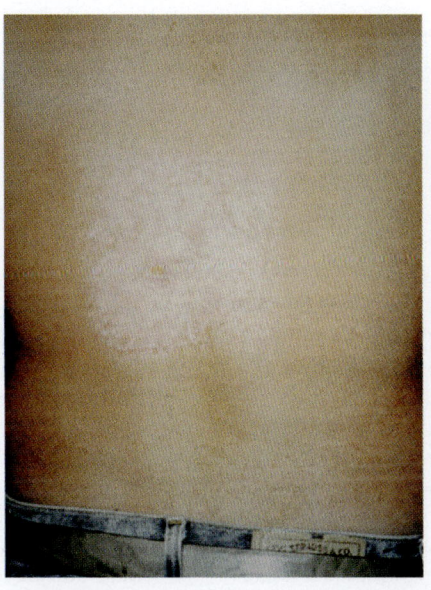

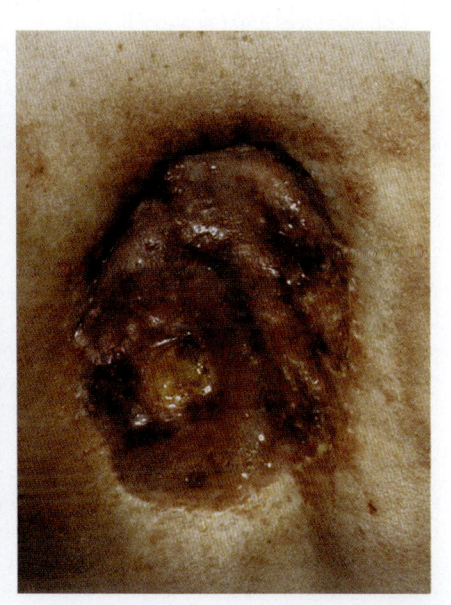

FIG. 2.6 • Skin injuries at 6 to 8 weeks, 12 to 16 weeks, and 18 to 21 weeks following a very high-dose interventional procedure. (Data extracted from NCRP. *Radiation Dose Management for Fluoroscopically-Guided Interventional Medical Procedures* (Report No. 169). Bethesda, MD: National Council of Radiaiton Protection and Measurement; 2010.)

the skin entrance dose. The dose at the interventional reference point along with the DAP and total fluoroscopy time is displayed throughout the procedure and may be used to estimate whether or not the threshold for deterministic skin effects is being approached or exceeded. If the apparent skin dose becomes very high during a procedure, it is sometimes possible to use a different view angle so that the dose to any one part of the skin is less likely to be seriously affected. The dose at the interventional reference point is nearly always an overestimate of the maximum skin dose because the X-ray field is not stationary during the entire procedure.

With the potential for skin injury resulting from interventional procedures, the Food and Drug Administration (FDA) advises that facilities develop procedures for managing dose and patient care in the event that the radiation dose does approach the threshold for skin injury. Facilities generally set a threshold level for dose at the interventional reference point that triggers follow-up care. A typical threshold dose that is used is 5 Gy. The follow-up procedures may include providing patients with information on what effects may occur, what to look for, and what precautions to take, contacting the patient either by phone or in person if they are in the clinic for follow-up care 1 week and 1 month after the procedure to determine if any reactions have occurred, and possible referral to dermatology services in an extreme case. Interventional reference doses at or near 5 Gy, however, rarely produce any discernable skin reactions. Efforts are underway to provide maps of skin dose because of the high level of uncertainty when using the interventional reference dose to estimate the skin entrance dose.

PERSONNEL SAFETY

Radiation safety practice in diagnostic imaging is not only needed for regulatory compliance but also essential to protect workers, patients, and members of general public from harmful exposures to ionizing radiation. For an excellent review on radiation safety practice for diagnostic radiology personnel, the reader should refer to The AAPM/RSNA Physics Tutorial for Residents.[63] In general, there are three guiding tenants of radiation safety:

1. Justification: no practice shall be carried out unless its introduction produces a net positive benefit.
2. Optimization: all exposures shall be kept as low as reasonably achievable, economic and social factors being taken into account.
3. Limitation: the dose received to individuals shall not exceed dose limits established by the individuals governing regulatory body.

Justification

It is generally assumed that the first tenant is often established for most medical procedures. However, one could argue that individual patient safety issues addressed in the previous section could be classified as justification concerns. Radiation safety practice in the hospital usually deals with optimization and limitation.

Optimization

Optimization of radiation exposures is of principle importance to radiation safety practice in diagnostic radiology. The concept of ALARA (as low as reasonably achievable) is based on minimizing the total *cost* of an operational procedure dealing with radiation or a design feature of a designated radiation room or facility, where the total *cost* is the sum of the cost of achieving a certain level of radiation protection and the cost of the corresponding detriment.

Cost is used here in a mathematical sense as an optimization parameter, which may or may not imply monetary cost.

In general, there are three parameters used to reduce the dose levels from ionizing radiation that include time, distance, and shielding. The duration of a diagnostic exam is proportional to the amount of occupational dose received by a worker in the vicinity of the examination. Therefore, it is desirable for both the patient and the worker to reduce the exposure times of the examination as much as possible without degrading the quality of the examination. For example, in fluoroscopy reduced personnel dose can be achieved by minimizing the total beam-on time by the optimal use of the exposure switch only during times when the operator is actively viewing the image. For interventional procedures, it is desirable to reduce the total amount of time the worker is near the interventional unit. When possible and feasible, workers should avoid using mobile units at patient beds when a room with a control booth is available.

Increasing the distance between the source of radiation and a worker decreases the amount of absorbed dose to the worker during a given scanning procedure. If the source under consideration can be approximated by a point source, then the intensity of radiation seen by the worker is inversely proportional to the square of the distance separating the source and the worker. In practice, most sources cannot be approximated by a point source so that the intensity of radiation falls off less rapidly than with a point source. There are multiple sources of radiation that contribute to the dose to a worker during an examination, which need to be considered in situations when personnel need to be in the room during a procedure (e.g., fluoroscopy) or when shielding is being designed. In general, the sources are classified as either the primary radiation or stray radiation. Stray radiation consists of the leakage radiation, patient scatter radiation, and secondary scatter radiation. Leakage radiation includes the small amount of radiation that leaks from the housing of the X-ray tube during a procedure. Patient scatter radiation results from primary beam scatter in the patient. While the amount will vary depending on beam energy, it can be assumed that roughly 5% to 15% of the primary beam is transmitted through the patient. The remaining portion of the beam is either absorbed or scattered. In addition, the transmitted beam can also scatter off barriers behind the patient leading to a source of secondary scatter radiation.

The third parameter to reduce dose levels from ionizing radiation is shielding. Shielding refers to the use of protective barriers that are used to attenuate radiation fields down to acceptable dose levels. The NCRP Report 147 provides several recommendations for shielding X-ray imaging facilities. The report recommends a shielding design goal of 0.1 mGy per week for controlled areas and 0.02 mGy per week for uncontrolled areas. Controlled areas are limited access areas in which the occupational exposure to a worker is under surveillance. These are typically areas in close proximity to where X-ray equipment is used. Uncontrolled areas are all other areas in the hospital or clinic and the surrounding environment. The shielding design process involves solving for an appropriate barrier thickness to reduce the dose levels down to these shielding design goals by making use of information regarding the imaging modality that is being shielded and radiation transmission data for a variety of different shielding barriers. Lead is often used as a primary shielding barrier although concrete and wallboard can sometimes provide adequate shielding for certain imaging modalities.

When it is necessary and justified to have medical personnel inside the room, such as in interventional radiology, the use of personal protective gear is recommended or required. Such gear includes lead aprons, skirts, thyroid shields, and lead-plated eyewear to reduce exposure levels to occupational workers. Note that the necessity of wearing protective gear depends on the workers daily responsibilities, institutional policies, and government regulations.

Limitation

The third tenant of radiation protection is limitation. Various dose limits have been established to ensure that exposures to medical personnel are kept below safe levels. In general, occupational safety from X-ray sources falls under the jurisdiction of the U.S. Occupational Safety and Health Administration. However, in most states, the enforcement of radiation safety and regulation is typically done by state regulatory agencies. The Nuclear Regulatory Commission (NRC) is in charge of regulating radioactive materials that are produced in nuclear reactors as well as the safety of those individuals who are exposed to these materials. It is not uncommon that workers who are exposed to diagnostic X-rays may also be exposed to radioactive materials in the workplace. Therefore, these workers are also regulated by NRC and must comply with NRC rules.

Given the complexity of federal, state, and local regulation of radiation exposures, a nonregulatory organization was created in 1968 to promote consistency in addressing and resolving radiation protection issues in the workplace. This organization is known as the Conference of Radiation Control Program Directors (CRCPD). The CRCPD, whose membership is made up of radiation professionals in the state and local government that regulate the use of radiation sources, has created Suggested State Regulations for Control of Radiation (SSRCR). This document combines all of the federal standards into one document, and it is left up to the states to adopt all or any of the suggested standards.

Most states adopt limitation requirements set forth by the NRC 10 CFR 20 for all occupational workers. These limits are provided in Table 2.2. The total effective dose equivalent is the sum of the deep-dose equivalent from external radiation sources and the effective dose equivalent from internally deposited radiation sources. The deep-dose equivalent is an operational quantity defined as the dose equivalent deposited in 10-mm of tissue. All occupational workers dealing with radiation are required to wear a radiation dosimeter at the location at which the individual will receive the largest dose, typically in the middle of the chest. These dosimeters usually include filters so that the deep-dose equivalent can be measured directly. Also, the dosimeter often includes additional filters that are used to measure the shallow dose equivalent, which is used to predict dose to the skin, and eye dose equivalent, which is used to predict dose to the lens of the eye. In addition, no organ shall receive a dose greater than 0.5 Sv.

Additional Considerations for Pregnant Workers

Given the sensitivity of the embryo or fetus to radiation, additional safety precautions are taken for pregnant workers. The occupational dose to an embryo or fetus must remain below 5 mSv during the entire pregnancy as shown in Table 2.2 with a recommended limit of no more than 0.5 mSv per month. This limit pertains to a woman who voluntarily informs her employer of her pregnancy and the estimated date of conception. Employers are also required to provide instruction on the health effects of exposure to ionizing radiation and precautions and procedures to minimize exposures. The U.S. Nuclear Regulatory Commission's Regulatory Guide 8.13 may be used for this purpose.[64] If applicable, the woman's radiation dose history should be reviewed to determine if her deep-dose equivalent and the dose equivalent to the embryo/fetus resulting from radionuclides are likely to exceed these limits. If not, then she may continue with her current radiation safety practices. A second radiation badge might also be issued that is to be worn at waist level beneath a protective lead apron to better monitor the dose to the embryo/fetus. Also, the worker should be aware that lead aprons are unshielded in the back so that workers should always be facing the radiation source.

DISCUSSION AND CONCLUSION

The primary goals of a radiation safety program for patients and personnel exposed to radiation during diagnostic imaging and image-guided interventional procedures are to limit the probability of stochastic effects and to prevent deterministic effects from occurring. For radiation protection purposes, it is prudent to assume that stochastic effects can occur even at low doses, and that the probability of an effect increases proportionally with the dose. Consequently, the conservative approach to using radiation safely is to keep all radiation doses as low as reasonably achievable (ALARA) while providing necessary care for patients.

In general, radiation dose to both the patient and occupational worker can be minimized by first ensuring that there is a clear medical benefit for each radiographic procedure, and if so, then to use the minimum radiation dose that achieves the objectives of the procedure. For the patient, image quality is often improved with increasing radiation dose, so there is a tradeoff between dose and image quality. The objective of each diagnostic imaging procedure or image-guided interventional procedure should be to use the minimum amount of radiation dose and image quality necessary rather than producing unnecessarily higher quality images by using an excessive amount of radiation in accordance with the ALARA principle.

Given the increased use of diagnostic imaging there has been a greater impetus for addressing and implementing patient safety practices in the clinic. The Image Gently campaign was established in 2007 to advocate for the safe and effective imaging care of pediatric patients. This was soon followed by the establishment of the Image Wisely campaign that was launched by the American College of Radiology (ACR) and the RSNA to raise awareness of opportunities to eliminate unnecessary imaging examinations and to lower the amount of radiation used during adult examinations

Table 2.2 DOSE LIMITS SET FORTH BY THE NRC FOR OCCUPATIONAL WORKERS AND MEMBERS OF THE GENERAL PUBLIC.

Application	Occupational (Sv)	Public (Sv)
Total effective dose equivalent (TEDE)	0.05	0.001
Total organ dose equivalent (TODE)	0.5	
Lens of eye	0.15	
Limbs below elbow or knees	0.5	
Skin averaged over 10 cm^2	0.5	
Fetus	0.005	

to only that needed to produce a useful medical image. Largely due to these efforts, vendors are starting to consider additional forms patient safety technology aimed at more accurately quantifying and reporting radiation dose in the products that they offer. For example, General Electric (GE) now offers a dose-tracking software called DoseWatch (General Electric Company, Waukesha, WI) and Siemens Healthcare offers a similar solution called DoseMAP (Siemens Healthcare GmbH, Erlangen, Germany). Also, the Joint Commission, which is the largest hospital accreditation body in the United States, has established much more stringent radiation dose management standards. It is clear patient safety concerns in diagnostic imaging will remain relevant in years to come.

Of course, the increased use of diagnostic imaging has also placed a greater emphasis on the safety of medical personnel that are exposed to radiation from these procedures. For these workers, it is important to remember that reducing exposure time, increasing distance from the radiation source, and using appropriate shielding can all help to keep dose levels low. These dose-reduction strategies are particularly relevant for the worker involved with fluoroscopy-guided interventions during which high doses can be received. During these interventions, the use of personal protective clothing and equipment should be employed.

With all the benefits radiation affords, there are serious risks to patients and personnel when radiation is not used safely. Radiation safety practices for diagnostic imaging have come a long way since the days when patients were developing severe skin burns following an exam and personnel were developing radiation-induced cancers following several years of occupational exposures from scans before key safety practices were established. However, it is more imperative now than ever to maintain a culture of safety in the clinic so that diagnostic imaging can continue to advance health care and improve the lives of millions of patients.

References

1. Daniel J. The X-rays. *Science.* 1896;3(67):562–563. doi:10.1126/science.3.67.562.
2. Scott N. X-ray injuries. *Am X-ray.* 1897;1:57–76.
3. Codman A. A study of the cases of accidental X-ray burns hitherto recorded. *Phil Med J.* 1902;9:438–442.
4. Tesla N. On the roentgen streams. *Electr Rev.* 1896. Epub December, 11896.
5. Thomson E. Roentgen rays act strongly on the tissues. *Electr Eng.* 1896;22:534.
6. Fuchs W. Simple recommendations on how to avoid radiation harm. *West Electr.* 1896;12.
7. Walsh D. Deep tissue traumatism from roentgen ray exposure. *Br Med J.* 1897;2(1909):272–273.
8. Pfahler G. Shield for the prevention of X-ray burns. *Am X-ray J.* 1901;8(6):917.
9. Pfahler G. Protection in radiology. *Am J Roentgenol Radium Ther.* 1922;9:467.
10. Frieben. Demonstrationveines Cancroid des rechten Handruckens, das sich nach langdauernder Einwirkungvvon Rontgenstrahlen entwickelt hatte. *Fortschr Rontgenstr.* 1902;6:106.
11. Hesse O. *Symptamologie, pathogenese an therapie die rontgenkarzinoms.* Leipzig, Germany: JA Barth; 1911.
12. Krause P. Ein Beitrag zur Kenntnis des Röntgenkarzinoms als Berufskrankheit. *Strahlentherapie.* 1930;35:210.
13. Feygin S. *Du Cancer Radiologique.* Paris: Rousset; 1915.
14. Ledoux-Lebard.*General Meeting of League Franco-Anglo-Americans against Cancer,*Paris; 1922.
15. Clarke R, Valentin J. The history of ICRP and the evolution of its policies. *Ann ICRP.* 2009;39:75. (Publication no. 109.)
16. Taylor L. *X-ray Measurements and Protection, 1913–1964: The Role of the National Bureau of Standards and the National Radiological Organizations.* Washington, DC: National Bureau of Standards, U.S. Government Printing Office;1981.
17. Dixon RL. A new look at CT dose measurement: beyond CTDI. *Med Phys.* 2003;30(6):1272–1280. doi:10.1118/1.1576952.
18. McCollough CH, Leng S, Yu L, et al. CT dose index and patient dose: they are not the same thing. *Radiology.* 2011;259(2):311–316. doi:10.1148/radiol.11101800.
19. Brenner DJ, Doll R, Goodhead DT, et al. Cancer risks attributable to low doses of ionizing radiation: assessing what we really know. *Proc Natl Acad Sci USA.* 2003;100(24):13761–13766. doi:10.1073/pnas.2235592100.
20. Council NR. *Health Risks from Exposure to Low Levels of Ionizing Radiation: BEIR VII—Phase 2.* Washington DC: National Academy of Sciences;2006.
21. Balter S, Hopewell JW, Miller DL, et al. Fluoroscopically guided interventional procedures: a review of radiation effects on patients' skin and hair. *Radiology.* 2010;254(2):326–341. doi:10.1148/radiol.2542082312.
22. Merriam G, Szechter A, Focht E. *The Effects of Ionizing Radiation on the Eye.* Vienna, Austria: International Atomic Energy Agency; 1972.
23. Nakashima E, Neriishi K, Minamoto A. A reanalysis of atomic-bomb cataract data, 2000–2002: a threshold analysis. *Health Phys.* 2006;90(2):154–160.
24. Neriishi K, Nakashima E, Minamoto A, et al. Postoperative cataract cases among atomic bomb survivors: radiation dose response and threshold. *Radiat Res.* 2007;168(4):404–408. doi:10.1667/RR0928.1.
25. Hodge WG, Whitcher JP, Satariano W. Risk factors for age-related cataracts. *Epidemiol Rev.* 1995;17(2):336–346.
26. Hamon MD, Gale RF, Macdonald ID, et al. Incidence of cataracts after single fraction total body irradiation: the role of steroids and graft versus host disease. *Bone Marrow Transplant.* 1993;12(3):233–236.
27. Notter G, Walstam R, Wikholm L. Radiation induced cataracts after radium therapy in children. A preliminary report. *Acta Radiol Diagn (Stockh).* 1966:254(Suppl):87–89.
28. Osman IM, Abouzeid H, Balmer A, et al. Modern cataract surgery for radiation-induced cataracts in retinoblastoma. *Br J Ophthalmol.* 2011;95(2):227–230. doi:10.1136/bjo.2009.173401.
29. Wilde G, Sjöstrand J. A clinical study of radiation cataract formation in adult life following gamma irradiation of the lens in early childhood. *Br J Ophthalmol.* 1997;81(4):261–266.
30. Ainsbury EA, Bouffler SD, Dörr W, et al. Radiation cataractogenesis: a review of recent studies. *Radiat Res.* 2009;172(1):1–9. doi:10.1667/RR1688.1.
31. Blakely EA, Kleiman NJ, Neriishi K, et al. Radiation cataractogenesis: epidemiology and biology. *Radiat Res.* 2010;173(5):709–717. doi:10.1667/RRXX19.1.
32. Ciraj-Bjelac O, Rehani MM, Sim KH, et al. Risk for radiation-induced cataract for staff in interventional cardiology: is there reason for concern? *Catheter Cardiovasc Interv.* 2010;76(6):826–834. doi:10.1002/ccd.22670.
33. Marbach JR, Sontag MR, Van Dyk J, et al. Management of radiation oncology patients with implanted cardiac pacemakers: Report of AAPM Task Group No. 34. American Association of Physicists in Medicine. *Med Phys.* 1994;21(1):85–90. doi:10.1118/1.597259.
34. McCollough CH, Zhang J, Primak AN, et al. Effects of CT irradiation on implantable cardiac rhythm management devices. *Radiology.* 2007;243(3):766–774. doi:10.1148/radiol.2433060993.
35. NCRP. *Ionizing Radiation Exposure of the Population of the United States.* Bethesda, MD;2009.
36. Shepard SJ, Wang J, Flynn M, et al. An exposure indicator for digital radiography: AAPM Task Group 116 (executive summary). *Med Phys.* 2009;36(7):2898–2914. doi:10.1118/1.3121505.
37. Goldman LW. Principles of CT: radiation dose and image quality. *J Nucl Med Technol.* 2007;35(4):213–225; quiz 26–28. doi:10.2967/jnmt.106.037846.
38. McCollough CH. CT dose: how to measure, how to reduce. *Health Phys.* 2008;95(5):508–517. doi:10.1097/01.HP.0000326343.35884.03.
39. McCollough CH, Bruesewitz MR, Kofler JM. CT dose reduction and dose management tools: overview of available options. *Radiographics.* 2006;26(2):503–512. doi:10.1148/rg.262055138.

40. McCollough CH, Primak AN, Braun N, et al. Strategies for reducing radiation dose in CT. *Radiol Clin North Am.* 2009;47(1):27–40. doi:10.1016/j.rcl.2008.10.006.
41. Coakley FV, Gould R, Yeh BM, et al. CT radiation dose: what can you do right now in your practice? *Am J Roentgenol.* 2011;196(3):619–625. doi:10.2214/AJR.10.5043.
42. Sodickson A. Strategies for reducing radiation exposure in multi-detector row CT. *Radiol Clin North Am.* 2012;50(1):1–14. doi:10.1016/j.rcl.2011.08.006.
43. Howlander N, Noone A, Krapcho M, et al. *SEER Cancer Statistics Review, 1975–2012*. Bethesda, MD: National Cancer Institute, 2015.
44. Food and Drug Administration (FDA) U.S. *MQSA National Statistics*. Silver Springs, MD: U.S. FDA;2016.
45. Hendrick RE. Radiation doses and cancer risks from breast imaging studies. *Radiology.* 2010;257(1):246–253. doi:10.1148/radiol.10100570.
46. Code of Federal Regulations (CFR) U.S. *Title 21—Food and Drugs; Chapter I—Food and Drug Administration, Department of Health and Human Services; Subchapter I—Mammography Quality Standards Act. Part 900: Mammography.* Silver Springs, MD: U.S. FDA; 2015.
47. Dachman AH, Kuniyoshi JK, Boyle CM, et al. CT colonography with three-dimensional problem solving for detection of colonic polyps. *Am J Roentgenol.* 1998;171(4):989–995. doi:10.2214/ajr.171.4.9762982.
48. Fenlon HM, Nunes DP, Schroy PC, et al. A comparison of virtual and conventional colonoscopy for the detection of colorectal polyps. *N Engl J Med.* 1999;341(20):1496–1503. doi:10.1056/NEJM199911113412003.
49. Hara AK, Johnson CD, Reed JE, et al. Detection of colorectal polyps with CT colography: initial assessment of sensitivity and specificity. *Radiology.* 1997;205(1):59–65. doi:10.1148/radiology.205.1.9314963.
50. Rex DK, Vining D, Kopecky KK. An initial experience with screening for colon polyps using spiral CT with and without CT colography (virtual colonoscopy). *Gastrointest Endosc.* 1999;50(3):309–313. doi:10.1053/ge.1999.v50.97776.
51. Johnson CD, Chen MH, Toledano AY, et al. Accuracy of CT colonography for detection of large adenomas and cancers. *N Engl J Med.* 2008;359(12):1207–1217. doi:10.1056/NEJMoa0800996.
52. Macari M, Milano A, Lavelle M, et al. Comparison of time-efficient CT colonography with two- and three-dimensional colonic evaluation for detecting colorectal polyps. *Am J Roentgenol.* 2000;174(6):1543–1549. doi: 10.2214/ajr.174.6.1741543.
53. Pescatore P, Glücker T, Delarive J, et al. Diagnostic accuracy and interobserver agreement of CT colonography (virtual colonoscopy). *Gut.* 2000;47(1):126–130.
54. Morrin MM, Farrell RJ, Raptopoulos V, et al. Role of virtual computed tomographic colonography in patients with colorectal cancers and obstructing colorectal lesions. *Dis Colon Rectum.* 2000;43(3):303–311.
55. Levin B, Lieberman DA, McFarland B, et al. Screening and surveillance for the early detection of colorectal cancer and adenomatous polyps, 2008: a joint guideline from the American Cancer Society, the US Multi-Society Task Force on Colorectal Cancer, and the American College of Radiology. *CA Cancer J Clin.* 2008;58(3):130–160. doi:10.3322/CA.2007.0018.
56. Boellaard TN, Venema HW, Streekstra GJ, et al. Effective radiation dose in CT colonography: is there a downward trend? *Acad Radiol.* 2012;19(9):1127–1133. doi:10.1016/j.acra.2012.04.013.
57. Berrington de González A, Kim KP, Knudsen AB, et al. Radiation-related cancer risks from CT colonography screening: a risk-benefit analysis. *Am J Roentgenol.* 2011;196(4):816–823. doi:10.2214/AJR.10.4907.
58. Chang KJ, Caovan DB, Grand DJ, et al. Reducing radiation dose at CT colonography: decreasing tube voltage to 100 kVp. *Radiology.* 2013;266(3):791–800. doi:10.1148/radiol.12120134.
59. Cohnen M, Vogt C, Beck A, et al. Feasibility of MDCT Colonography in ultra-low-dose technique in the detection of colorectal lesions: comparison with high-resolution video colonoscopy. *Am J Roentgenol.* 2004;183(5):1355–1359. doi:10.2214/ajr.183.5.1831355.
60. Iannaccone R, Catalano C, Mangiapane F, et al. Colorectal polyps: detection with low-dose multi-detector row helical CT colonography versus two sequential colonoscopies. *Radiology.* 2005;237(3):927–937. doi:10.1148/radiol.2373041747.
61. Chang KJ, Yee J. Dose reduction methods for CT colonography. *Abdom Imaging.* 2013;38(2):224–232. doi:10.1007/s00261-012-9968-1.
62. NCRP. *Radiation Dose Management for Fluoroscopically-Guided Interventional Medical Procedures* (Report No. 168). Bethesda, MD: National Council of Radiaiton Protection and Measurement;2010.
63. Brateman LF. Radiation safety considerations for diagnostic radiology personnel. *Radiographics.* 1999;19(4):1037–1055. doi:10.1148/radiographics.19.4.g99jl231037.
64. Nuclear Regulatory Commission (NRC) US. *Instruction Concerning Prenatal Radiation Expsure, Regulatory Guide 8.13.* Washington DC: NRC;1999.

SELF-ASSESSMENT QUESTIONS

1. What relationship between dose and solid cancer risk is generally assumed in radiation protection?

   A. Linear–quadratic
   B. Hormesis
   C. Linear no-threshold
   D. Supralinearity
   E. Linear threshold

2. What scanning protocol factors influence the absorbed dose from a CT scan?

   A. Tube current
   B. Slice scan time
   C. Tube peak voltage
   D. Pitch
   E. All of the above

Answers to Chapter Self-Assessment Questions

1. C. For radiation protection purposes, it is generally assumed that a linear no-threshold (LNT) relationship exists between dose and solid cancer risk.

2. E. The tube current, slice scan time, tube peak voltage, and pitch all impact the absorbed dose.

Patient Satisfaction 3

Jeffrey P. Kanne

LEARNING OBJECTIVES

1. Describe approaches to gauging patient satisfaction in radiology
2. List specific aspects of patient experience in radiology and list specific metrics that can be used to evaluate those aspects

Consumer-driven health care has led to patient satisfaction becoming a major point of focus for health-care providers, hospitals and clinics, health-care systems, and even health insurance companies. The Institute of Medicine's 2011 report advocates promoting patient-centered care to deliver more effective health care with fewer errors.[1] In recent years, the radiology profession has made an effort to improve the public's perception of radiology, conveying that radiologists are highly trained physicians who play a significant role in the delivery of health care.[2] Furthermore, the radiology community has been advocating for more patient-centered radiology to maintain the value that radiologists add to human health.[3]

ASSESSING PATIENT SATISFACTION

Patient satisfaction has become a major indicator for hospitals because of the Centers for Medicare and Medicaid Services (CMS) Value-Based Purchasing Program. Beginning in October 2012, CMS instituted a 1% withhold from inpatient payments to participating hospitals, with a gradual increase to 2% by fiscal year 2017.[4] The participating hospitals can recoup their withhold and can potentially earn additional incentive payments from CMS on the basis of performance rankings. Performance scores derived from clinical quality indicators and patient satisfaction metrics account for 70% and 30%, respectively. Patient satisfaction metrics include provider communication, pain management, and overall impression.

The Hospital Consumer Assessment of Healthcare Providers and Systems (HCAHPS) is used in hospitals to survey patients on their inpatient experiences and report results to CMS. In its current form, the HCAHPS survey is designed for patients to evaluate their entire inpatient experience, with focus on communication, pain control, and response times.[5] Specific information for radiology departments is rather lacking. Furthermore, because radiology procedures consist of multiple steps, any of which could impact patient satisfaction, identifying specific practices affecting the patient experience can be difficult using the HCAHPS instrument.

In order for radiologists and radiology administrators to get a better sense of patient satisfaction within their own practices, well-designed survey instruments are necessary to gauge patients' attitudes toward their experience in a radiology department (Table 3.1).[6] While ready-to-use surveys are available, a customized survey will most likely provide the most benefit to an individual practice, as questions can be tailored to the specifics of a radiology department or facility.

When developing projects to improve patient satisfaction, it is best to assess metrics related to patient perception and emotion. Factors such as image quality, quality of interpretation, and health outcomes, while all important to the practice of radiology, are not relevant to the immediate experience of the patient in the radiology department.[6] Rather, quality improvement projects should focus on improving patient perception.

Table 3.1 **COMMON SURVEY METRICS FOR RADIOLOGY DEPARTMENTS.**

Aspect of Patient Experience	Specific Metrics
Registration	Wait time
	Ease of registration
	Helpfulness of front desk staff
Facility	Waiting area comfort
	Cleanliness
Examination	Technology courtesy
	Concern for patient comfort and safety
	Explaining of test
	Answered questions
Personal items	Protecting privacy
	Response to patient needs and complaints

From Kadom N, Nagy P. Patient satisfaction: opportunities for quality improvement. *J Am Coll Radiol*. 2014;11(8):830–831.

Two key points regarding patient perceptions need to be recognized. First, patients may use perceptions as proxies for rating quality of care. For example, in studies of patient satisfaction, Cleveland Clinic reported that when metrics of service quality were lacking, patients used dirty rooms as a proxy for poor-quality care.[7] Second, narration can be used to influence perceptions.[7,8] One example given is surveying patient perception of employee hand washing. If the question is asked, "To what extent did employees wash their hands?" and the sinks are out of view, patients may report a very poor perception of employee hand washing. In contrast, employees can use narration and indicate to patients that a strict guideline is in place across all departments for hand washing and that it is strictly enforced.[6]

CHALLENGES IN RADIOLOGY

One of the major challenges in radiology is a persistent misperception by the public as to what a radiologist is and what he or she does.[9] Several studies have shown that only about half of patients recognize that radiologists are physicians, with the rest often mistaking radiologists for technologists or nurses.[9-11] In contrast to breast imagers and interventional radiologists who have regular patient contact, most radiologists have only limited or no patient contact in their respective practices.[12] A widespread adoption of picture archiving and communication systems (PACS) has resulted in a distributed model of radiology workflow, and the radiologist interpreting a diagnostic imaging study may be located far away from the patient being imaged.[13] Other factors influencing public perception of radiologists is the primary consultant role of the radiologist and the traditional reporting of results to the ordering provider.[14]

References

1. Institute of Medicine CoQoHCiA. *Crossing the Quality Chasm: A New Health System for the 21st Century.* Washington, DC: National Academies Press; 2001.
2. Neiman HL. Face of radiology campaign. *Acad Radiol.* 2009;16(5):517–520.
3. Carlos RC. Patient-centered radiology: the time is now. *Acad Radiol.* 2009;16(5):515–516.
4. Centers for Medicare and Medicaid Services. Hospital value-based purchasing 2014. http://www.cms.gov/Medicare/Quality-Initiatives-Patient-Assessment-Instruments/hospital-value-based-purchasing/index.html?redirect=/hospital-value-based-purchasing/. Accessed May 31, 2016.
5. Centers for Medicare and Medicaid Services. Hospital Consumer Assessment of Healthcare Providers and Systems. Baltimore, MD: Centers for Medicare and Medicaid Services; 2014. http://www.hcahpsonline.org/. Accessed May 31, 2016.
6. Kadom N, Nagy P. Patient satisfaction: opportunities for quality improvement. *J Am Coll Radiol.* 2014;11(8):830–831.
7. Merlino JI, Raman A. Health care's service fanatics. *Harvard Bus Rev.* 2013;91(5):108-16, 50.
8. Lee F. *If Disney ran your hospital: 9 1/2 things you would do differently.* Bozeman, Montana: Second River Healthcare; 2004. 216 p.
9. Miller P, Gunderman R, Lightburn J, Miller D. Enhancing patients' experiences in radiology: through patient-radiologist interaction. *AcadRadiol.* 2013;20(6):778–781.
10. American College of Radiology. The Face of Radiology Campaign Presentation. http://www.mypatientconnection.com/Resources.aspx. Accessed May 31, 2016.
11. Kuhlman M, Meyer M, Krupinski EA. Direct reporting of results to patients: the future of radiology? *Acad Radiol.* 2012;19(6):646–650.
12. Fritzsche PJ. Communication: the key to improved patient care. *Radiology.* 2005;234(1):13–14.
13. Gunderman RB. Commodity or profession? *J Am Coll Radiol.* 2008;5(4):540–543.
14. Margulis AR, Sostman HD. Radiologist-patient contact during the performance of cross-sectional examinations. *J Am Coll Radiol.* 2004;1(3):162–163.

SELF-ASSESSMENT QUESTIONS

1. Which is the single *biggest* contributor to hospital performance scores in the CMS Value-Based Purchasing Program?

   A. Patient satisfaction metrics
   B. Clinical quality indicators
   C. Case mix index
   D. Number of malpractice claims

2. Which of the following metrics is commonly used to measure *patient satisfaction* in a radiology department?

   A. Report turn-around time
   B. Radiation exposure
   C. Protection of privacy
   D. Availability of newest technology

Answers to Chapter Self-Assessment Questions

1. B. Seventy percent of performance scores for the CMS Value-Based Purchasing Program are derived from clinical quality indicators, and 30% comes from patient satisfaction scores. Case mix indices are used to define the acuity and complexity of a hospital's patient population to use for benchmarking. Malpractice claims are not taken into consideration in the CMS Value-Based Purchasing Program.

2. C. Patient privacy is an important satisfaction metric for any health-care practice, not only for regulatory (HIPAA) reasons but also for patient perception. Although patients expect results in a timely manner, results of diagnostic imaging tests usually come from the ordering provider, who may or may not be the rate-limiting step in conveying results to patients. Patients may be concerned about radiation exposure, but this metric is better focused on patient safety than on satisfaction. Patients may be interested in new technology but satisfaction is more focused on having the right test.

Report Turn-Around Time

4

Jeffrey P. Kanne

LEARNING OBJECTIVES

1. Define report turn-around time and describe its importance in the context of all stakeholders
2. Describe the advantages and disadvantages of voice recognition software in radiology
3. List methods to improve report turn-around time

For many stakeholders, the major work product of a radiology department is the official or final radiology report. Referring health-care providers rely on diagnostic imaging test results to diagnose patients and make treatment decisions,[1] and delays in result reporting can lead to dissatisfaction among referring providers and their patients.

Radiology report turn-around time (TAT) is one metric that is frequently used as marker of radiologist efficiency. The definition of TAT varies and must be viewed in the eyes of the primary stakeholder (Table 4.1). For example, the referring health-care provider may consider TAT as the time from when an order for diagnostic imaging study is placed until the time when results are received. In contrast, the radiologist typically views TAT as the time from when a study is complete and available for interpretation until final signature.

Traditionally, medical transcriptionists typed the dictated report and returned a hardcopy for the radiologist's signature. Edits were made by hand, and the corrected reports were retyped and then resubmitted for signatures. Signed reports were then delivered, by hand or mail, to referring physicians, who subsequently discussed results with patients in person or by telephone. With the widespread adoption of fax machines in the 1980s, final reports could be delivered more quickly to referring physicians, avoiding the inherent delays in hand delivery and mail. As computer technology evolved, transcribed reports could be entered into computer systems and queued for radiologists to sign electronically. Electronic reports could even be transmitted to some fledgling electronic health records (EHRs).

Rapid adoption of picture archiving and communication systems (PACS) in the 2000s and improved integration between radiology information systems (RIS) and hospital information systems (HIS) over the past two decades have led to near-universal electronic archiving and transmission of diagnostic imaging studies and their respective reports. Because one of the goals of the EHR is to improve patient safety through effective communication,[2] notifications are typically sent to referring health-care providers when imaging or laboratory test results are available so that they can be reviewed and appropriately acted upon. More sophisticated implementations of PACS or EHR include electronic notification applications for critical or urgent results.[3]

VOICE RECOGNITION TRANSCRIPTION

Voice recognition (VR) software for radiology, first described in 1981,[4] also benefited from advancing computer technology and became a core part of the informatics revolution in diagnostic radiology in the 2000s.[5] Growth in VR technology was also fueled by increasing demands from patients, referring physicians, and administrators for faster TAT.[6]

Advantages of VR include decreased radiologist TAT because final reports can be issued immediately following interpretation of the diagnostic examination. In one study performed at a 150-bed community hospital, investigators found a 24-fold decrease in median report TAT following implementation of VR without significant effect on normalized radiologist productivity.[7] Other studies have also showed improved report TAT from implementation of VR.[8–10] At one large urban hospital, implementation of VR not only resulted in decreased radiology report TAT but also increased referring physician satisfaction scores and Hospital Consumer Assessment of Healthcare Providers and Systems (HCAHPS) scores rating patient satisfaction. Furthermore, the practice reduced transcription costs from US$30,000 per month to fewer than US$300 per month.[11]

Table 4.1 **DEFINITIONS OF REPORT TURN-AROUND TIME IN THE CONTEXT OF DIFFERENT STAKEHOLDERS.**

Stakeholder	Start time	End time
Radiologist	Completion of examination	Final report signature
Referring provider	Order for examination placed	Receipt of final report
Patient	Time of examination	Communication of results
Administrator	Time of examination	Claim or bill submitted

The ability to use templates and structured reporting has also been touted as an advantage of VR,[12] potentially reducing diagnostic and transcription errors and improving radiologist productivity. Newer software packages allow practices to link specific dictation templates to procedural codes,[13] enabling the reporting radiologist to use a standard report format with prepopulated text, the latter of which can be edited to reflect abnormal or additional findings on the examination being interpreted. In one single-institution study investigating the impact of standardized reporting templates, researchers found that the use of prepopulated report templates did not significantly affect dictation time or error rates. Interestingly, the authors did note that radiologists in the study showed a strong preference for using the standardized templates, contradicting previous arguments that standardized reporting goes against the radiologist's professional autonomy to dictate freely.[14]

Nevertheless, despite all of the potential advantages of employing VR for diagnostic radiology reporting, some radiologists remain dissatisfied with the technology. One of the major criticisms of VR is real or perceived negative impact on radiologist productivity. Because VR transitions editing tasks from transcriptionist to radiologist, more physician time is spent on tasks other than image interpretation. One study demonstrated a 50% increase in report dictation time despite a 24% decrease in report length.[15] Furthermore, the authors also estimated a US$6.10 increase in cost per case using VR as compared with traditional transcription, on the basis of the fact that radiologist time, rather than transcriptionist time, was being used for editing.

Another criticism of VR is high rate of transcription errors in diagnostic radiology reports. One study of two radiologists dictating 100 magnetic resonance imaging (MRI) reports, 50 with VR and 50 with standard transcription, showed that 30% to 42% of the VR reports contained errors in contrast to only 6% to 8% of transcription-generated reports. Furthermore, the authors showed a decline in productivity to 8.6 MRI reports an hour using VR, down from 13.3 MRI reports an hour using transcription.[16] Another study showed that 22% of reported imaging studies had potentially confusing transcription errors and, more importantly, that radiologists greatly underestimated the rate of errors in their reports.[17] Not only can these errors imply that the radiologist was not paying attention to detail,[14] but also the meaning of a report could dramatically change. For example, "There is no pulmonary embolism" could be incorrectly transcribed "There is pulmonary embolism."

Some commercial VR systems have included a "send-to-editor" function as a solution for problems with report editing and radiologist productivity. This allows the radiologist to dictate a report into the VR system, with or without the use of templates, and send the transcribed report and accompanying audio file to an editor, who can review the report for errors compared against the audio recording, make any necessary corrections, and return the report to the radiologist for final review and signature.[18] However, this workflow requires the added expense of employing transcriptionists, and TAT may be adversely affected (Table 4.2).

MEASURING TAT

A radiology practice can decide to define and measure TAT. Reports can usually be run from data derived from the RIS or from VR software databases. Minimum, maximum, mean, and median report TATs can be extracted (Figs. 4.1 and 4.2). Using median TAT may be preferable over mean TAT because the former avoids penalizing radiologists who report on studies performed afterhours

Table 4.2 **ADVANTAGES AND DISADVANTAGES OF VOICE RECOGNITION SOFTWARE.**

Advantages	Disadvantages
Final signature at time of imaging study review	Higher rate of transcription errors
Decreased report turn-around time	Radiologist time used for clerical tasks instead of image interpretation
Use of templates and structured reports	Real or perceived decrease in radiologist productivity

or those reports that may be delayed because of postprocessing such as cardiac MRI. Comparison of radiologist TAT should be limited to members of groups with similar workflows. For example, a hospital-based radiologist reporting on a large percentage of routine inpatient studies performed afterhours will likely have a longer TAT than a radiologist working exclusively at an outpatient center reporting on studies as they are performed.

Specific subspecialties require certain considerations, as well. Report TAT in interventional radiology should not be benchmarked against TAT for diagnostic imaging given the complexity of the former's cases, complexities of coding requirements, and detail required in reports. Instead of report TAT, promptness of procedure notes in the EHR can be measured for interventional radiology. Likewise, measuring TAT in breast imaging can be complicated because screening mammograms are often interpreted in batches, sometimes at a central location, and results of diagnostic mammograms and breast ultrasound are often communicated directly to the patient at the time of the examination.

Benchmarks for diagnostic imaging report TAT can vary depending on the type of patient being imaged. For example, radiology report TAT is extremely important in the emergency department (ED), where length of stay (LOS) is an important quality metric to hospitals and ED physicians.[19] Imaging results are often used in the ED to assist in triaging patients, and delays in radiology TAT can result in increased LOS. Many radiology practices set an expected TAT for ED examination, usually between 20 and 60 min, depending on the type of study (Fig. 4.3). In contrast, routine outpatient imaging studies are usually less urgent, and a 12-to-24-hour TAT may be sufficient. However, with increasing focus on patient-centered care, many patients, particularly those with chronic medical conditions such as cancer, go straight from their diagnostic imaging appointment to their clinic appointment, where lab and imaging results are expected to be available so that patients can be informed of the results and subsequent treatment decisions can be made.

IMPROVING TAT

The impetus to reduce radiology report TAT may come from hospital administrators, referring health-care providers, or practice managers. However, before embarking on a performance improvement project to reduce radiology report TAT, a practice must first measure its current performance, looking at overall, section or practice group, and individual data. To successfully implement a project to reduce TAT, a project team consisting of stakeholders should first be assembled. The team may consist of departmental physician leaders, technologists, information technology personnel, transcriptionists,

Radiologist Turn-Around-Time (TAT) in Hours (2014)

	Jan	Feb	Mar	Apr	May	Jun	Jul	Aug	Sep	Oct	Nov	Dec
Diagnostic Section												
Abdominal	3.10	3.43	2.84	3.42	3.18	3.03	3.64					
Chest and cardiovascular	2.71	2.26	2.17	2.16	2.15	2.05	2.86					
Community	0.97	1.11	1.04	1.14	1.05	0.96	1.03					
Musculoskeletal	2.28	2.22	2.85	3.78	1.43	1.97	3.01					
Neuroradiology	7.70	6.19	7.80	6.48	4.91	6.37	4.42					
Nuclear medicine	2.42	2.30	2.23	2.26	2.17	2.38	2.60					
Pediatric	2.33	1.41	1.78	1.57	1.80	1.69	3.26					

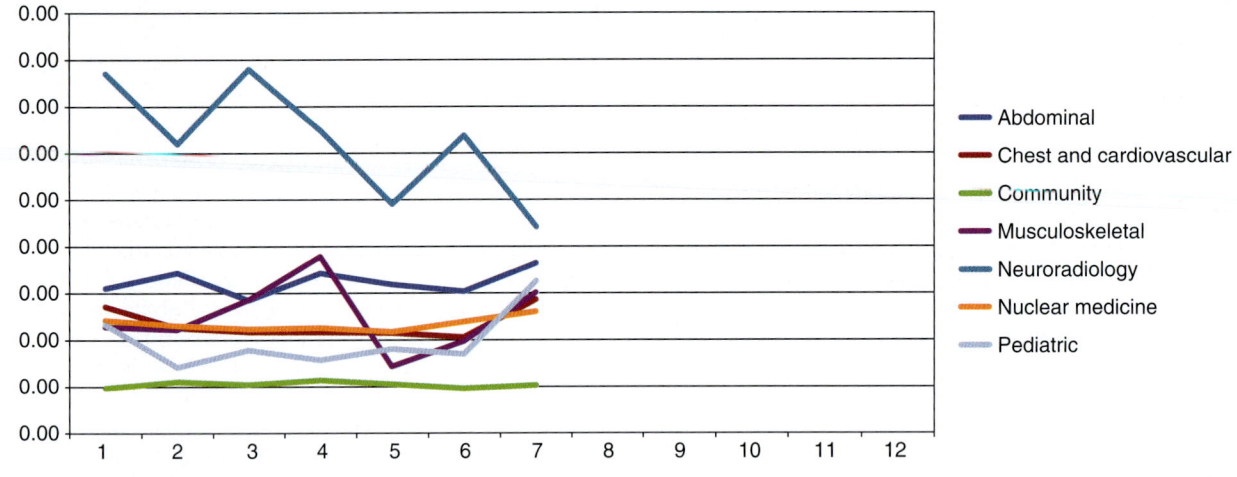

FIG. 4.1 • Sample TAT report comparing median TAT for an academic subspecialty diagnostic radiology department. *Note:* The slight uptick in median TAT in July, corresponding to the start of new residents and fellows.

Radiologist Turn-Around-Time (TAT) in Hours

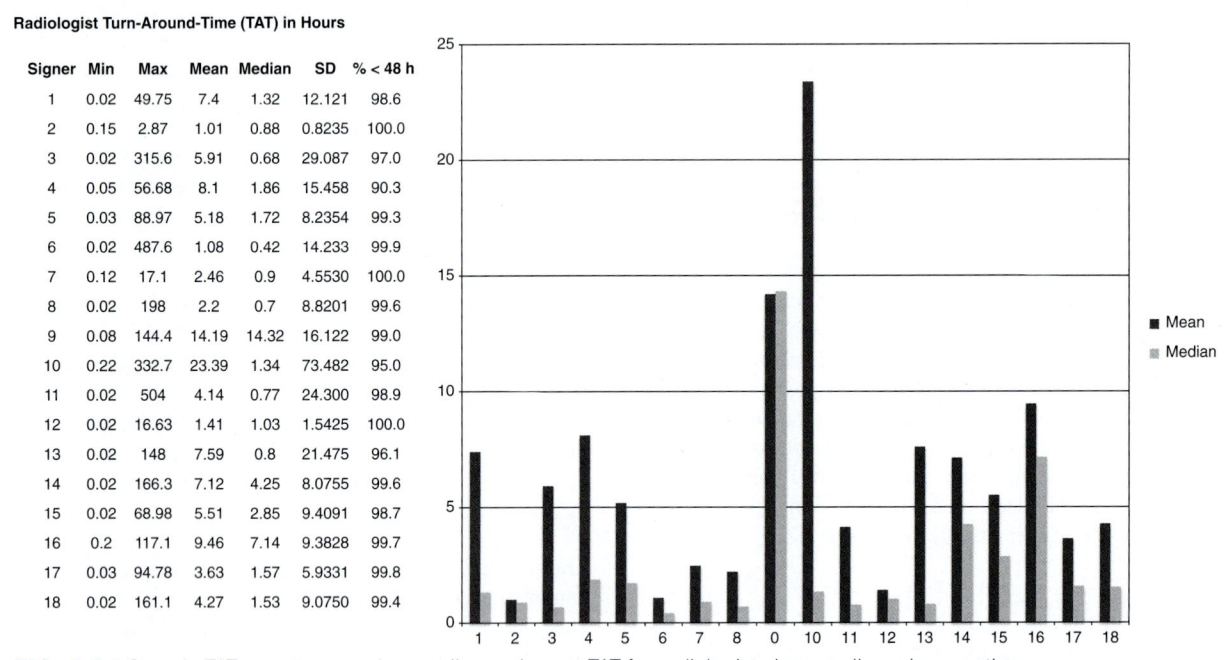

Signer	Min	Max	Mean	Median	SD	% < 48 h
1	0.02	49.75	7.4	1.32	12.121	98.6
2	0.15	2.87	1.01	0.88	0.8235	100.0
3	0.02	315.6	5.91	0.68	29.087	97.0
4	0.05	56.68	8.1	1.86	15.458	90.3
5	0.03	88.97	5.18	1.72	8.2354	99.3
6	0.02	487.6	1.08	0.42	14.233	99.9
7	0.12	17.1	2.46	0.9	4.5530	100.0
8	0.02	198	2.2	0.7	8.8201	99.6
9	0.08	144.4	14.19	14.32	16.122	99.0
10	0.22	332.7	23.39	1.34	73.482	95.0
11	0.02	504	4.14	0.77	24.300	98.9
12	0.02	16.63	1.41	1.03	1.5425	100.0
13	0.02	148	7.59	0.8	21.475	96.1
14	0.02	166.3	7.12	4.25	8.0755	99.6
15	0.02	68.98	5.51	2.85	9.4091	98.7
16	0.2	117.1	9.46	7.14	9.3828	99.7
17	0.03	94.78	3.63	1.57	5.9331	99.8
18	0.02	161.1	4.27	1.53	9.0750	99.4

FIG. 4.2 • Sample TAT report comparing median and mean TAT for radiologists in a medium-size practice.

Report Turn-Around Time

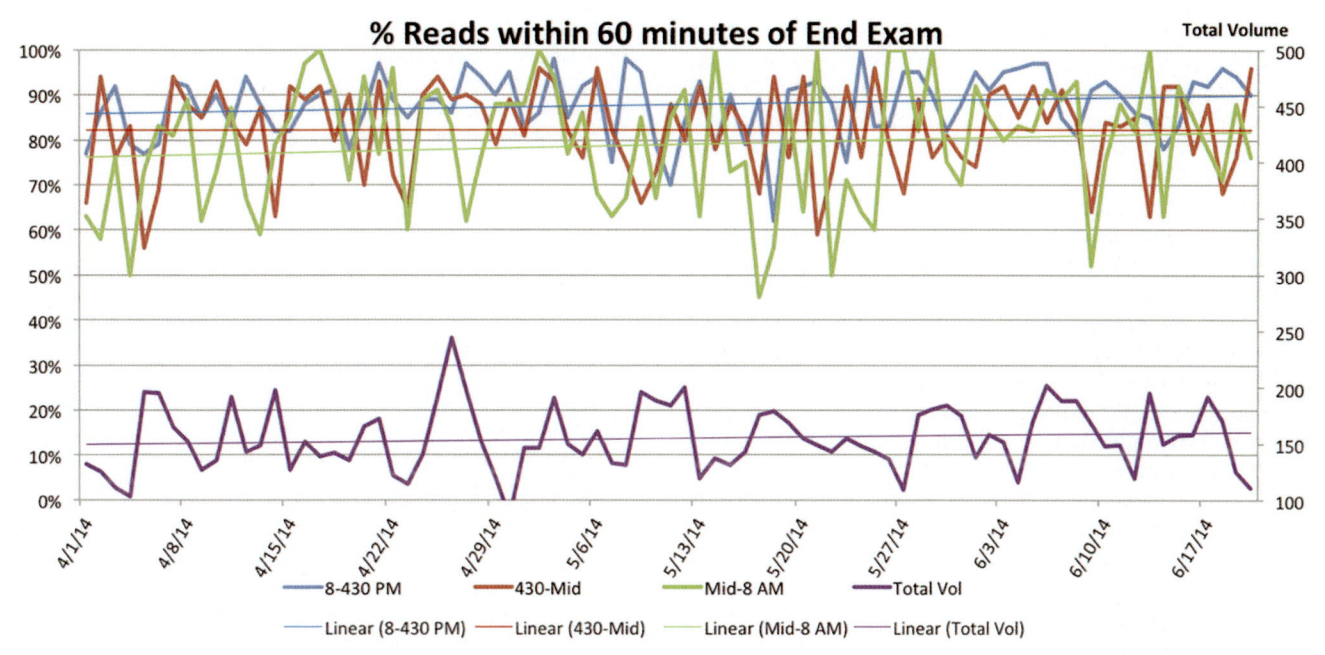

FIG. 4.3 • Sample TAT report specifically tracking emergency department examinations. In this report, TAT is compared across shifts and is compared with volume.

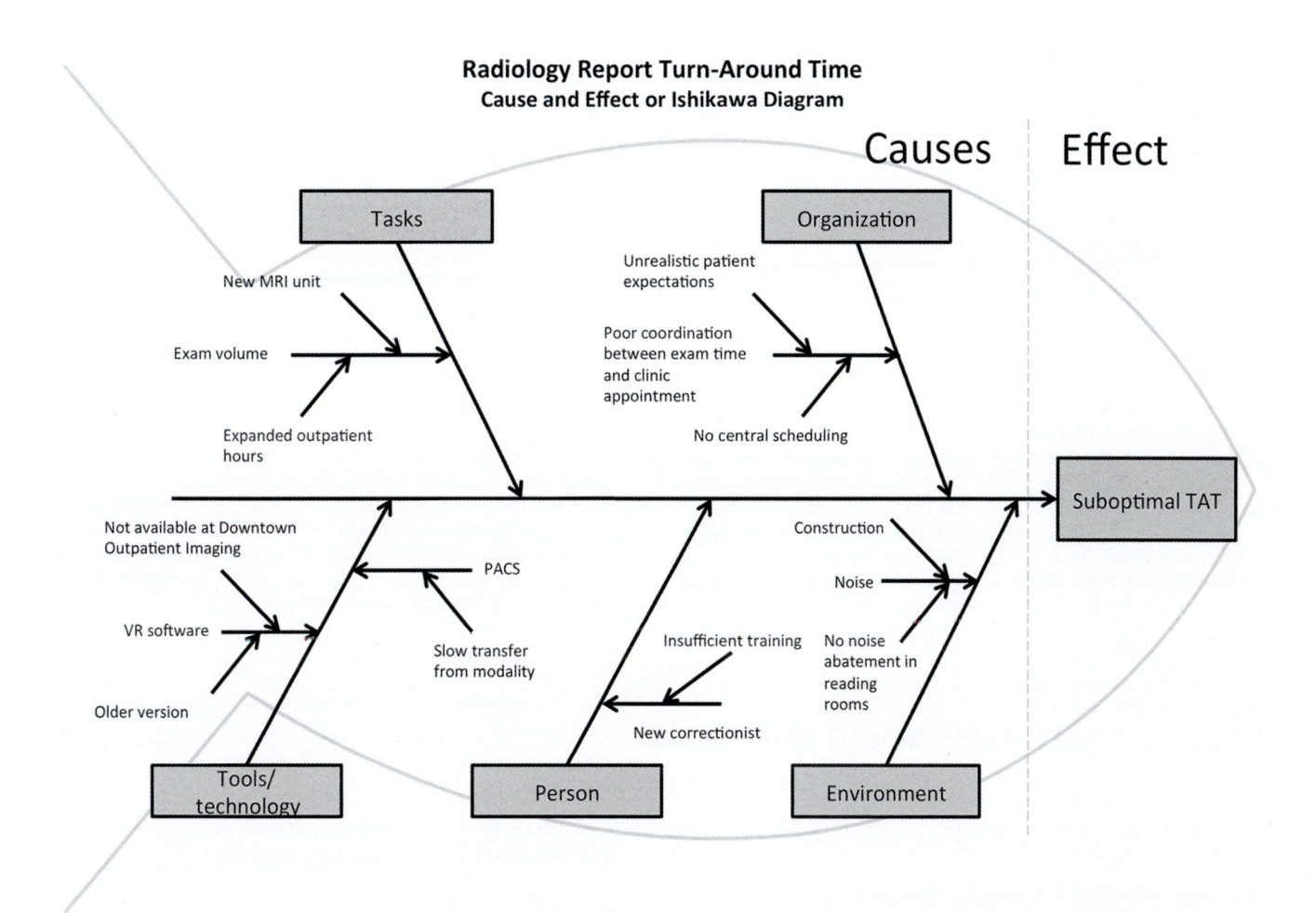

FIG. 4.4 • Sample Ishikawa or cause-and-effect diagram for determining causes of radiology report TAT underperformance for a hypothetical radiology practice.

and administrators. The team should review the current state of report TAT, determine the cause or causes for underperformance, propose practice changes to improve performance, and define the goals of the improvement project. The team should then present the improvement project plan to all relevant individuals so as to define rationale, methodology, and expectations up front.

Identifying the source of underperforming TAT may be the most difficult component of the improvement project (Fig. 4.4). In a private practice setting, report TAT is frequently used as a service and quality metric, and so the incentive to reduce TAT is tangible to radiologists in these practices. Unhappy referring providers and patients will send their business elsewhere.[1,20,21] However, in many large academic centers where the business environment is relatively noncompetitive, faculty radiologists may not have the same sense of urgency as their counterparts in the community. Moreover, many imaging studies have preliminary reports dictated by fellows or residents that contain the information discussed when the study was reviewed in conjunction with the faculty radiologist.[22]

One study performed at an academic medical center assessed the impact of implementing a pay-for-performance program on radiology report TAT.[22] The authors showed that mean TATs from completed exam to final report (C-F), completed exam to preliminary report (C-P), and preliminary report to final report (P-F) all decreased with the implementation of the pay-for-performance program. The P-F metric, for which the faculty radiologist had direct control, showed the greatest reduction in mean TAT. Another study assessing the impact of e-mail notification and off-site signing capabilities on final signatures in an academic medical center showed that providing off-site access and reminders resulted in a decrease in P-F time.[23]

At times, improving report TAT requires adjusting radiology staffing models. Large academic and private institutions may employ dedicated emergency radiologists around the clock in order to provide continuous coverage to reduce report TAT and provide prompt final radiology interpretations for ED patients.[24] Practices with subspecialty radiology services may include extended or staggered-hours coverage.[25]

References

1. Boland GW. Stakeholder expectations for radiologists: obstacles or opportunities? *J Am Coll Radiol.* 2006;3:156–163.
2. Institute of Medicine. *Key Capabilities of an Electronic Health Record System: Letter Report.* Washington, DC: National Academies Press; 2003.
3. Hayes SA, Breen M, McLaughlin PD, et al. Communication of unexpected and significant findings on chest radiographs with an automated pacs alert system. *J Am Coll Radiol.* 2014;11:791–795.
4. Leeming BW, Porter D, Jackson JD, et al. Computerized radiologic reporting with voice data-entry. *Radiology.* 1981;138:585–588.
5. Mehta A, McLoud TC. Voice recognition. *J Thorac Imaging* 2003;18:178–182.
6. Boland GW, Guimaraes AS, Mueller PR. Radiology report turnaround: expectations and solutions. *Eur Radiol.* 2008; 18:1326–1328.
7. Prevedello LM, Ledbetter S, Farkas C, et al. Implementation of speech recognition in a community-based radiology practice: effect on report turnaround times. *J Am Coll Radiol.* 2014;11:402–406.
8. Bhan SN, Coblentz CL, Norman GR, et al. Effect of voice recognition on radiologist reporting time. *Can Assoc Radiol J.* 2008;59:203–209.
9. Kauppinen T, Koivikko MP, Ahovuo J. Improvement of report workflow and productivity using speech recognition—a follow-up study. *J Digit Imaging.* 2008;21:378–382.
10. Krishnaraj A, Lee JK, Laws SA, et al. Voice recognition software: effect on radiology report turnaround time at an academic medical center. *Am J Roentgenol.* 2010;195:194–197.
11. Kelley L. Improving satisfaction performance through faster turnaround times. *Radiol Manag.* 2011;33:38–41.
12. Larson DB, Towbin AJ, Pryor RM, et al. Improving consistency in radiology reporting through the use of department-wide standardized structured reporting. *Radiology.* 2013;267:240–250.
13. Hawkins CM, Hall S, Hardin J, et al. Prepopulated radiology report templates: a prospective analysis of error rate and turnaround time. *J Digit Imaging.* 2012;25:504–511.
14. Reiner BI, Knight N, Siegel EL. Radiology reporting, past, present, and future: the radiologist's perspective. *J Am Coll Radiol.* 2007;4:313–319.
15. Pezzullo JA, Tung GA, Rogg JM, et al. Voice recognition dictation: radiologist as transcriptionist. *J Digit Imaging.* 2008;21:384–389.
16. Strahan RH, Schneider-Kolsky ME. Voice recognition versus transcriptionist: error rates and productivity in MRI reporting. *J Med Imaging Radiat Oncol.* 2010;54:411–414.
17. Quint LE, Quint DJ, Myles JD. Frequency and spectrum of errors in final radiology reports generated with automatic speech recognition technology. *J Am Coll Radiol.* 2008;5:1196–1199.
18. Williams DR, Kori SK, Williams B, et al. Journal club: voice recognition dictation: analysis of report volume and use of the send-to-editor function. *Am J Roentgenol.* 2013;201:1069–1074.
19. Paul JA, Lin L. Models for improving patient throughput and waiting at hospital emergency departments. *J Emerg Med.* 2012;43:1119–1126.
20. Boland GW, Guimaraes AS, Mueller PR. The evolving radiology landscape: the importance of effective leadership. *Eur Radiol.* 2009;19:2321–2325.
21. Thrall JH. Changing relationships between radiologists and hospitals. Part I. Background and major issues. *Radiology.* 2007;245:633–637.
22. Boland GW, Halpern EF, Gazelle GS. Radiologist report turnaround time: impact of pay-for-performance measures. *Am J Roentgenol.* 2010;195:707–711.
23. Deitte LA, Moser PP, Geller BS, et al. Email notification combined with off site signing substantially reduces resident approval to faculty verification time. *Acad Radiol.* 2011;18:774–781.
24. Lamb L, Kashani P, Ryan J, et al. Impact of an in-house emergency radiologist on report turnaround time. *CJEM.* 2014; 16:1–6.
25. Sellers A, Hillman BJ, Wintermark M. Survey of after-hours coverage of emergency department imaging studies by US Academic Radiology Departments. *J Am Coll Radiol.* 2014;11:725–730.

SELF-ASSESSMENT QUESTIONS

1. Which of the following best defines report turn-around time for the radiologist?

    A. Time from study completed to final report signature
    B. Time from study ordered to final report signature
    C. Time from study ordered to results received
    D. Time from study completed to bill submitted

2. Which of the following is **true** regarding implementation of voice recognition software for radiology reporting?

    A. Direct transcription costs increase
    B. Patient satisfaction decreases
    C. Report turn-around time increases
    D. Referring physician satisfaction decreases

Answers to Chapter Self-Assessment Questions

1. C. The definition of report turn-around time (TAT) varies by stakeholder. For most radiologists, report TAT is the time an imaging study is completed and available for review to final report signature. For the ordering physician, report TAT may be time from study ordered until results received. For a finance administrator, report TAT may be time from study completed until bill submitted, whereas an operations administrator may be more interested in time from study ordered to final report signature.

2. D. Studies have shown that implementation of voice recognition (VR) software for radiology reporting reduces transcription costs, increases patient satisfaction (HCAHPS) scores, reduces radiologist report turn-around time (TAT), and improves referring physician satisfaction.

Image Quality Assurance Programs

5

Jeffrey P. Kanne

LEARNING OBJECTIVES

1. Describe modality-specific image quality management strategies
2. State methods for integrating quality management into radiologists' workflow
3. List the steps of the medical imaging chain and state the relevant stakeholders of each step

Image quality is a critical component of diagnostic medical imaging because suboptimal quality can result in error and uncertainty in interpretation.[1,2] Image quality control (QC) and quality assurance (QA) have been longstanding parts of the practice of radiology and primarily have been the responsibilities of the radiology technologist. However, radiologist involvement in image quality management remains critical to ensure that examinations are acceptable for interpretation, and ultimately medical decision making.

IMAGE QUALITY MANAGEMENT

Before the widespread adoption of digital imaging, QC and QA for image quality fell primarily on radiology technologists. In the era of film-screen radiography, dark rooms, processing equipment, and film quality had to be rigorously maintained. A radiology department typically employed a senior technologist to oversee the QC/QA process. This individual would provide feedback to technologists when studies were suboptimal because of exposure, positioning, artifact, or processing. This oversight helped ensure that examinations submitted to radiologists for interpretation were of acceptable and of consistent quality. Additionally, the QC/QA lead served as the liaison between radiologists and technologists. However, as digital radiography and picture archiving and communications systems (PACS) became standard in the practice of radiologist, interactions between technologists and radiologists have waned, both as a result of higher throughput and subsequent increased volumes, as well as distributed imaging studies and resultant increased physical distances between radiologists and technologists. Therefore, the paucity or absence of opportunities for radiologists and technologists to confer on issues of image quality can been seen as lost opportunities for engaging in image QA programs.[3]

Monitoring image quality and repeat rates should be a regular practice in a radiology department (Fig. 5.1 A–C).[4] With film-screen radiography, rejected films could easily be gathered and analyzed for QC purposes (as well as to reclaim silver on the film).[5] However, because of the widespread adoption of digital radiography over the past decade, tracking repeat rates has become more complicated. Technologists can simply delete images that they deem inadequate. Additionally, the impetus to track repeat rates has waned with disappearance of the cost of film. Furthermore, the transition from film screen to digital radiography was also associated with a documented decrease in repeat rates because incorrect exposure became less of an issue,[5–8] and with fewer suboptimal studies related to exposure, positioning becomes the primary reason for a repeat acquisition.[8] Nevertheless, because of the ease with which technologists can simply discard a suboptimal image and acquire

Number of repeat exposures

Jan–Feb	21.0%
Jun–Jul	7.3%

A

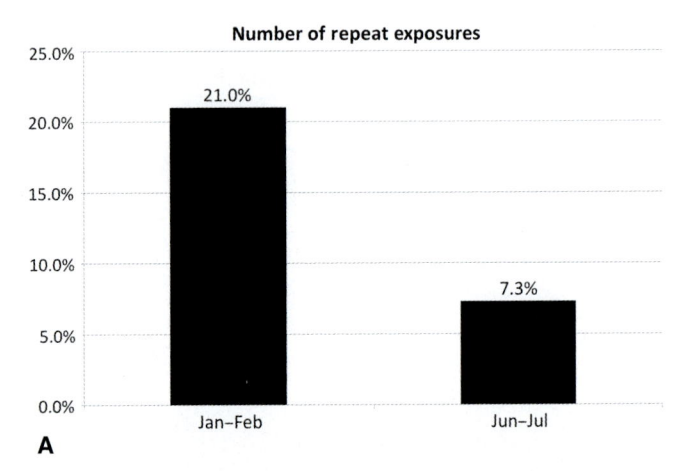

FIG. 5.1 • **Sample data from a quality improvement project assessing digital radiography (DR) repeat rates in a single X-ray room.** Education on patient positioning for knee radiographs was provided to technologists between the two time periods. **A:** Graph showing DR repeat rates over the two examined time periods. Note the marked drop in repeat rates from 21% to 7.3% after the action plan was initiated. **B:** Graph detailing reason for DR repeat rates over two examined periods. Note that patient positioning is the dominant cause for DR repeat in both time periods. **C:** Graph from initial time period showing repeat rates by examination, highlighting that positioning for chest and knee radiographs are the major contributors to DR repeats.

Reason for repeat exposure

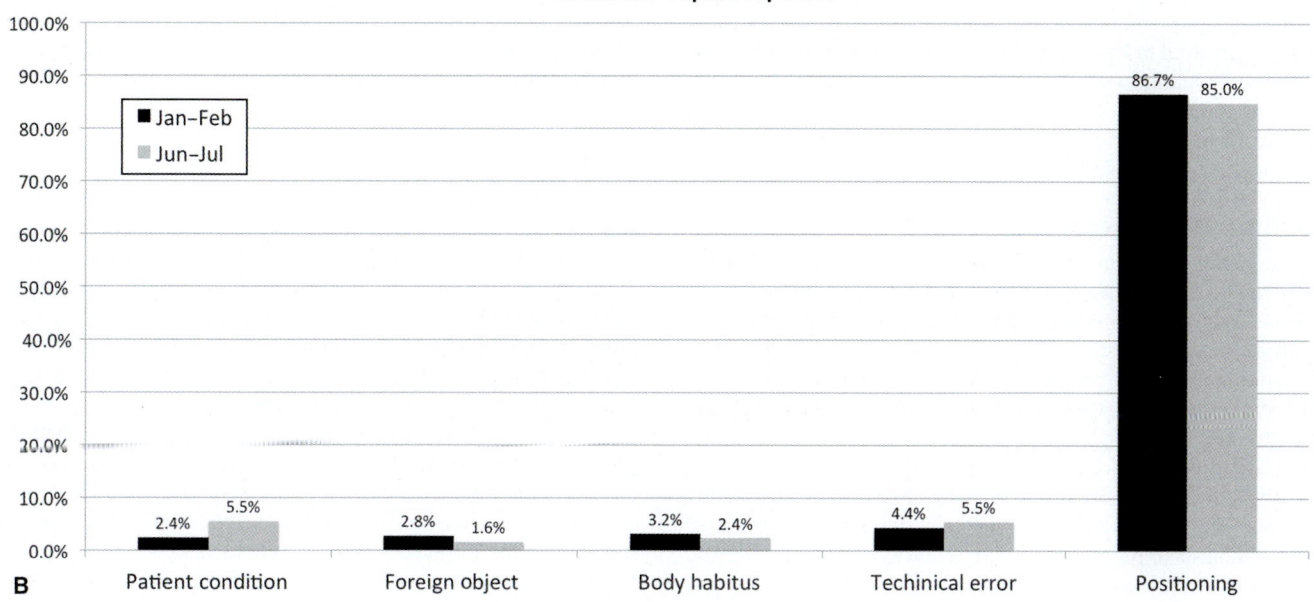

■ Jan–Feb
■ Jun–Jul

	Patient condition	Foreign object	Body habitus	Techinical error	Positioning
Jan–Feb	2.4%	2.8%	3.2%	4.4%	86.7%
Jun–Jul	5.5%	1.6%	2.4%	5.5%	85.0%

B

Reason for repeat exposure by body part
Jan–Feb

Number of repeat exposures

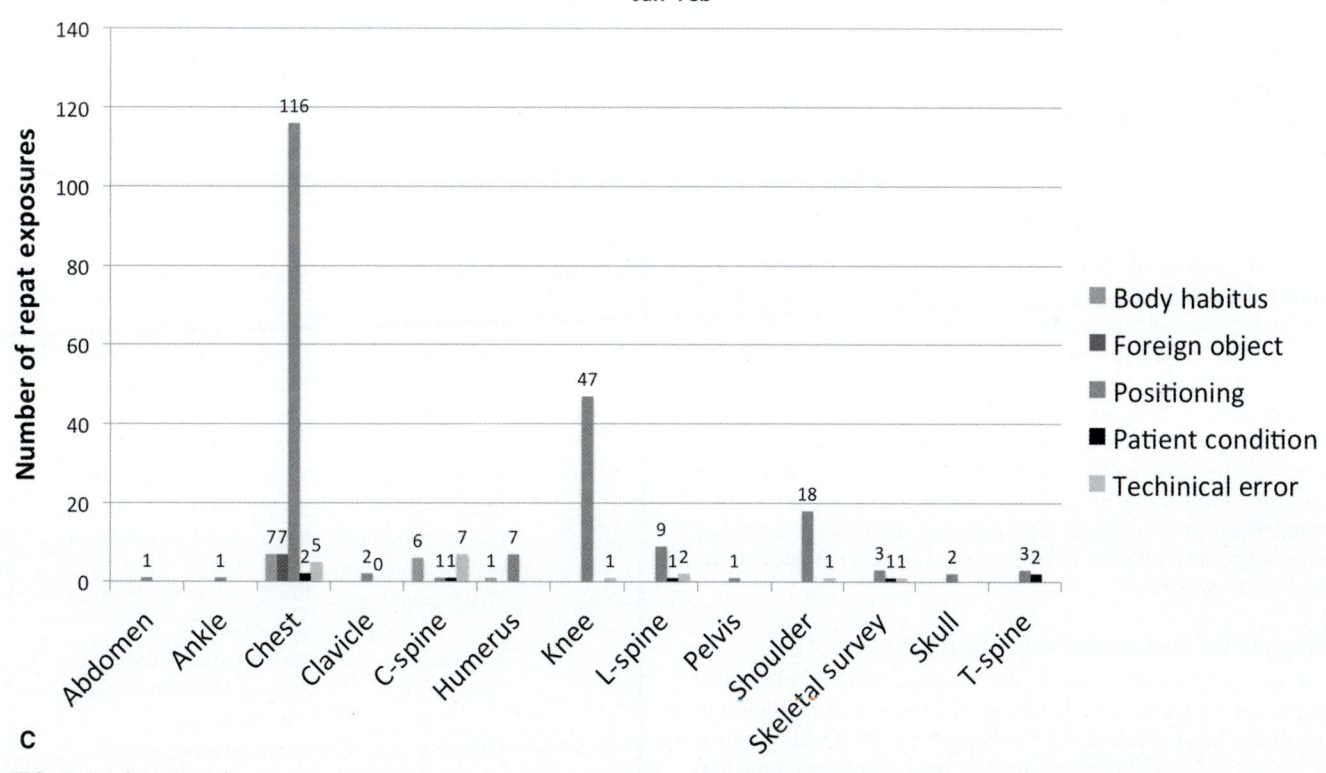

- Body habitus
- Foreign object
- Positioning
- Patient condition
- Techinical error

Chest: 116, 77, 2, 5
Knee: 47
Shoulder: 18
Abdomen: 1
Ankle: 1
Clavicle: 2, 0
C-spine: 6, 1, 1
Humerus: 7, 1
L-spine: 9, 1, 2
Pelvis: 1
Skeletal survey: 3, 1, 1
Skull: 2
T-spine: 3, 2

C

FIG. 5.1 • (*continued*)

a new one, there is potential for repeat rates to rise, especially as a younger generation of technologists who train exclusively on digital equipment enters the workforce.

The American Association of Physicists in Medicine (AAPM) first published QA guidelines for radiography in 1977,[9] followed by updated guidelines in 2002.[10] The guidelines advocate for instituting a QC program designed to ensure that radiography studies were obtained with acceptable image quality. The QC program should focus on equipment, processing, and technologist performance.

Specifically, the AAPM states in the 2002 report that the repeat rate analysis should be performed at least quarterly, preferably by the same individual to ensure consistency in analysis. To understand repeat rate data, the AAPM suggests that the report contain the following data points: patient positioning, patient motion, artifacts, film fog (for film screen), equipment malfunctions, over- or underexposed films, examination room, technologist, and the anatomical view.

Image quality management extends beyond radiography into other imaging modalities such as computed tomography (CT), ultrasound (US), magnetic resonance imaging (MRI), fluoroscopy, mammography, and nuclear medicine. Radiologists may be more directly involved in image QA and QC for these modalities because of the lower volumes as compared with radiography, close proximity to technologists such as with US and mammography (especially diagnostic mammography), and extensive involvement in protocol development such as in CT and MRI.

Computed Tomography

Image quality management in CT not only ensures that image quality is adequate but also can help protect patients from unnecessarily high exposures to ionizing radiation. CT operators typically work with medical physicists and vendors to ensure that equipment is functioning properly and scheduled maintenance is performed. Specific features of image quality that require assessment, typically by a trained medical physicist, include CT number, image noise, contrast-to-noise ratio, and spatial resolution.[11]

The radiologist also plays an important role in CT image quality management. CT protocols are typically developed or modified by radiologists to reflect practice preferences and specific clinical indications. A radiologist or group of radiologists should review CT protocols regularly to confirm that the protocols are still appropriate for the designated clinical indication(s) and that they meet the needs of interpreting radiologists while minimizing patient exposure to ionizing radiation. Additionally, radiologists should regularly monitor scans for higher-than-expected radiation exposure, artifacts, appropriate patient positioning and scan range, and adherence to prescribed protocols.

Ultrasound

Quality management in the United States can be challenging because the US units are becoming increasingly common in hospitals, medical centers, and private offices, and not all US equipment falls under the purview of radiology. The first step in developing an US quality management program is to inventory all ultrasound equipment, including transducers and handheld units. Second, equipment needs to be evaluated by a medical physicist for performance. Specific tests include system sensitivity, uniformity, spatial accuracy, and contrast and spatial resolution. Additionally, the medical physicist should work closely with users of the equipment to ensure that settings are optimized for image quality. Aside from image quality management, US equipment should be evaluated by an appropriate individual such as a clinical engineer for mechanical and electrical safety.[12]

Magnetic Resonance Imaging

Because of the complexities of MRI, image QC requires substantial technical expertise. The American Association of Physicists in Medicine has published AAPM Report No. 28 "Quality Assurance Methods and Phantoms for Magnetic Resonance Imaging" to "describe a standard set of test procedures, which can be used to evaluate the performance of clinical magnetic resonance imaging systems."[13] Not only must MR units themselves be evaluated, but coils used in clinical scans must also be evaluated. As with CT, a specialized medical physicist is typically delegated the responsibility for managing MRI image quality management.

Radiologist involvement in MRI image quality management focuses on developing acquisition protocols and regularly evaluating the performance of these protocols as well as providing ongoing feedback to MRI technologists regarding the quality of clinical MRI examinations. Consultation with a medical physicist may be warranted when artifacts persist across multiple patients or when images continue to be suboptimal.

MEDICAL IMAGING CHAIN

While image quality may be thought of as the result of the single action of image acquisition, it is actually part of a sequence of events (Table 5.1) that begins with exam ordering and ends with communication of results.[14] Each step involves multiple technologies and individuals beyond the imaging modality and the technologist. Other technologies include computerized physician order entry (CPOE), radiology information systems, postprocessing software, PACS, and radiology reporting systems.

Reiner describes the imaging chain as having two distinct phases: preexam archival and postarchival. The preexam archival phase begins with ordering of the imaging exam and ends with archiving of the image. The radiology technologist is the primary stakeholder in this phase, but other individuals' contributions also play part, beginning with the ordering provider and also including scheduling staff, administrators, supervising technologists, and the radiologist. These steps affect image quality because they involve selecting the appropriate examination, scheduling, assessing clinical indication, review of previous imaging results, protocol selection and optimization, image acquisition, and image processing.[14]

Table 5.1 **MEDICAL IMAGING CHAIN.**

Step Number	Description	Stakeholder(s)
1	Exam ordering	Ordering provider
2	Scheduling	Clerical staff (scheduling), radiology administrator
3	Data retrieval	Radiologist, technologist, administrator
4	Protocol selection	Radiologist, technologist
5	Image acquisition	Technologist
6	Image review and quality assurance	Technologist, technologist supervisor
7	Image processing	Technologist, technologist supervisor
8	Archiving	Technologist, informatics
9	Distribution	Technologist, radiologist, informatics
10	Display	Informatics, radiologist
11	Interpretation	Radiologist
12	Reporting	Radiologist, informatics, clerical staff (transcription)
13	Communication	Radiologist, ordering provider, informatics

Adapted from Reiner BI. Hidden costs of poor image quality: a radiologist's perspective. *J Am Coll Radiol.* 2014;11(10):974–978.

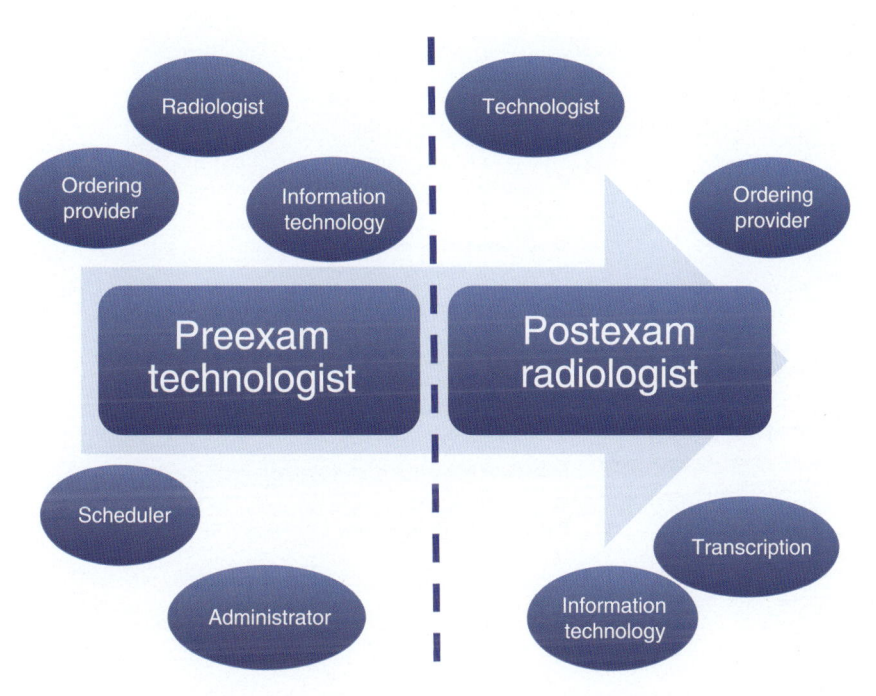

FIG. 5.2 • **Schematic of the medical imaging chain.** Although the technologist is the primary stakeholder in the preexam phase and the radiologist is the primary stakeholder in the postexam phase, other individuals have a stake in the medical imaging chain.

During the second phase of the imaging chain, after the image has been archived, image quality is already established. Occasionally, the radiologist may request that the patient return for additional imaging (e.g., prone images on chest CT or additional sequences on MRI). The radiologist is the primary stakeholder in this phase, although other individuals such as technologists and information technology and clerical staff are also involved (Fig. 5.2).

INTEGRATION OF IMAGE QA INTO THE RADIOLOGY WORKFLOW

Recent initiatives in radiology quality improvement have proposed incorporating image quality management in their frameworks,[15,16] likely reflecting on the fact that as radiology has moved from film and paper to a purely digital environment, many image quality management programs have failed to make the transition to the digital era.[3] In addition to increased volume and distributed workflows, the decline in image quality management may also be a reflection of the relatively increased complexity of building a digital solution for image QA as compared with designing and filling out a paper form.

Because radiologists primarily function in the second phase of the imaging chain, radiologist participation in image QA primarily occurs at the time of image interpretation. With most, if not all, radiologic studies being interpreted on PACS, it makes the most sense for the image quality feedback mechanism to be integrated into the PACS workflow. The ability to build this type of workflow will depend on the specific PACS software used, information technology resources, and institutional policies.

An integrated point-of-care application for image quality management benefits both radiologists and technologists. Radiologist can provide useful feedback to technologists, with little disruption to workflow (Fig. 5.3). Technologists receive documented feedback about specific examinations, and supervisors can review aggregate data to identify trends in quality deficiency, assess technologist performance, and identify opportunities for education.

A key part of any image quality management program is the ability of the technologist or supervisor to respond to the radiologist's comments. As imaging examination requisitions have disappeared, technologists typically log any comments about the examination into PACS or the radiology information system (RIS), potentially not coming to the attention of the radiologist, depending on software functionality and configuration. By having a "closed loop" system of image quality management, the communication lines between radiologists and technologists remain open (Fig. 5.4).

The number of reported QA issues in a radiology department will vary greatly depending on the method of reporting, radiologist workflow, and the overall culture of quality in the department. For example, one study using a paper-based QA process reported that 0.04% of the annual volume of examinations had quality issues.[17] Another study using a web-based reporting system reported an adjusted annual volume of 0.2% exams with quality issues.[18] Finally, a study of a highly integrated electronic QA system showed 0.85% of imaging examinations had a reported quality issue.[3]

A proposed, more comprehensive approach to image QA includes rating every diagnostic imaging study with an image quality score (Table 5.2).[14] Analysis of these aggregate data can help drive improvement by identifying strengths and weaknesses and enable detection of potential problems with personnel performance and training, equipment, and other variable that may affect image quality.

Whichever approach to image QA is taken, it remains incumbent on the radiologist to ensure that optimal patient care is delivered by performing routine image quality management across all modalities. A robust image QA program positions the medical imaging service to add value to the health-care enterprise and to optimize clinical outcomes.

38 QUALITY AND SAFETY IN MEDICAL IMAGING

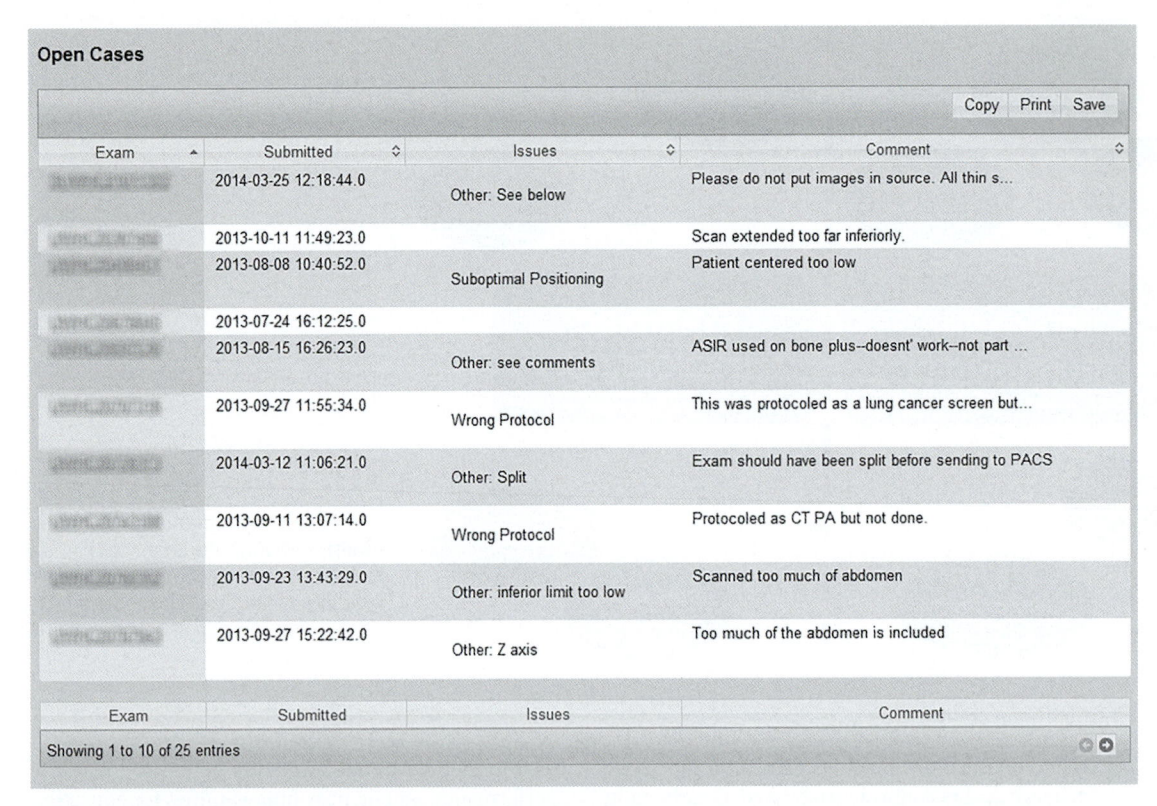

FIG. 5.3 • Sample radiologist's dashboard of cases submitted for review because of quality concerns.

FIG. 5.4 • Sample radiologist's dashboard showing cases that have been reviewed by the supervising technologist, including documentation of what actions were taken.

Table 5.2 IMAGE QUALITY RATING SCALE.

Rating	Image Quality Criteria	Example
1	Image quality deficiency of high magnitude, precluding diagnostic evaluation and requiring the imaging exam to be repeated for diagnosis	Severe motion artifact on CT pulmonary angiogram precluding interrogation of the pulmonary arteries
2	Image quality deficiency of intermediate magnitude and resulting in limited diagnostic evaluation, which may or may not require repeating the exam, depending on the clinical context	IV contrast extravasation during CT scan of the neck for possible mass, resulting in partial contrast delivery
3	Image quality deficiency of low magnitude and not significantly limiting diagnostic evaluation	Mildphase encoding artifact on liver MRI exam
4	Barely perceptible image quality deficiency, which has no impact on clinical interpretation and diagnosis	Processor artifact on periphery of portable abdominal, away from the imaged body part
5	No image quality deficiency identified; exam of superior quality and diagnostic value	Well positioned, full inspiration PA and lateral chest radiographs

Adapted from Reiner BI. Hidden costs of poor image quality: a radiologist's perspective. *J Am Coll Radiol.* 2014;11(10):974–978.

References

1. Alpert HR, Hillman BJ. Quality and variability in diagnostic radiology. *J Am Coll Radiol.* 2004;1:127–132.
2. Reiner B. Uncovering and improving upon the inherent deficiencies of radiology reporting through data mining. *J Digit Imaging.* 2010;23:109–118.
3. Nagy PG, Pierce B, Otto M, et al. Quality control management and communication between radiologists and technologists. *J Am Coll Radiol.* 2008;5:759–765.
4. Fintelmann F, Pulli B, Abedi-Tari F, et al. Repeat rates in digital chest radiography and strategies for improvement. *J Thorac Imaging.* 2012;27:148–151.
5. Nol J, Isouard G, Mirecki J. Digital repeat analysis; setup and operation. *J Digit Imaging.* 2006;19:159–166.
6. Weatherburn GC, Bryan S, West M. A comparison of image reject rates when using film, hard copy computed radiography and soft copy images on picture archiving and communication systems (PACS) workstations. *Br J Radiol.* 1999;72:653–660.
7. Peer S, Peer R, Giacomuzzi SM, et al. Comparative reject analysis in conventional film-screen and digital storage phosphor radiography. *Radiat Prot Dosimetry.* 2001;94:69–71.
8. Lau S-L, Mak AS-H, Lam W-T, Chau C-K, Lau K-Y. Reject analysis: a comparison of conventional film–screen radiography and computed radiography with PACS. *Radiography.* 2004;10:183–187.
9. American Association of Physicists in Medicine. *Basic Quality Control in Diagnostic Radiology.* New York: American Association of Physicists in Medicine; 1977.
10. American Association of Physicists in Medicine. *Quality Control in Diagnostic Radiology.* Madison, WI: American Association of Physicists in Medicine; 2002
11. International Atomic Energy Agency. *Qualtiy Assurance Programme for Computed Tomography: Diagnostic and Therapy Applications.* Vienna, Austria: International Atomic Energy Agency; 2012
12. Boote EJ. *Current Ultrasound Quality Control Recommendations and Techniques.* Philadelphia, PA: American Association of Physicists in Medicine; 2010
13. American Association of Physicists in Medicine. *Quality Assurance Methods and Phantoms for Magnetic Resonance Imaging.* Colchester, Vermont: American Association of Physicists in Medicine; 1990
14. Reiner BI. Hidden costs of poor image quality: a radiologist's perspective. *J Am Coll Radiol.* 2014;11(10):974–978.
15. Dunnick NR, Applegate KE, Arenson RL. Quality—a radiology imperative: report of the 2006 Intersociety Conference. *J Am Coll Radiol.* 2007;4:156–161.
16. Johnson CD, Swensen SJ, Applegate KE, et al. Quality improvement in radiology: white paper report of the Sun Valley Group meeting. *J Am Coll Radiol.* 2006;3:544–549.
17. Glenn L. IRQN award article: labeling defects in radiology. *J Am Coll Radiol.* 2007;4:720–722.
18. Kruskal JB, Yam CS, Sosna J, et al. Implementation of online radiology quality assurance reporting system for performance improvement: initial evaluation. *Radiology.* 2006;241:518–527.

SELF-ASSESSMENT QUESTIONS

1. Which of the following has contributed most to the declining impetus to track radiography image repeat rates?

    A. Transition to digital radiography
    B. Increased volume
    C. New practice parameters
    D. Declining reimbursements

2. Which of the following regarding CT protocols is **true**?

    A. Medical physicists are responsible for protocol development.
    B. A "one size fits all" for CT acquisition is the best way to reduce error.
    C. Tracking patient radiation exposure is primarily the responsibility of the technologist.
    D. CT protocols should be reviewed regularly by a radiologist or group of radiologists.

Answers to Chapter Self-Assessment Questions

1. A. The transition from film-screen to digital radiography has been the single largest reason for the waning impetus to track radiography image repeat rates. With digital acquisition, the cost of film has gone away. Also, technologists can easily delete suboptimal images, and so radiologists only see images deemed adequate. Furthermore, PACS has enabled distributed workflows, which can increase the physical distance between radiographer and radiologist. Although imaging volumes have increased and reimbursements have declined, neither of these is not a primary reason for the decline in radiography quality control programs. The American Association of Physicists in Medicine (AAPM) updated its QA guidelines for radiography and currently maintains these guidelines.

2. D. Regular review of CT protocols by a radiologist or group of radiologists is important to ensure that image quality is adequate for radiologist interpretation, patient radiation exposure is minimized while maintaining adequate image quality, and the protocols are still appropriate for the designated clinical indications. Medical physicists may help develop CT protocols but still rely on radiologists for designating the appropriate clinical indications and for ensuring that image quality is adequate for interpretation. The "one size fits all" approach to CT acquisition can lead to unnecessary radiation exposure or use of contrast or reduce the utility of the scan by not tailoring the acquisition to the clinical question. Although technologists who operate CT scanners control the output of ionizing radiation from the scanner, the supervising radiologist is ultimately responsible for ensuring that the amount of ionizing radiation in the CT protocol is appropriate.

Monitoring and Reporting of Complications

6

Jeffrey P. Kanne

LEARNING OBJECTIVES

1. Define sentinel event and near miss
2. List causes of errors in medical imaging interpretation
3. Describe types of medical error reporting systems

In 2000, the Institute of Medicine (IOM) published its 1999 report, "To Err Is Human: Building a Safer Health System," drawing attention to medical errors.[1] Complications and injuries associated with the delivery of health care continue to face scrutiny from various stakeholders, including patient advocacy groups, government agencies, accrediting and certifying organizations, insurance companies, employers, and patients. Not only do complications from medical treatment result in patient harm, but they also result in increased costs to the health-care enterprise. The IOM estimated that 98,000 patients died each year as a result of medical errors.

Adverse events are those that are associated with patient harm as a result of the administration of health care. A preventable adverse event is one that is the result of a medical error, which is defined as a behavior that falls below the standard of care.[2] Adverse events occur in approximately 3% of hospitalizations, and around 10% of adverse events lead to patient deaths.[1,3]

A core mission of quality improvement in health care is to identify medical errors and their causes for improving patient safety by reducing the number of errors. Risk management in health care has shifted from a reactive process to one of prevention.[4]

TYPES OF ERRORS

Sentinel Events

The Joint Commission (TJC) defines a sentinel event as a patient safety event that reaches the patient and results in death, permanent harm, or severe temporary harm requiring intervention to sustain life (Table 6.1). Other events considered sentinel include suicide of any patient receiving care, treatment, or services in a staffed around-the-clock care setting or within 72 hours of discharge, including from the organization's emergency department (ED); unanticipated death of a full-term infant; discharge of an infant to the wrong family; and abduction of any patient receiving care, treatment, or services. Although accredited organizations are not required to report sentinel events to TJC, they are strongly urged to do so.

Table 6.1 **SENTINEL EVENTS.**

Death
Permanent harm
Severe temporary harm requiring life-sustaining intervention
Suicide of patient in facility continuously staffed or within 72 h of discharge
Unanticipated death of full-term infant
Discharge of infant to wrong family

Near Misses

Near misses are safety events that do not reach a patient or result in minimal harm (Table 6.2). A more positive term is "good catch," reflecting that the error was detected and corrected before reaching the patient. Unfortunately, near misses tend to receive less attention than sentinel events despite the fact that a number of opportunities for improvement can be garnered from studying processes and practices that result in near misses.

Table 6.2 **EXAMPLE OF NEAR MISSES IN RADIOLOGY DEPARTMENT.**

Wrong exam ordered
Wrong protocol selected
Incorrect patient identifiers
Contraindication to scheduled examination
Medication stocking or labeling error
Patient allergy not documented

CAUSES OF ERRORS

Medical errors can be caused by single or multiple contributing factors that include limited or lack of knowledge, insufficient experience, fatigue, carelessness, and faulty judgment.[5]

In radiology, errors can lead to delay in diagnosis and treatment, failure to recognize treatment-related complications, performing a study that is contraindicated or not indicated, or failure to adequately supervise and monitor an examination.[6] Errors in diagnostic radiology are common and are often multifactorial (Table 6.3). Environmental factors such a room lighting, available clinical information, index of suspicion, comparison studies, old radiology reports,[7] and psychophysiologic characteristics of human visual perception[8] all play into the complex process of medical imaging interpretation.[9]

For image interpretation, three types of errors have been described.[10] Scanning error is the failure to fixate on the area of the abnormality. Various factors can contribute to scanning error, including lack of search pattern, eye fatigue, and interruptions. Recognition error is failure to recognize the abnormality. Factors that can contribute to scanning error include eye fatigue, room ambience, lack of experience, and technical limitations (artifact, noise, etc.). Decision-making error, the most common, is the incorrect interpretation of abnormal finding as normal or a normal finding as abnormal. Another important type of observational error in diagnostic radiology is satisfaction of search, which occurs when an abnormality is overlooked because another one is found. Satisfaction of search can be associated with scanning error, recognition error, or decision-making error.

ERROR REPORTING SYSTEMS

Error reporting systems can be defined as mandatory or voluntary. Some organizations may contract with third-party vendors while other organizations develop their own error reporting systems.

Mandatory Reporting Systems

Mandatory reporting systems have the primary purpose of holding providers accountable. These focus on errors that contribute to serious injury or death. State regulatory agencies and programs typically oversee these reporting systems and have the authority to investigate specific cases and issue penalties for wrongdoing. Mandatory reporting systems serve three main functions. First, they provide a minimal level of protection to the public by ensuring that serious errors are reported, investigated, and followed up on. Second, they incentivize health-care organizations to improve patient safety under the pressure to avoid penalties and public exposure. Third, require all health-care organizations to make an investment in patient safety. Although errors reported through mandatory reporting systems represent those with greatest severity and resulting in greatest harm, these errors and complications constitute only a small fraction of errors.

Voluntary Reporting Systems

In contrast to mandatory reporting systems, which focus on accountability and corrective actions, voluntary reporting systems attempt to identify gaps in health-care delivery with the intention of fostering a culture of quality improvement. Voluntary reporting systems typically provide for event reporting into a closed system, and penalties are not assessed around a specific case.[11] Near misses or events with only minimal harm are the primary focus of voluntary reporting systems. Analysis of these aggregated reports provides organizations with comparison data from their peers and can help organizations identify underlying systems problems that can contribute to patient harm. For voluntary reporting systems to be effective, attention to reported events and adequate resources dedicated to process improvement are required.

Components of an Event Report

The details of an event report will vary on the basis of the reporting system used. A basic report, however, should include patient demographics, time and place of the event, a description of the event and any responses taken, type and extent of harm (if any), the reporter's information, and the perceived level of harm. Furthermore, the report should indicate which personnel were involved and who was notified of the event. More sophisticated systems can prepopulate demographics and automatically route reports to the appropriate supervising individual for review (Table 6.4).

When reviewing an event report, all factors that may have contributed to the event should be noted. These factors could include the environment of care, personnel, patient factors, and technology. Once the event has been fully evaluated, an action plan should be defined. Action plans could include staff education, process changes, or changes to the environment of care.

Table 6.3 CAUSES OF ERRORS IN DIAGNOSTIC RADIOLOGY.

Environmental	Lighting
	Disruptions (phone calls, other people in the work area)
	Ergonomics
Information	Provided clinical data
	Access to comparison examinations and reports
	Index of suspicion
Physiologic	Eye strain
	Fatigue
	Psychophysiology of human vision
	Satisfaction of search
	Inherent biases

Table 6.4 MINIMUM COMPONENTS OF AN EVENT REPORT.

Patient demographics
Time and place of the event
Description of the event
Description of action(s) taken
Type and extent of harm, if any, reaching the patient
Personnel involved or who witnessed event
Personnel notified of event
Personnel reporting event

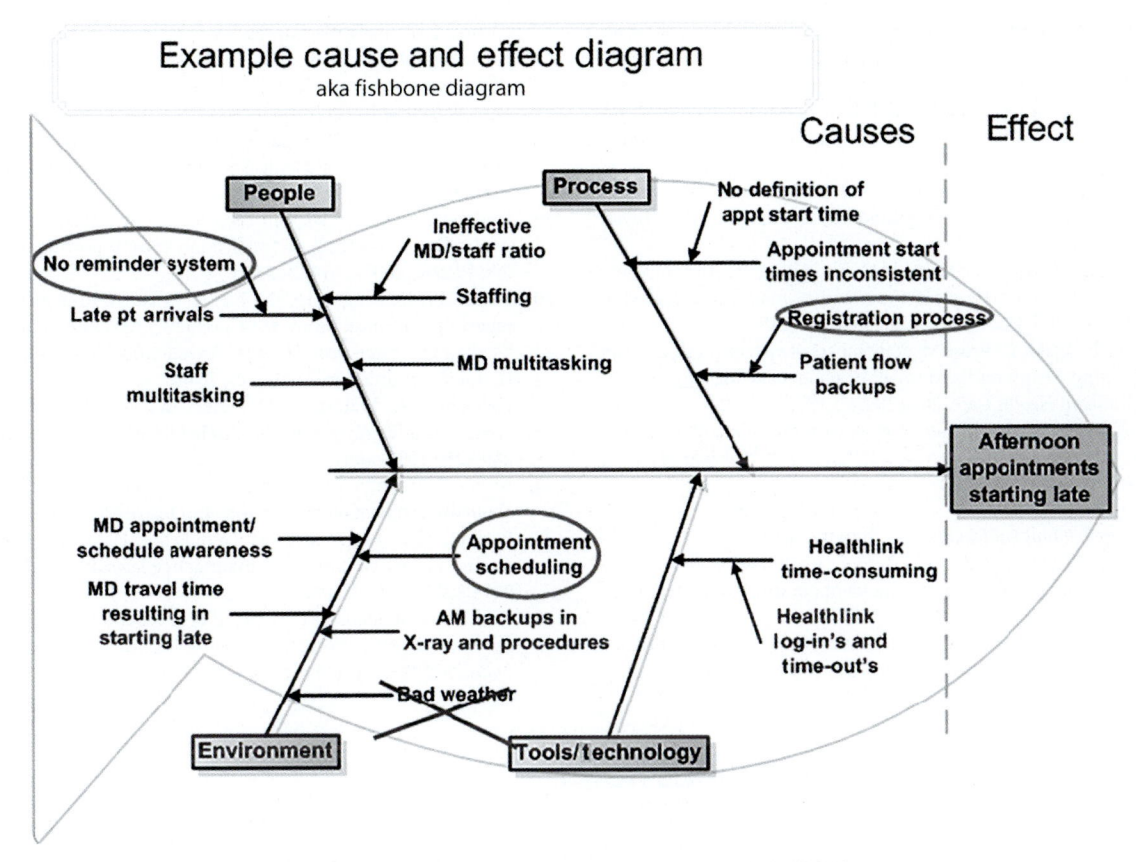

Example cause and effect diagram
aka fishbone diagram

FIG. 6.1 • Example fishbone or Ishikawa diagram showing root cause analysis (RCA) process.

Root Cause Analysis

Root cause analysis (RCA) is a formal process by which the basic or causal factors that contribute to variation in performance are identified. RCAs are frequently used in health-care organizations following a sentinel event or when another significant patient safety concern is brought to light. The RCA team typically consists of a physician or manager team leader, team members from relevant disciplines, and a facilitator.

RCAs are performed with a nonpunitive intent, with the goal of identifying causes contributing to the sentinel event and making recommendations to help avoid similar events in the future.

The findings of an RCA can be mapped onto a fishbone or Ishikawa diagram (Fig. 6.1). These diagrams visually depict all potential contributors to an event or outcome and assist RCA team members in identifying the major contributing factors.

Improving Quality of Reporting

One of the challenges with event reporting is establishing a culture in which all members of the health-care team embrace reporting. Limited research has shown that implementing electronic event reporting systems[12–14] and integrating reporting into regular clinical workflows[13,15,16] can increase participation. Furthermore, reporting that is anonymous[17,18] and reviewed by multidisciplinary safety teams[19] can improve reporting quantity and quality. Moreover, providing educational feedback to health-care providers closes the loop on event reporting and can potentially lead to improved quality of care.[12,17,20]

DISCLOSURE OF ERRORS

Disclosure of errors to patients and caregivers is a complex and challenging process. Because TJC currently requires that accredited facilities inform patients of unexpected outcomes,[21] many hospitals have developed formal processes for disclosure of errors to patients. However, health-care providers may still be hesitant to discuss mistakes with patients. Some evidence suggests that full disclosure can actually enhance patient satisfaction and trust[22,23] as well as possibly reduce the likelihood of malpractice litigation.[24,25]

References

1. Institute of Medicine. *To Err Is Human: Building a Safer Health System.* Washington, DC: National Academy Press; 1999.
2. Guillod O. Medical error disclosure and patient safety: legal aspects. *J Public Health Res.* 2013; 2: e31.
3. Weiler P, Hiatt H, Newhouse JP, et al. *A Measure of Malpractice: Medical Injury, Malpractice Litigation, and Patient Compensation.* Boston: Harvard University Press; 1993.
4. Yarmohammadian MH, Mohammadinia L, Tavakoli N, et al. Recognition of medical errors' reporting system dimensions in educational hospitals. *J Educ Health Promot.* 2014;3:76.
5. Goldberg RM, Kuhn G, Andrew LB, et al. Coping with medical mistakes and errors in judgment. *Ann Emerg Med.* 2002;39:287–292.
6. Brenner RJ, Lucey LL, Smith JJ, et al. Radiology and medical malpractice claims: a report on the practice standards claims survey of the Physician Insurers Association of America and the American College of Radiology. *Am J Roentgenol.* 1998;171:19–22.
7. Berlin L. Malpractice issues in radiology. Alliterative errors. *Am J Roentgenol.* 2000;174:925–931.

8. Yerushalmy J. The statistical assessment of the variability in observer perception and description of roentgenographic pulmonary shadows. *Radiol Clin N Am.* 1969;7:381–392.
9. Pinto A, Acampora C, Pinto F, et al. Learning from diagnostic errors: a good way to improve education in radiology. *Eur J Radiol* 2011;78:372–376.
10. Kundel HL, Nodine CF, Carmody D. Visual scanning, pattern recognition and decision-making in pulmonary nodule detection. *Invest Radiol.* 1978;13:175–181.
11. Richter JP, McAlearney AS, Pennell ML. Evaluating the effect of safety culture on error reporting: a comparison of managerial and staff perspectives. *Am J Med Qual.* 2015;30(6):550–558.
12. Fukuda H, Imanaka Y, Hirose M, et al. Impact of system-level activities and reporting design on the number of incident reports for patient safety. *Qual Saf Health Care.* 2010;19:122–127.
13. Haller G, Myles PS, Stoelwinder J, et al. Integrating incident reporting into an electronic patient record system. *J Am Med Inform Assoc.* 2007;14:175–181.
14. Tuttle D, Holloway R, Baird T, et al. Electronic reporting to improve patient safety. *Qual Saf Health Care.* 2004;13:281–286.
15. Wang SC, Li YC, Huang HC. The effect of a workflow-based response system on hospital-wide voluntary incident reporting rates. *Int J Qual Health Care.* 2013;25:35–42.
16. Welsh CH, Pedot R, Anderson RJ. Use of morning report to enhance adverse event detection. *J Gen Intern Med.* 1996;11:454–460.
17. Abstoss KM, Shaw BE, Owens TA, et al. Increasing medication error reporting rates while reducing harm through simultaneous cultural and system-level interventions in an intensive care unit. *BMJ Qual Saf.* 2011;20:914–922.
18. Grant MJ, Larsen GY. Effect of an anonymous reporting system on near-miss and harmful medical error reporting in a pediatric intensive care unit. *J Nurs Care Qual.* 2007;22:213–221.
19. Costello JL, Torowicz DL, Yeh TS. Effects of a pharmacist-led pediatrics medication safety team on medication-error reporting. *Am J Health-Syst Pharm.* 2007;64:1422–1426.
20. Force MV, Deering L, Hubbe J, et al. Effective strategies to increase reporting of medication errors in hospitals. *J Nurs Admin* 2006;36:34–41.
21. The Joint Commission. *Hospital Accreditation Standards.* Oakbrook, IL: Joint Commissoin Resources; 2014.
22. Gallagher TH, Waterman AD, Ebers AG, et al. Patients' and physicians' attitudes regarding the disclosure of medical errors. *JAMA.* 2003;289:1001–1007.
23. Mazor KM, Simon SR, Yood RA, et al. Health plan members' views about disclosure of medical errors. *Ann Intern Med.* 2004;140:409–418.
24. Berlin L. Medicolegal-malpractice and ethical issues in radiology. Will saying "I'm sorry" prevent a malpractice lawsuit? *Am J Roentgenol.* 2014;202:W503–W504.
25. Kachalia A, Shojania KG, Hofer TP, et al. Does full disclosure of medical errors affect malpractice liability? The jury is still out. *Jt Comm J Qual Saf* 2003;29:503–511.

SELF-ASSESSMENT QUESTIONS

1. What percentage of adverse events during hospitalization is estimated to lead to patient deaths?

   A. 1.0%
   B. 5.0%
   C. 10.0%
   D. 15.0%

2. Which of the following would be classified as sentinel event in radiology?

   A. Wrong exam ordered
   B. Patient allergy not documented
   C. Mislabeled medication
   D. Radiation burn from fluoroscopy

Answers to Chapter Self-Assessment Questions

1. C. It is estimated that 10% of adverse events that occur during hospitalization result in patient death.

2. D. A sentinel event is a patient safety event that reaches the patient and results in death, permanent harm, or severe temporary harm requiring intervention to sustain life. Ordering the incorrect examination, failure to document a patient allergy, and mislabeling of a medication are considered near misses since harm has not occurred.

Agencies and Programs

Jeffrey P. Kanne

LEARNING OBJECTIVES

1. List agencies that regulate health care in the United States
2. Describe current programs focusing on quality improvement and safety in health care as a whole and in radiology

Health-care delivery in the United States is regulated by several governmental agencies that are part of the US Department of Health and Human Services (DHHS). The agencies run a variety of programs that affect public health, individual patients, and individual practitioners. Furthermore, each state, the District of Columbia, and the US territories have medical boards that regulate the practice of medicine within their respective jurisdictions (Table 7.1). Additionally, various health-care delivery programs focused on diagnostic imaging have been developed by professional not-for-profit groups and are targeted to professionals and the general public alike (Table 7.2).

AGENCIES

Centers for Medicare and Medicaid Services

The Centers for Medicare and Medicaid Services (CMS) is an agency in the DHHS. CMS oversees and regulates all federal health-care programs, including Medicare, Medicaid, Children's Health Insurance Program (CHIP), and Health Insurance Marketplaces. Some programs such as Medicaid, CHIP, and Health Insurance Marketplaces are operated jointly with individual states.

Table 7.1 **SUMMARY OF GOVERNMENTAL AGENCIES REGULATING HEALTH CARE.**

Agency	Roles
Centers for Medicare and Medicaid Services	1. Oversee Medicare program 2. Oversee Medicaid programs jointly with respective states
Centers for Disease Control and Prevention	1. Detect and respond to new public health threats 2. Confront biggest health problems that cause death and disability for Americans 3. Promote disease prevention through science and advanced technology 4. Promote health and safe behaviors, communities, and environments 5. Develop public health leaders and train the public health workforce 6. Assess the health status of the United States
Food and Drug Administration	1. Ensure safety of US food supply 2. Ensure safety of human and veterinary drugs, vaccines, and other biologic products and medical devices 3. Protect public from electronic product radiation 4. Ensure that cosmetics and dietary supplements are safe and properly labeled 5. Regulate tobacco products 6. Advance public health by helping speed product innovations
State medical boards	1. Issue licenses to practice medicine 2. Investigate complaints against physicians 3. Supervise and facilitate rehabilitation of impaired physicians

Table 7.2 **SUMMARY OF GOVERNMENTAL AND PROFESSIONAL PROGRAMS RELATED TO DIAGNOSTIC IMAGING.**

Program	Primary Sponsor	Goal(s)
Imaging 3.0	American College of Radiology	1. Increase the value of the radiologist to health-care team 2. Improve the quality of health care through appropriate imaging
Image Gently	Image Gently Alliance	Provide safe, high-quality imaging for children while minimizing exposure to ionizing radiation
Image Wisely	American College of Radiology Radiological Society of North America American Society of Radiologic Technologists American Association of Physicists in Medicine	1. Raise public and professional awareness about the risks and benefits of the use of ionizing radiation in medical imaging 2. Advocate for lowering the amount of ionizing radiation used in medically necessary diagnostic imaging studies 3. Eliminating unnecessary procedures
Choosing Wisely	American Board of Internal Medicine Foundation	Promote conversations between patients and providers regarding value of diagnostic tests, procedures, or treatments in the context of scientific evidence and potential for harm
Accountable Care Organizations	Centers for Medicare and Medicaid Services	Provide high-quality care to Medicare beneficiaries while reducing costs
Medicare and Medicaid Electronic Health Care Record (EHR) Incentive Programs	Centers for Medicare and Medicaid Services	Promote adoption, implementation, expansion, and meaningful use of EHR technology

CMS sets reimbursement rates for medical services provided, including technical and professional fees for imaging studies. Furthermore, CMS's fee schedules often affect reimbursement rates for local private insurance carriers. CMS requirements also dictate requirements for providers and facilities. For example, CMS requires that all outpatient facilities that bill CMS for the technical component for advanced imaging studies (CT, MRI, and PET) be accredited by an organization with deeming authority.[1]

Centers for Disease Control and Prevention

The Centers for Disease Control and Prevention (CDC) is a large agency of the DHHS. The CDC is charged with detecting and responding to new and emerging health threats; confronting the biggest health problems that cause death and disability for Americans; using science and advanced technology to prevent disease; promoting health and safe behaviors, communities, and environments; developing leaders and training the public health workforce; and assessing the health status of the United States.[2]

The CDC provides educational materials for providers and the public on specific diseases, healthy lifestyles, travel risks and recommendations, emergency preparedness, and other public health topics. Furthermore, through the National Center for Health Statistics, the CDC provides a wealth of public health data.

The National Institute for Occupational Safety and Health (NIOSH) is a unit of the CDC that conducts research and makes recommendations to prevent worker injury and illness. NIOSH runs the B Reader Program, which began in 1974 in response to the need to identify physicians qualified to serve in national pneumoconiosis programs directed at coal miners.[3] The Federal Mine Safety and Health Act of 1977 mandated the creation of the Coal Workers' X-ray Surveillance Program, which requires B reader certification for interpreters of worker radiographs. B reader certification is also required for the Asbestos Medical Surveillance Program, which is administered by the Navy and Marine Corps Public Health Center.

Food and Drug Administration

The Food and Drug Administration (FDA) is an agency in the DHHS and is responsible for protecting public health by assuring the safety of the food supply (certain animal products such as meat are regulated by the US Department of Agriculture); ensuring that human and veterinary drugs, vaccines, and other biologic products and medical devices for human use are safe and effective; protecting the public from electronic product radiation; assuring cosmetics and dietary supplements are safe and properly labeled; regulating tobacco products; and advancing public health by helping speed product innovations.[4] For example, CT and MRI scanners, contrast agents, intravascular catheters, and computer-aided detection (CAD) software all must receive FDA clearance before being routinely implemented in health-care delivery. The FDA also administers the Mammography Quality Standards Act (MQSA) (see Chapter 8).

State Medical Boards

All the 50 US states, the District of Columbia, and US territories have laws that regulate the practice of medicine and define the responsibility of the state or territorial medical board. Depending on state or territorial law, medical boards are either independent agencies or part of a larger umbrella such a state health department. There are currently 70 medical and osteopathic medical boards in the United States and its territories, which are represented by the not-for-profit Federation of State Medical Boards (FSMB).

State medical boards grant licenses for the general practice of medicine and do not limit practice to specific medical specialties.

Furthermore, physicians are not required to hold board certification in a medical specialty to be granted a license. Requirements for licensure, including postgraduate training requirements, number of attempts at licensing examination (United States Medical Licensing Examination), and time limit for completing licensure examination sequence, vary by jurisdiction. In some jurisdictions, licenses for other health-care practitioners such as physician assistants, physical therapists, and acupuncturists are issued by state medical boards.

State medical boards are also responsible for investigating complaints against practitioners, disciplining practitioners who violate state laws, and evaluating and facilitating rehabilitation for impaired physicians.[5]

PROGRAMS
Imaging 3.0

Imaging 3.0 is a campaign developed and promoted by the American College of Radiology (ACR), with the strategic goals of preserving radiologist relevance while improving patient care in the era of US health-care reform.[6] For patients, Imaging 3.0 focuses on providing better care at lower cost, improving population health, and empowering patients to make informed decisions regarding their own personal health care. For radiologists, Imaging 3.0 promotes practice patterns that increase radiologist relevance, develops tools that enhance the value of radiologists to all stakeholders, and seeks alternatives to continued reduction in fee-for-service (FFS) payments. One of the main thrusts of Imaging 3.0 is the role of the radiologist beyond image interpretation. The ACR seeks to redefine the radiologist's role to one that begins when imaging is considered and does not end until both the patient and referring physician fully understand the results of the imaging test and any recommendations based on the findings of the imaging study.

Coordinating Care

Before an imaging examination is performed, the radiologist plays an important role as consultant. First, the results of any previous imaging studies should be reviewed, as sometimes information on early examinations may be sufficient to answer the current clinical question. Second, published guidelines including white papers and the ACR Appropriateness Criteria should be consulted, either manually or through the use of decision support software integrated with the electronic health record. Radiation safety should be considered by all stakeholders. Finally, the radiologist should ensure that the most appropriate imaging study is ordered.

Acquisition and Interpretation

Image acquisition and interpretation have traditionally been the core practice of the radiologist. Imaging 3.0 expands on this role in several ways. First, the imaging facility should be accredited by an appropriate body to ensure that defined technical standards are met. Accreditation is currently mandated for outpatient (nonhospital) advanced imaging including CT, MRI, and PET. Second, imaging facilities should have established quality and safety programs, including information on radiation safety for providers and patients. Third, Imaging 3.0 advocates for American Board of Radiology certification for radiologists, as this reflects achievement of a certain level of professional competence in addition to ongoing maintenance of this competence. Fourth, Imaging 3.0 increases the focus on patient-centered care, which includes tailoring the examination appropriately to the specific patient and clinical indication. This approach to patient-centered care includes appropriate selection and use of contrast agents, appropriate choice of imaging sequences, and optimizing patient radiation exposure. Finally, the ACR advocates for making imaging examinations and their reports easily available to patients, with the goal of improving communication among providers and patients regarding imaging results and recommendations.

Results Reporting

The traditional radiology report is a text-only description of the imaging study performed, the findings, an impression of the findings, and, when appropriate, recommendations for further management. In Imaging 3.0, stress is placed on using evidence-driven recommendations, improving the quality of diagnostic reporting through standardization and developing methods to integrate images and other media into the report, making imaging test and reports readily available to patients and providers (personal imaging records and image exchange networks), and for registry reporting as appropriate.

Image Gently

Image Gently is a program created in 2007 by the Society of Pediatric Radiology, the ACR, the American Society for Radiologic Technologists (ASRT), and the American Association of Physicists in Medicine (AAPM), with the goal of "providing safe, high quality pediatric imaging worldwide" through raising awareness "of the need to adjust radiation dose when imaging children."[7] The campaign is supported by the Image Gently Alliance, which includes the founding organization and dozens more from across the globe. Image Gently provides parents, technologists, physicians and other providers, and medical physicists with tools to minimize children's exposure to ionizing radiation, including image acquisition protocols, educational materials, and quality improvement projects.

Image Wisely

Similar to Image Gently, Image Wisely was developed to raise public and professional awareness about the risks and benefits of the use of ionizing radiation in medical imaging and to advocate for lowering the amount of ionizing radiation used in medically necessary diagnostic imaging studies and eliminating unnecessary procedures.[8] Image Wisely was formed from the ACR and Radiological Society of North America Joint Task Force on Adult Radiation Protection. Other participating organizations include ASRT and AAPM. The Image Wisely campaign provides information to radiologists on vendor-specific equipment and dose information, information to referring practitioners regarding radiation safety and appropriateness of diagnostic imaging studies, and links to information on diagnostic imaging and radiation concerns.

Choosing Wisely

Choosing Wisely is an initiative of the American Board of Internal Medicine Foundation that aims to promote conversations between patients and providers by helping patients choose care that is supported by evidence, not duplicative of other tests or procedures already performed, free of harm, and truly necessary. The campaign has led to a number of professional medical organizations, including the ACR, publishing lists of five things physicians and patients should question (Table 7.3). Choosing Wisely has partnered with Consumer Reports, an independent, nonprofit consumer organization, to coordinate with consumer-oriented organizations to help disseminate information and provide education to patients on making informed decision regarding health care.[9]

48 QUALITY AND SAFETY IN MEDICAL IMAGING

> **Table 7.3 THE AMERICAN COLLEGE OF RADIOLOGY'S CHOOSING WISELY—TOP 5.**
>
> 1. Don't do imaging for uncomplicated headaches.
> 2. Don't image for suspected pulmonary embolism without moderate or high pretest probability.
> 3. Avoid admission or preoperative chest X-rays for ambulatory patients with unremarkable history and physical exam.
> 4. Don't do computed tomography for the evaluation of suspected appendicitis in children until after ultrasound has been considered as an option.
> 5. Don't recommend follow-up imaging for clinically inconsequential adnexal cysts.

Accountable Care Organizations

CMS created the voluntary Accountable Care Organization (ACO) program as a way to provide high-quality care to Medicare patients while reducing health-care spending. An ACO is a group of doctors, hospitals, and other health-care providers that functions as a single medical entity to provide coordinated, high-quality care to Medicare beneficiaries. ACOs that meet CMS quality metrics are eligible to share any cost savings with CMS.

Currently, three ACO programs are in effect. The Medicare Shared Savings Program is designed to improve Medicare patient outcomes and increase value of care by promoting accountability, requiring coordinated care for all services provided under Medicare FFS, and encouraging investment in infrastructure and redesigned care processes. The Advance Payment ACO program is designed to provide physician-based and rural providers, who frequently lack the capital to make investments required to successfully coordinate care as required by an ACO, with both upfront and monthly payments (depending on historically assigned beneficiaries) so that initial and ongoing investments in infrastructure and care coordination programs can be made in order to improve the quality of care delivery while reducing costs. The Pioneer ACO program, which is no longer open for enrollment, was designed for organizations with established coordinated care programs across care settings so that they could more rapidly transition from a shared savings program to a population-based payment model. Although CMS has reported nearly 2-year savings of US$100 million in 2012 to 2013, only 19 of the original 32 pioneer ACOs remain in the program.[10]

Medicare and Medicaid Electronic Health Care Record Incentive Programs

The CMS's Electronic Health Record (EHR) Incentive Programs are designed to promote adoption, implementation, expansion, and meaningful use (MU) of EHR technologies. The CMS's MU program began in 2011 and currently consists of three stages. Stage 1 addresses EHR implementation and capturing and sharing of health-care data. Stage 2 focuses on continuous quality improvement and sharing of information in a structured format. Stage 3, which as of now has not been implemented, centers on improved outcomes through leveraging the EHR infrastructure built around stages 1 and 2. Other goals include patient health portals, clinical decision support, and improvement of population health.

The CMS's MU program consists of one program for eligible professionals and one for eligible hospitals. The requirements of each program are different, but there is some overlap. Furthermore, there is one incentive plan for Medicare and one for Medicaid. For a radiologist to be eligible, more than 10% of reported studies billed under CMS must be performed in the outpatient setting (point-of-service code 22). In the first 4 years of the program (2011 to 2014), eligible providers and hospitals that met EHR MU requirements were eligible to receive incentive payments from CMS. Beginning in federal fiscal year 2015, reduction in CMS payments for professional services rendered will begin for providers and hospitals not meeting program requirements. Additional penalties may be imposed in the future for eligible, nonexempt professional and hospitals not participating in the MU program.[11,12]

References

1. Centers for Medicare & Medicaid Services. http://www.cms.gov. Accessed June 1, 2016.
2. Centers for Disease Control and Prevention. http://www.cdc.gov/about/organization/mission.htm. Accessed June 1, 2016.
3. Centers for Disease Control and Prevention. Chest Radiography: The NIOSH B Reader Program. http://www.cdc.gov/niosh/topics/chestradiography/breader.html. Accessed June 1, 2016.
4. U.S. Food and Drug Administration. http://www.fda.gov. Accessed June 1, 2016.
5. Federation of State Medical Boards. 2014. http://www.fsmb.org. Accessed June 1, 2016.
6. Allen B Jr. ACR Informatics Summit; 2013.
7. Goske MJ, Applegate KE, Bell C, et al. Image gently: providing practical educational tools and advocacy to accelerate radiation protection for children worldwide. *Semin Ultrasound CT MR.* 2010;31:57–63.
8. Brink JA, Amis ES Jr. Image Wisely: a campaign to increase awareness about adult radiation protection. *Radiology.* 2010;257:601–602.
9. Consumer Reports. Choosing Wisely. http://consumerreports.org/cro/health/doctors-and-hospitals/choosing-wisely/index.htm. Accessed June 1, 2016.
10. Centers for Medicare & Medicaid Services. Accountable Care Organizations (ACO); 2014. http://www.cms.gov/Medicare/Medicare-Fee-for-Service-Payment/ACO/index.html. Accessed June 1, 2016.
11. Krishnaraj A, Siddiqui A, Goldszal A. Meaningful use: participating in the federal incentive program. *J Am Col Radiol.* 2014;11:1205–1211.
12. Centers for Medicare & Medicaid Services. EHR Incentive Progams; 2014. http://www.cms.gov/Regulations-and-Guidance/Legislation/EHRIncentivePrograms/index.html. Accessed June 1, 2016.

SELF-ASSESSMENT QUESTIONS

1. Which of the following agencies must approve a new MRI scanner for use in human health?

   A. The Centers for Medicare and Medicaid Services
   B. National Institute for Occupational Safety and Health
   C. Food and Drug Administration
   D. American College of Radiology

2. Which of the following is true regarding state medical licenses?

   A. Licensees must hold specialty board certification
   B. Issued by the Department of Health and Human Services
   C. Requirements are dictated by individual jurisdictions
   D. Licenses must be US citizens or permanent residents

Answers to Chapter Self-Assessment Questions

1. **C.** The Food and Drug Administration (FDA) is responsible for ensuring that medical devices, including imaging equipment, are safe and effective for use in human health. The Centers for Medicare and Medicaid Services and National Institute for Occupational Safety and Health do not issue approval for medical device use. Although the American College of Radiology (ACR) provides accreditation for MRI and other advanced diagnostic imaging modalities, use in human health is not incumbent on ACR accreditation.

2. **C.** Each state medical board determines its own requirements for licensure. Licensees are not required to hold board certification in their respective specialty. The Department of Health and Human Services does not issues medical licenses. Licenses can be issued to non-US nationals, but exact requirements vary by jurisdiction.

Quality and Safety in Breast Imaging

8

Mai A. Elezaby

LEARNING OBJECTIVES

At the end of this chapter, readers will be able to:

1. List the requirements for quality health-care services in a breast imaging practice
2. List the timing and requirements for the FDA (MQSA) and ACR accreditation in mammography
3. Be familiar with the requirements for ACR accreditation for breast ultrasound, breast MRI, and stereotactic breast biopsy programs
4. Be familiar with the acceptable physician performance metrics for screening and diagnostic mammography

INTRODUCTION

The Institute of Medicine (IOM) has defined quality in health care as "safe, effective, patient-centered, timely, efficient and equitable."[1] To fulfill these six aspects of health-care performance in breast imaging, the scope of quality and safety initiatives should extend across the entire imaging continuum (Fig. 8.1). This entails embracing a quality environment that emphasizes the role of each member of the health-care team, including technologists, radiologists, radiology nursing, information technology (IT) personnel, staff members, and administrators.

Through the next chapter, with this framework in mind, we will discuss the specifics and resources available for promoting safety and quality in a breast imaging practice and identify potential areas for improvement that our readers can address at their individual institution.

APPROPRIATE UTILIZATION OF IMAGING—EXAMINATION ORDERING AND SCHEDULING PROCESS

The role of radiologic imaging in screening, diagnosis, and treatment of diseases, including those of the breast, has no doubt exponentially increased over the last few decades. Although this has resulted in earlier and more accurate diagnosis of diseases and better assessment of therapy responses, it has been coupled with the increase of inappropriate imaging, leading to increased radiation exposure and health-care costs.[2] The American College of Radiology (ACR), as a leader in promoting the delivery of evidence-based appropriate imaging, has created the ACR appropriateness criteria (ACR AC) to guide referring clinicians on the most appropriate imaging decision for a specific clinical scenario, while eliminating unnecessary "wasteful" health-care expenses.[3]

The ACR AC embodies the first three initiatives of health-care quality—safe, effective, and patient centered—by emphasizing evidence-based utilization of imaging and promoting value-based care over volume-based care. The ACR AC provides a nine-point scoring system, ranging from most appropriate (=9) to least appropriate (=1), for some of the most common clinical and imaging scenarios routinely encountered in a clinical breast practice (Fig. 8.2).

Promoting appropriate utilization of imaging is one of the primary goals of the radiology community and can be achieved only through the reinforcement of the value of ACR AC at every educational and clinical opportunity, when possible. From an educational perspective, they should be incorporated in radiology curricula for medical students, radiology residents, and fellows. From a clinical perspective, they should be integrated into scheduling templates and guidelines utilized by radiology department administrators and schedulers or through the utilization of clinical decision support systems (CDSSs) in the examination ordering process by referring clinicians.

Clinical Decision Support Systems

CDSSs are one of the IT tools that have been proposed to promote value-based health care and have been increasingly incorporated into the common clinical practice. These systems are generally designed to integrate patient-specific characteristics and match them to a computerized knowledge base for the purpose of generating patient- and task-specific recommendations that are then presented to the clinicians to assist in patient management decisions.[4] These can be stand-alone platforms or embedded within the electronic medical record (EMR) ordering process. According to the Protecting Access to Medicare Act of 2014 (PAMA 2014, H.R), starting in January 2017 Medicare reimbursements for advanced imaging will be contingent upon confirmation that physicians requesting advanced imaging (CT, MRI, nuclear medicine, and PET) consulted

Quality and Safety in Breast Imaging 51

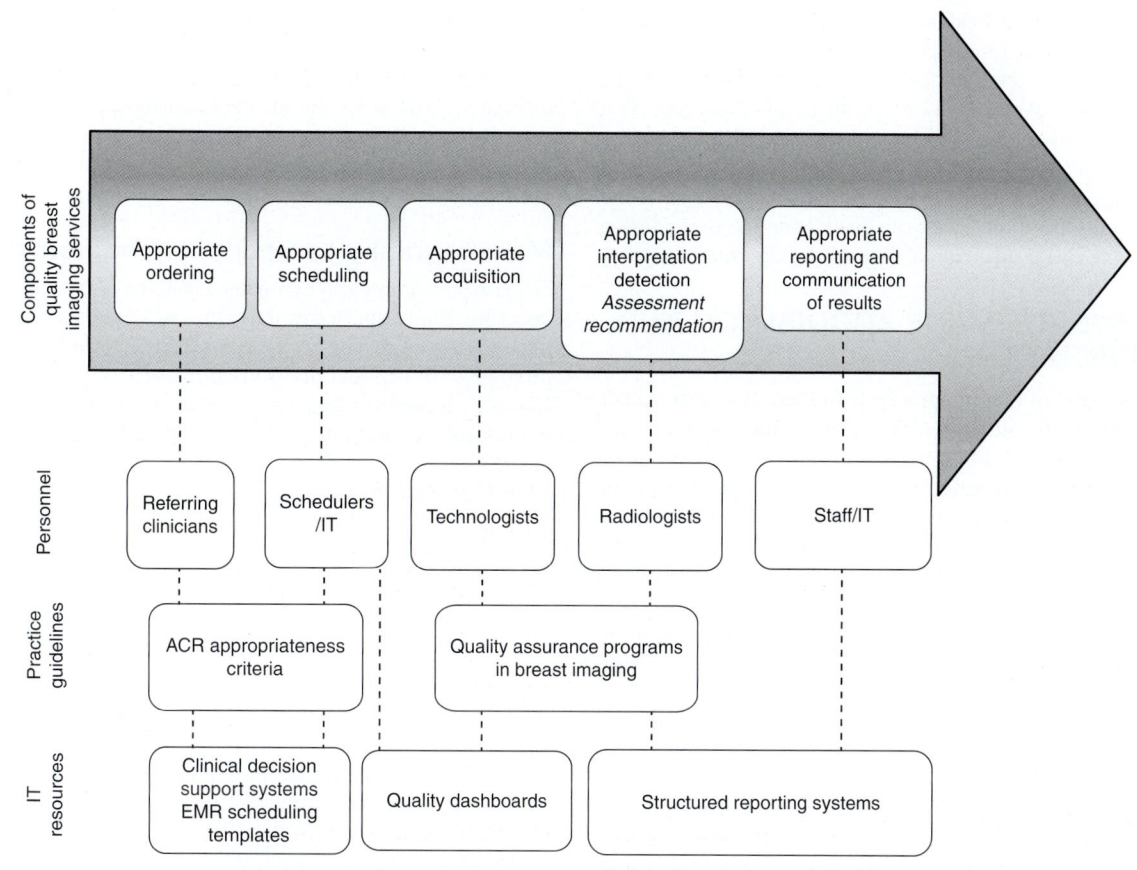

FIG. 8.1 • Components and resources to ensure quality services along the breast imaging continuum.

A

Breast Cancer Screening
- Average risk
- Intermediate risk
- High risk

Breast Pain
- Cyclical, uni or bilateral. Age < 40 lateral
- Cyclical, uni or bilateral. Age ≥ 40
- Non-cyclical, uni or bilateral. Age < 30
- Non-cyclical, uni or bilateral. Age ≥ 30 lateral
- Non-cyclical, uni or bilateral. Age < 40
- Non-cyclical, uni or bilateral. Age ≥ 40

Palpable Breast Masses
- Initial evaluation. Age ≥ 40
- Suspicious for malignancy on mammography. Age ≥ 40
- Probably benign on mammography. Age ≥ 40
- Benign on mammography. Age ≥ 40
- Negative on mammography. Age ≥ 40
- Initial evaluation. Age < 30
- Suspicious for malignancy on ultrasound. Age < 30
- Probably benign on ultrasound. Age < 30
- Benign on ultrasound. Age < 30
- Negative on ultrasound. Age < 30
- Initial evaluation. Age 30–39

Stage 1 Breast Cancer: Initial Work-up and Surveillance for Local Recurrence and Distant Metastases in Asymptomatic Women
- Newly diagnosed. Initial work-up. Rule our metastases
- Surveillance. Rule out metastases
- Surveillance. Rule out local recurrence

Symptomatic Male Breast
- Male patient with symptoms and signs consistent of gynecomastia or pseudo-gynecomastia
- Male patient with palpable breast lump. Age < 25
- Male patient with palpable breast lump. Age ≥ 25
- Male patient with palpable breast lump. Age ≥ 25. Mammography suspicious

Nonpalpable Mammographic Findings (Excluding Calcifications)
- Architectural distortion on screening, no history of surgery or trauma
- Architectural distortion on screening, prior history of surgery or trauma
- Mass on screening with suspicious mammographic features
- Mass on screening with probably benign mammographic features
- Multiple bilateral masses on screening with no suspicious mammographic features
- Multiple bilateral masses on screening with suspicious or dominant mass
- Focal asymmetry or asymmetry on baseline exam
- Focal asymmetry or asymmetry, new or enlarging from prior exam

B

Radiologic Procedure	Rating	RRL*
Mammography diagnostic	9	0.1–1 mSv
Image-guided core biopsy breast	1	Varies
Mammography short interval follow-up	1	0.1–1 mSv
MRI breast without and with contrast	1	O 0 mSv
MRI breast without contrast	1	O 0 mSv
Return to screening mammography	1	0.1–1 mSv
US breast	1	O 0 mSv

Rating Scale: 1,2,3 usually not appropriate; 4,5,6 may be appropriate; 7,8,9 usually appropriate

*Relative Radiation Level

FIG. 8.2 • **A:** List of the ACR appropriateness criteria (ACR AC) in breast imaging. **B:** Example of ratings for radiologic procedures for initial work-up of new or enlarging nonpalpable focal asymmetry. (Adapted from the ACR AC: https://acsearch.acr.org/list.)

a government-approved, evidence-based appropriate–use criteria through a CDSS prior to ordering examinations.[5,6] Thus far, the published data from other radiology subspecialties that introduced CDSSs in their clinical practice have identified a significant reduction in inappropriate imaging.[7-11] Although advanced imaging studies constitute a smaller proportion of a breast imaging practice volumes, the use of CDSS that incorporates ACR AC for common clinical and imaging conditions of the breast can be extended to the ordering process for the entire spectrum of breast imaging examinations.

APPROPRIATE IMAGE ACQUISITION AND INTERPRETATION

The ultimate goal of mammography is to identify breast cancer at earlier stages of the disease, which with advancement in treatments has been shown to have good prognosis and decreased mortality.[12] Since its introduction as an imaging technique of the breast, the radiology community realized that ensuring the quality of image acquisition and interpretation of mammography was essential for its success. Improving quality has the potential of decreasing missed cancers (false negative) as well as decreasing unnecessary call backs (false positives).[13] The ACR was at the forefront of these quality initiatives and, in 1987, initiated the ACR voluntary Mammography Accreditation Program (MAP).[14] Initially, participation in this program was encouraged and not mandated. However, soon it became standard of care and even a requirement for health insurance reimbursement in some states.[15] The MAP program addressed four categories of quality assurance (QA): *equipment specifications, equipment performance, facility QA procedures*, and *personnel qualifications*. The variability in adoption and implementation of the MAP program by various states was the impetus for the Mammography Quality and Standards Act (MQSA), which was enacted by Congress in 1992 and reauthorized and amended in 1998 and 2004, respectively. This legislation mandated that mammography facilities have to be certified by the federal government. The specifics of this mandate, primarily based on the MAP program, nevertheless further standardized the process of certification and accreditation. The inspection and certification of mammography facilities was delegated to the Department of Health and Human Services (HHS), which in turn delegated the task of annual certification of mammography facilities to the U.S. Food and Drug Administration (FDA). The MQSA legislation also mandated oversight and accreditation of mammography facilities by an FDA-approved accreditation body; this is typically on a 3-year cycle. Given the experience that the ACR had in quality accreditation process, it was intuitively chosen as the primary FDA-approved accreditation body for mammography facilities. The Arkansas, Iowa, and Texas departments of state health services were also approved as accreditation bodies for facilities in their respective states.[16]

THE COMPREHENSIVE ACCREDITATION IN BREAST IMAGING

Initially, the MQSA was enacted to ensure performance of quality mammographic imaging and interpretation. However, the rapid technologic advancement in breast imaging necessitated that the Breast Imaging Quality Assurance Programs expand to include accreditation programs for breast ultrasound, ultrasound- and stereotactic-guided breast procedures, and breast MRI. These additional accreditation programs are not mandated by MQSA; however, they are conducted through the ACR, and enrollment in these programs is encouraged to maintain quality of breast imaging services. Currently, a designation of *ACR Imaging Center of Excellence* is provided to imaging centers that not only pass the mandated ACR MAP, but also voluntarily apply to and pass the accreditation programs for other provided breast imaging services. In the next few sections, we will provide a general overview of the accreditation programs for each of the breast imaging technologies

Mammography Accreditation Programs

To perform mammography, imaging facilities are required by law to be certified and inspected by the FDA, and accredited by an accrediting body. As we review the specifics of each of these accreditation programs, we will identify overlap in some of the requirements. However, in combination, they cover all aspects of quality and safety in performance and interpretation of mammography.

FDA Certification
Timing
- Initial certification any time new mammography equipment is installed or equipment replaced.
- Yearly renewal for the already certified facilities and equipment

Components

A separate certification process has to be initiated for each clinic or imaging center that performs mammography, even when belonging to the same organization or radiology group. Of note, the FDA certification is a collective certification for the individual geographic locations or clinics.

The certification process involves the following:

A. Submitting an application for certification (initial or renewal) that includes:
   a. The name and qualifications of the designated lead interpreting radiologist who is ultimately responsible that the quality control (QC) tests and measures have been met
   b. The name and qualifications of the designated lead mammography technologist who oversees the performance of the QC tests
   c. The name and qualifications of the designated lead physicist who performs the required annual tests and produces the annual report
   d. The information on each mammography unit used for clinical imaging at that location (vendor, make, and model)
   e. Types and number of mammographic examinations performed (screening versus diagnostic) in the last 12 months
   f. The names and qualifications (educational background, training, and professional experience) of all the radiologists interpreting the mammographic examinations
   g. The names and qualifications of all the technologists performing the mammography examinations
B. Application fees for the facility and each mammography unit
C. A physical site visit by a designated state or FDA mammography inspector. During this site visit, the inspector will review:
   a. Records of completing the recommended QC tests for each mammography unit in that facility for the past 12 months
   b. Records of initial certification and maintenance of certification requirements for each radiologist interpreting mammographic examinations at that facility
   c. Records of initial certification and maintenance of certification requirements for each mammography technologist acquiring mammographic examinations
   d. Records of the medical outcomes audit

Quality and Safety in Breast Imaging

Key Points Every Radiologist Should Know Regarding Quality Control Program in Mammography
- There are some general QC requirements that are common between the different imaging acquisition techniques (screen-film versus digital imaging) and between different commercially available manufacturers, while other requirements or timing of tests will be specific to individual systems (Table 8.1).
- Manufacturers will routinely provide technologists training on the specifics of QC tests, with the installation or upgrade of their equipment. Additionally, they will provide detailed QC manuals and checklists that can guide the technologists during routine QC tests.
- The role of the *lead mammography technologist* is to perform mammography or identify key technologists who will be delegated the specific QC tests and checklists as well as to ensure that all the QC

Table 8.1 **EXAMPLE OF MAMMOGRAPHY QC TESTS FOR ONE OF THE COMMERCIALLY AVAILABLE DIGITAL IMAGING SYSTEMS.**

Category	Location of Test	Name of QC Test or Procedure	Description/Objective	Frequency	Tools
Image viewing	Reading room	Monitor cleaning/viewing conditions	To assure cleanliness of the monitors from dust, finger print, or particles	Daily	Specific cleaning instructions per manufacturer
		Diagnostic review workstations QC—display calibration check	To assure consistency and calibration of brightness and contrast of the diagnostic workstation	Daily (or monthly depending on vendor)	Society of Motion Picture and Television Engineers (SMPTE) pattern
		Display phantom	To assure quality and consistency of mammographic image	Weekly	ACR phantom
Image printing	Tech work area	DICOM printer QC	To assure consistency of DICOM printer performance	Weekly; after PM service; after software change	SMPTE pattern printed from imaging equipment (for density measurement and artifacts); densitometer
Image acquisition	Examination room	Detector flat field calibration	To assure proper system calibration	Weekly	Flat field phantom
		System artifact	To assure lack of artifact during image acquisition	Weekly	Flat field phantom analyzed on the diagnostic review workstation
		SNR and contrast-to-noise ratio (CNR)	To assure consistency of the image receptor	Weekly	ACR phantom analyzed on the acquisition workstation
		Compression thickness indicator	To assure the indicated compression thickness is within tolerance	Biweekly (every 2 wk)	
		Visual check of equipment	To assure all equipment in the examination room and system are mechanically stable (system indicator lights, displays, mechanical locks, cones, collimators, hand switch, angulation indicator, control booth)	Monthly	
		Repeat analysis	To assure technologists are adequately trained on patient positioning	Quarterly	Checking records for percentage of examinations requiring additional views; should be between 2% and 5%
		Compression force	To assure the system can provide adequate compression through manual or power-assisted mode and that compression is controlled	Semiannually	Bathroom scale, towels
System analysis		Routine service PM by the manufacturer		Semiannually	The vendor's service team

tests are performed according to the timing and technique specified by individual manufacturers and are well documented. Prior studies have estimated that the time involvement in maintaining the QC tests is approximately 160 hours per year.[17]

- The role of the *lead interpreting physician* is to work in close collaboration with lead mammography technologist in oversight of the QC process and documentation, in creation of QA policies, procedures, and workflow strategies to fulfill the MQSA regulations (Table 8.2), and to identify areas for workflow improvement. Additionally, one of the key roles of the lead interpreting radiologists is to closely review the medical outcomes audit for the entire practice and for individual radiologists and to compare these metrics to national benchmarks. This is crucial for identifying trends or outlying performers and facilitating practice improvement measures. This will further be discussed in the Medical Outcomes Audit section.

Personnel Qualifications

For the success of a QA program, the individuals involved in acquiring and interpreting the mammographic examinations have to meet minimal requirements that ensure their ability to perform their delegated tasks up to predefined quality standards. There are specific requirements for initial certification and maintenance of certification. Tables 8.3 to 8.5 list the initial certification and maintenance of certification requirements for radiologists, technologists, and physicists in a mammography facility.

The designated FDA inspector who conducts the onsite visit also has to meet certain certification requirements; however, this is beyond the scope of this chapter.

For radiologist and technologist who rotate between the various satellite clinics that belong to the same organization or breast imaging practice, a travelling book with copies of the initial certification and maintenance of certification records is required at each imaging facility during the inspection visit.

Equipment Specifications and Physicist Mammography Equipment Evaluations

There are specific hardware and software requirements for mammography equipment that the FDA mandates for clinical care and can be reviewed at http://www.fda.gov/Radiation-EmittingProducts/MammographyQualityStandardsActandProgram/default.htm.

Routine preventative maintenance (PM) for each mammography unit by qualified service engineers is also a requirement. Reports of these PM checks as well as any deficiencies identified and corrective action should be kept for records.

Mammography equipment evaluation (MEE) is an extensive process performed by an MQSA qualified physicists, and assures that the equipment installed meets FDA technical specifications and its performance passes the FDA QA program (the medical physicist's survey).

The MEE evaluation must be conducted after:

1. A new unit is installed
2. A previously accredited unit moved from one location to another
3. Major repair or upgrades

The Medical Physicist's Survey: These are checklists of QA tests that are conducted by the lead physicists at initial certification, then at least annually or after every major equipment repair. After completion of this inspection, the physicist generates a report indicating that the unit passed all QC tests and is eligible for clinical care.

Table 8.2 EXAMPLES OF DIFFERENT STANDARD OPERATING POLICIES (SOP) AND PROCEDURES TO MEET REQUIREMENTS FOR MQSA ACCREDITATION FOR MAMMOGRAPHY.

- SOP for technically suboptimal mammograms
- SOP for consumer complaint mechanism
- SOP for health-care provider result notification
- SOP for communication of mammograms with BI-RADS 4 or 5
- SOP for patient result notification—patient letter
- SOP for medical outcomes audit and procedure
- SOP for medical records and film retention

Table 8.3 MAMMOGRAPHY PROGRAM: MQSA AND ACR REQUIREMENTS FOR INITIAL AND CONTINUED CERTIFICATION FOR INTERPRETING RADIOLOGISTS.

	Initial Certification	Maintenance of Certification
Licensure	Licensed to practice medicine and Board certified by: • ABR or • American Osteopathic Board of Radiology (AOBR) or • Royal College of Physicians and Surgeons of Canada	Maintain his or her medical license and Board certification
Continued experience (volumes of examination interpreted)	Must have read 240 mammograms in any 6 mo within the last 2 y prior to board certification under the direct supervision of a certified radiologist	Must have read 960 mammograms over the last 24-mo period
Continued education (category 1 CME hours in mammography)	Category 1 CME in mammography (15 h have to be acquired in the 3 y immediately prior to qualification date) • 40 h (if qualified before April 28, 1999) • 60 h (if qualified after April 28, 1999) and • 8 h in mammographic modality before beginning to use that modality (e.g., digital or DBT)	Must have documented: • 12 h of CME in mammography in the last 12-mo period or • 15 h of CME in mammography in the last 36-mo period

Table 8.4 **MAMMOGRAPHY PROGRAM: MQSA AND ACR REQUIREMENTS FOR INITIAL AND CONTINUED CERTIFICATION FOR TECHNOLOGISTS.**

	Initial Certification		Maintenance of Certification
Licensure	*If Qualified before April 28, 1999* Certified by: • American Registry of Radiologic Technologists (ARRT) *or* • American Registry of Clinical Radiologic technologists *or* Licensed to perform general radiographic procedures in a state	*If Qualified after April 28, 1999* Certified by: • American Registry of Radiologic Technologists (ARRT) *or* • American Registry of Clinical Radiologic technologists *or* Licensed to perform general radiographic procedures in a state	Maintain his or her board certification
Continued experience (performing examinations)	40 h of training in mammography *and* 8 h in mammographic modality before beginning to use that modality (e.g., digital or DBT)	40 h of training in mammography *Specifically:* • Performed 25 examinations under direct supervision of a qualified individual • Training in anatomy, physiology, positioning general & with implants, compression, QA/QC procedures *and* 8 h in mammographic modality before beginning to use that modality (e.g., digital or DBT)	Perform 200 mammographic examinations over a 24-mo period
Continued education (category 1 CEU credit hours)			Must have documented 15 h in the last 36-mo period

Table 8.5 **MAMMOGRAPHY PROGRAM: MQSA AND ACR REQUIREMENTS FOR INITIAL AND CONTINUED CERTIFICATION FOR PHYSICISTS.**

	Initial Certification		Maintenance of Certification
Licensure	*Master's degree or higher* Certified by: • American Registry of Radiologic Technologists (ARRT) *or* • American Registry of Clinical Radiologic technologists *or* Licensed to perform general radiographic procedures in a state	*Bachelor's degree* Certified by: • American Registry of Radiologic Technologists (ARRT) *or* • American Registry of Clinical Radiologic technologists *or* Licensed to perform general radiographic procedures in a state	Maintain his or her board certification
Continued experience (performing examinations)	40 h of training in mammography *and* 8 h in mammographic modality before beginning to use that modality (e.g., digital or DBT)	40 h of training in mammography *Specifically:* • Performed 25 examinations under direct supervision of a qualified individual • Training in anatomy, physiology, positioning general & with implants, compression, QA/QC procedures *and* 8 h in mammographic modality before beginning to use that modality (e.g., digital or DBT)	Survey 2 mammography facilities and 6 mammography units over a 24-mo period
Continued education (category 1 CME or CEU credit hours)			15 h CME or CEU in mammography in the last 36-mo period

This constitutes part of the MEE and is included with certification paperwork and kept with the QC documents (www.fda.gov/RegulatoryInformation/Guidances/ucm094405.htm).

Additional requirements for MQSA certification include the following:

- Facilities must ensure that final mammography reports are sent to the referring physicians as well as a summary of these results sent to the patient in lay terms as soon as possible, no longer than 30 days.
- Facilities must keep patients' prior mammograms as part of their permanent medical records somewhere between 5 and 10 years.

ACR Accreditation

- The majority of mammography facilities across the United States will need to be accredited by the ACR. The exceptions are the facilities in Texas, Arkansas, or Iowa, which can be accredited by their respective state departments of HHS.
- The ACR certification process has to be initiated for each clinic or imaging center that performs mammography, even when belonging to the same organization or radiology group, and it entails the certification of each imaging unit within that location.
- The ACR accreditation for mammography adheres to the same requirements as the FDA certification. In addition, it assures the quality of images acquired at each facility by reviewing an example of the facility's clinical images, which are submitted at the time of certification.
- Although onsite visit is not mandatory for ACR accreditation, the ACR will conduct onsite survey to random sample of mammography facilities across the United States. If a facility is chosen for a random site visit, it will be notified in advance. The survey team will include the ACR radiologist, medical physicist, and ACR staff technologist, and items that will be reviewed during their visit include:
  1. Documentation of personnel qualifications
  2. Documentation of the QA program
  3. Documentation of the policies and procedures
  4. Mammography images and reports from clinical cases

Timing

- Initial certification any time new mammography equipment is installed or equipment replaced.
- Renewal process for the already certified equipment. This is conducted on a 3-year accreditation cycle. The ACR will send a notification of renewal 8 months prior to the expiration of the accreditation cycle.

Components

The ACR accreditation is a two-step process:

First, the application for equipment certification can be filled online or sent by mail. The information included in the initial application is as follows:

A. Basic facility information, including detailed equipment information and personnel information
B. The detailed medical physicist's MEE; summary report detailing that all the equipment meets FDA specifications and have passed all required FDA QA tests, as detailed in the FDA Certification section.
C. Certification fees

Second, if all the initial application paperwork is complete, the ACR will send the facility access to online *testing package*. This package will have details on additional paperwork, additional forms to be completed, and instructions on how to send and label copies of actual clinical images that are acquired by the facility after the initial application approval. Once the testing package paperwork and images are completed, they should be sent back to the ACR within 45 days of receipt of the testing package.

The testing package that is sent back to the ACR will include the following:

- Personnel information and qualifications (physicians, technologists, physicist)
- Facility policies and QA procedures, including reporting mechanism
- Medical outcomes audit
- QC results
- Clinical images

Personnel Qualifications

Facilities should have documentation of the requirements for initial and continued certification for mammography for all interpreting radiologists, technologists, and medical physicists who follow the same guidelines and requirements as the FDA certification (Tables 8.3 to 8.5).

Equipment Specifications and Quality Control

The equipment specifications and QC procedures required for ACR accreditation adhere to the same requirements discussed in the FDA Certification section for mammography. Part of the ACR application packet is submitting the FDA renewal letter for the facility that ensures adherence to these requirements.

ACR Phantom Image

The ACR phantom is used by mammography technologists and physicists to conduct their QC testing. The phantom simulates a 4.2-cm compressed breast of average density. It includes various sized semi-radiopaque wax inserts, fibers (six), specks groups (five), and masses (five).

This phantom is used by technologists to assess optical density, contrast uniformity, and image quality of the imaging system to fulfill the MQSA and ACR mandated QC tests. The phantom is imaged on the mammography equipment being tested. In digital systems, the image of the ACR phantom is reviewed on the digital monitor used in clinical interpretation. For screen-film system, the film is printed and read on the view box used for clinical interpretation. To pass the phantom test, the image must show a minimum of four fibers, three speck groups, and three masses (Fig. 8.3). And, the average glandular dose should not exceed 300 mrad (3 mGy).

For ACR accreditation, a copy of the phantom image is sent with the application packet and will be reviewed by two ACR physicists.

Quality Assurance
Procedures and Policies

These are documents that detail the facility workflow strategies and steps taken to assure quality of the provided clinical services in adherence to the MQSA regulations. They are typically created by the lead interpreting physician and lead QC technologist taking into account the facility's resources (Table 8.2). These constitute a great opportunity for workflow improvement projects, and should be routinely reassessed and updated for optimal efficiency and performance.

The Medical Outcomes Audit

Medical outcomes audit of mammography facilities is a significant component of the comprehensive mammography QA program. The process of medical audit has four major components: an initial step

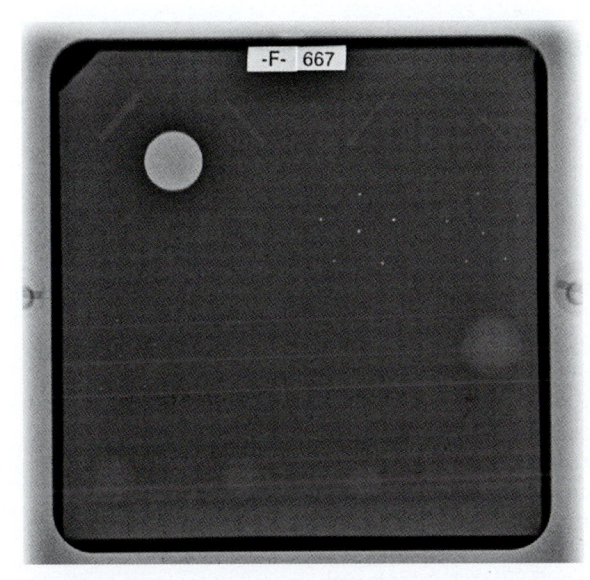

FIG. 8.3 • Digital image of the ACR phantom: technically adequate imaging system with at least four (4) fibers, three (3) speck groups, and three (3) masses are identified.

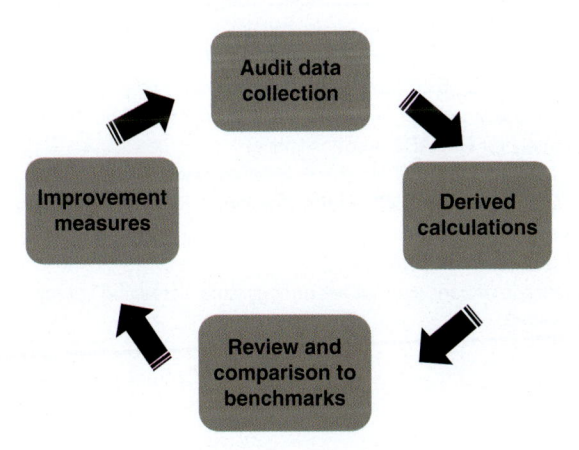

FIG. 8.4 • Medical outcomes audit cycle.

of accurate data accrual, a second step of calculations of derived data, a third step of reviewing and analyzing the outcomes data and comparing it to national benchmarks, and lastly, the fourth step of introducing practice improvement measures (Fig. 8.4). The initial three steps can then be repeated for assessing the impact of the introduced practice improvement measure.

For this comprehensive process to take place, breast imaging facilities must have a mammography medical outcomes audit program in place to follow positive mammography assessments and to correlate pathology results with the interpreting physician's findings.[18] The process of maintaining an accurate and meaningful medical audit program is lengthy and time consuming. Nonetheless, it is crucial in providing feedback to interpreting radiologists on their individual performance in detecting early cancers as well as their collective performance as a group in comparison to national standards with the ultimate goal of improved patient care.[19–21]

Step 1—Data accrual: The initial step of data accrual had historically been done manually. However, after the introduction of structured mammography reporting systems, this process has become semiautomated. These reporting systems typically have a medical outcomes audit package that tracks the total number of examinations based on indication, the interpreting radiologist, and the BI-RADS assessment category of each examination. Additionally, the majority of these systems will have a pathology reporting interface that allows manual entry of pathology results for each biopsy recommended and performed by the facility. These results (positive or negative) are in turn attributed to the interpreting physician for each of the screening and diagnostic mammogram, a step required in the process of outcomes calculation. Some of the newer commercially available systems also have the capability of linkage to the patients' EMRs and automating the process of importing pathology results, thus eliminating the manual entry of pathology data and potentially avoiding human errors and saving resources.

Each facility should have a QA process in place for follow-up on patients with mammograms coded as BI-RADS 4 or 5 that do not schedule or show up for biopsy at their institution. From a safety and quality standpoint, this process is to ensure that every attempt has been made to avoid missing cancers due to patient noncompliance, through contacting the patient's referring physician. Additionally, if the patient decides to receive care outside of the initial imaging facility, then this process would allow for the collection of pathology results for outcomes calculation.

Step 2—Calculation of derived data: Guidance on the methods of calculation of the medical outcomes audit is included in the BI-RADS atlas.[22] These calculations can be automatically generated through the structured reporting systems that generate comprehensive reports that include all the collected and calculated data recommended for accreditation. These reports can be performed on aggregate facility numbers or for individual radiologists.

Under MQSA regulations, conducting a minimal audit is required by facilities for accreditation purposes. However, the ACR recommends mammography facilities to conduct a more detailed audit to accurately assess the clinical performance of its interpreting physicians (Table 8.6).

Step 3—Data review and analysis: Review of the medical outcomes audit is the responsibility of the lead interpreting physician. This entails review of the aggregate facility and individual radiologist data. Data analysis and comparison to national benchmarks (based on data from national data repositories as well as modeling studies) identifies areas for potential improvement (Tables 8.7 and 8.8). Most importantly, as most of the statistical calculations of the derived data are based on correlation between the prospectively assigned BI-RADS assessment categories and the clinical outcome of mammograms, the interpreting radiologists should have a clear understanding and strong adherence to the ACR guidelines and the ACR BI-RADS terminology, assessment categories, and management recommendations.[23]

Step 4—Practice improvement measures: Through this comprehensive medical review process, areas of deficiencies should be addressed by the lead interpreting physician and practice improvement measures should be put in place. Some of the interventions that could improve performance recommended in previously published studies include additional education for technologists or interpreting radiologists, ensuring availability of prior comparisons, routine review and group discussion of false-negative cases, and workflow changes to allow uninterrupted reading sessions.[24–28]

Table 8.6 THE BASIC CLINICALLY RELEVANT AUDIT THAT IS MANDATED BY MQSA AND THE COMPLETE AUDIT RECOMMENDED BY THE ACR.

Data Collected for the Basic Clinically Relevant Audit	Additional Data Collected for the Complete Audit
1. Modality 2. Dates of audit period 3. Total number of examinations in that time range, and separated by indication (screening versus diagnostic) 4. Number of recommendations for additional imaging (BI-RADS 0) 5. Number of recommendations for short-interval follow-up (BI-RADS 3) 6. Number of recommendations for tissue diagnosis (BI-RADS 4 and 5) 7. Tissue diagnosis results (benign, high risk, or malignant) for BI-RADS 0, 3, 4, and 5 8. MQSA requires analysis of the false-negative examinations that become known, through attempts to retrieve pathology results and review of the examination given a negative assessment	1. Patient risk factors for breast cancer (age at time of examination, menopausal status, personal or family history of breast and ovarian cancer, previous breast biopsies yielding atypia, hormone replacement therapy, breast density estimated at mammography) 2. Has the patient had prior breast imaging studies 3. Number of recommendations for routine screening (number of negative examinations [BI-RADS 1] and number of benign examinations [BI-RADS 2]) 4. Tissue diagnosis results should be separated depending on mode of tissue sampling (fine needle aspiration, core biopsy, or surgical biopsy 5. Imaging findings identified on mammogram (masses, calcifications, architectural distortion, asymmetries) of imaging finding type 6. Palpable versus nonpalpable at time of imaging 7. Cancer staging: histologic type, invasive cancer size, nodal status, and tumor grade
Derived Data Calculated for the Basic Clinically Relevant Audit	**Derived Data Calculated for the Complete Audit**
1. True positive[a] (TP) 2. False positive (FP) 3. Positive predictive value of screening examinations recommended for anything other than routine screening (BI-RADS 0, 3, 4, or 5)—PPV1[b] 4. Positive predictive value based on recommendations for biopsy (BI-RADS 4 or 5)—PPV2 5. Positive predictive value based on biopsy actually performed, positive biopsy rate [PBR])—PPV3 6. Cancer detection rate (CDR) 7. Percentage of invasive cancers that are node negative 8. Percentage of minimal cancers (invasive cancer ≤ 1cm, or ductal carcinoma in situ [DCIS]) 9. Percentage of cancers that are stage 0 or 1 10. Abnormal interpretation (recall) rate for screening examinations—AIR	1. Sensitivity (if linked to tumor registry) 2. Specificity (if linked to tumor registry) 3. Positive predictive value of recommendation for biopsy should be done separately for screening versus diagnostic and done separately for BI-RADS 4 subdivisions 4. CDR for screening and diagnostic examinations 5. Incident and prevalent CDR for screening 6. CDR based on indication of diagnostic examination 7. CDR in different age groups 8. Percentage of cancers that are nonpalpable (screening versus diagnostic)

[a] Ascertainment of malignant results will require follow-up of biopsy results, surgical excision results, or through linkage to the regional tumor registry.
[b] PPV1 is only required calculation for facilities that are only providing screening services.
Adapted from the ACR BI-RADS Atlas 5th Edition.

Table 8.7 MINIMALLY ACCEPTABLE PERFORMANCE CRITERIA FOR SCREENING MAMMOGRAPHY.

Performance Metrics	Acceptable Ranges (%)
Cancer detection rate (per 1,000 examinations)	≥2.5
Abnormal interpretation (recall) rate	5–12
PPV1 (abnormal interpretation)	3–8
PPV2 (recommendation for tissue diagnosis)	20–40
Sensitivity (if measurable)	≥75
Specificity (if measurable)	88–95

Adapted from the ACR BI-RADS Atlas 5th Edition.

National Mammography Database

Despite the presence of the BI-RADS atlas as a comprehensive guide to radiologists, significant variability in practices still exists. Prior studies documenting and examining these variabilities attributed them partly to subspecialty training, years of experience, volumes of yearly interpreted examinations, and degree of adherence to BI-RADS recommendations.[29–34] And, since then, there has been a consorted effort by the radiology community to collect data on radiologists' performance through large national data repositories. These data repositories allowed for multi-institutional studies that focused on establishing national benchmarks and interpretative criteria, to minimize the variability in practices among radiologists and improve performance.[20,35–37] These set of performance metrics, as detailed in the ACR BI-RADS atlas,[22] are well-established quality measures in qualifying the collective success of a mammography practice as well as providing feedback to interpreting

Table 8.8 MINIMALLY ACCEPTABLE PERFORMANCE CRITERIA FOR DIAGNOSTIC MAMMOGRAPHY BASED ON EXAM INDICATION.

Performance Metrics	Work-up of Abnormal Mammogram (%)	Work-up of Palpable Lump (%)
Cancer detection rate (per 1,000 examinations)	≥20	≥40
Abnormal interpretation (recall) rate	8–25	10–25
PPV1 (abnormal interpretation)	15–40	25–50
PPV2 (recommendation for tissue diagnosis)	20–45	30–50
Sensitivity (if measurable)	≥80	≥85
Specificity (if measurable)	80–95	83–95

Adapted from the ACR BI-RADS Atlas 5th Edition

radiologists on their individual performance in comparison to national standards.[18–21,38]

The National Mammography Database (NMD) is one of the largest national mammography data repositories and part of the ACR's National Radiology Data Registry (NRDR). This registry allows for ongoing feedback on performance to individual mammography facilities that participate in this registry. It not only allows comparison to national published benchmarks, but also allows facilities to compare their performance to peers with similar practice type and regional location. Mammography facilities that become a member of the NMD can directly upload their medical outcomes audit data from their structured reporting systems. Data can be uploaded on a quarterly or semiannually timeline, and subsequently, the NMD provides to facilities semiannual reports that compare their collective performance as well as the individual performance of their radiologists against comparable practices across the country.[39]

Given the tremendous potential for improving performance of radiology practices through these tailored feedback reports, the American Board of Radiology (ABR) has designated participation in the NMD as practice quality improvement (PQI) that would fulfill the ABR Maintenance of Certification (MOC) program requirements.[40] Additionally, the NMD, and NRDR in general, has been approved by the CMS as a qualified clinical data registry (QCDR) for the physician quality reporting system (PQRS). Thus, by participating in the NMD, facilities would fulfill the PQRS quality reporting requirement under the Medicare Physician Fee Schedule Rule.

Clinical Images for Accreditation

Critical review of the clinical images acquired by a facility is an important facet of the accreditation process conducted by the ACR. This is a peer-review process by two ACR radiologist reviewers who score each submitted examination according to eight parameters (Table 8.9). Each facility is required to submit two clinical cases (one from a patient with fatty breast and one from a patient with dense breast). It is important to note that to submit images with patient information to the ACR, there should be a HIPAA Business Associate Agreement (BAA) between the facility and the ACR. This is an agreement of confidentiality that is in accordance with the standard HIPAA regulations.

The specific requirements for the submitted examinations are as follows:

- Actual clinical patients
- Must have been formally interpreted and assigned a BI-RADS assessment category 1 (*negative*)
- Should be an example of the facilities best work
- Should be of cases where the entire breast is imaged in a single exposure per projection (i.e., not multiple images per projection)

Table 8.9 THE *EIGHT* PARAMETERS FOR THE ACR CLINICAL IMAGE REVIEW PROCESS.

Parameters for ACR Clinical Images' Review

A. Positioning
B. Compression
C. Exposure levels
D. Sharpness
E. Contrast
F. Noise
G. Artifact
H. Exam identification

- Should have been reviewed and approved by the lead interpreting physician
- For digital images, no magnification or minification
- Should be labeled according to the MQSA required identification process (Table 8.10). Additionally, if they are submitted electronically, they should be labeled "For Presentation."

ACR Accreditation Approval Process

Once the facility and units have passed accreditation, a final report is sent to the lead interpreting physician within 60 days of receipt of testing package. This will include details on the results of the accreditation process and any comments including potential areas for improvement. The final approval package will also include the 3-year accreditation certificate and decal to be displayed in a visible place in every respective examination room.

ACR ACCREDITATION PROGRAMS OTHER THAN MAMMOGRAPHY

The ACR has created additional voluntary accreditation programs for breast imaging modalities and interventions that follow the same framework as the MAP. These programs represent a peer-review evaluation process to assure quality standards are met, provide constructive feedback to facilities, and identify areas for improvement.

Breast Ultrasound Accreditation Program

Timing

A 3-year accreditation cycle, starting from the date the unit passed the full evaluation

60 QUALITY AND SAFETY IN MEDICAL IMAGING

Table 8.10 IMAGE IDENTIFICATION REQUIREMENTS FOR ACR (PLUS MQSA FOR MAMMOGRAPHY) ACCREDITATION PROGRAMS BASED ON MODALITY.

Mammographic and Stereotactic Image Identification	Ultrasound Image Identification	MRI Image Identification
1. Patient's name (first and last)	1. Patient's name (first and last)	1. Patient's name (first and last)
2. Other patient's identifier (medical record number, or social security number, or date of birth)	2. Other patient's identifier (medical record number, or social security number, or date of birth)	2. Other patient's identifier (medical record number, or social security number, or date of birth)
3. Date of examination	3. Date of examination	3. Date of examination
4. Facility name and location (city, state, zip code)	4. Facility name and location (city, state, zip code)	4. Facility name and location (city, state, zip code)
5. Laterality (left or right breast)	5. Laterality (left or right breast)	5. Laterality (left or right breast)
6. Mammographic view (in mammography should be on the image in a position near the axilla)	6. Anatomic location using clock face or labeled diagram, and distance from the nipple in millimeters or centimeters	
7. Technologist identification	7. Technologist or physician performing the exam identification	
8. Cassette/screen identification (if screen/film technique)		
9. Mammography unit identification		

Components

Similar to the MAP, the ultrasound accreditation program includes personnel qualifications, equipment specifications, QC, and QA.

The ultrasound-guided breast biopsy program is an accreditation module that is supplementary to the breast ultrasound program and will be addressed in the section for Accreditation Programs for Breast Interventional Procedures.

Personnel Qualifications

Requirements for initial and continued accreditation to perform and interpret breast ultrasound by radiologist are listed in Table 8.11. However, the ACR identifies that breast ultrasound may be interpreted by physicians other than radiologists and lists the specific requirements in these practice settings.

Additional information on requirements for nonradiologist physicians, ultrasound technologists, and medical physicist can be reviewed on the ACR website: www.acr.org/~/media/ACR/Documents/Accreditation/BreastUS/Requirements.pdf

Equipment Specifications

The ACR mandates that breast ultrasound should be performed with:
- High-resolution technique
- Real-time linear array transducers with center frequency at least at 10 MHz (preferably higher)
- An equipment that allows for electronic focal zone adjustment

Quality Control

The breast ultrasound QC program has some optional (although highly recommended) components as well as required components. All these components should be performed on each unit by a qualified medical physicist or under his or her direct supervision by trained personnel. Some of the tests are done on phantoms through objective computer-based testing or subjective assessment.

The optional components include:
- *Acceptance testing* at the initial installation of new units, after equipment replacement, or after major hardware/software upgrades
- *Semiannual QC tests* that include physical inspection of the unit and evaluate the image uniformity, artifacts, geometric accuracy, and image display

The required component includes:
- *Annual survey*, which includes physical inspection of the unit and evaluates the image uniformity, artifacts, geometric accuracy, system sensitivity, contrast and spatial resolution, and image display. There should be a period of no longer than 14 months between surveys. An annual survey report is generated by the medical physicist and included in the application paperwork. This report should be reviewed by the lead interpreting physician.
- *PM*, which should be performed by qualified equipment service engineers per vendor recommendations.

As of June 1, 2014, the ACR requires documentation of the QC tests and corrective actions for accreditation.

Quality Assurance

To ensure quality of clinical breast ultrasound program, there should be a routine review process of the quality of examinations from a technical standpoint and an interpretative standpoint. This process should typically be put in place and supervised by the lead interpreting physician. There should be routine assessment of outcomes of the review process, and any areas of concerns should be documented and addressed, and quality improvement measures put in place.

Each facility should have QA policies similar to those in mammography. These, for example, could address consumer complaints, recording of adverse events, infection control, and appropriate communication of significant findings.

One of the QA measures to ensure quality interpretations of examinations is the presence of a *physician peer-review* process. This requirement can be achieved through an internal peer-review program or through participation in a national program such as RADPEER.

If the facility elects an internal program, it should include the following:
- Regular selection of random examinations to be double read by a second radiologist
- These examinations should be from routine clinical practice.
- A classification system of the review outcome in regards to agreement/disagreement/quality of the initial interpretation
- Policies for action to be taken on significant discrepancies in interpretation after peer review for quality improvement
- Summary data per facility and per radiologist

Quality and Safety in Breast Imaging

Table 8.11 ACR BREAST ULTRASOUND ACCREDITATION PROGRAM: REQUIREMENTS FOR INITIAL AND CONTINUED CERTIFICATION FOR INTERPRETING RADIOLOGISTS IN AN INDEPENDENT SETTING.

	Initial Certification	Maintenance of Certification
Licensure	Licensed to practice medicine *and* Board certified by: • ABR *or* • American Osteopathic Board of Radiology (AOBR) *or* • Royal College of Physicians and Surgeons of Canada *or* If radiology resident graduating after *June 30, 2014:* • Must be board eligible as defined by the ABR If not Board certified: • Must have completed an American College of Graduate Medical Education (ACGME)–approved radiology residency • Performance/interpretation of 300 breast ultrasound in the prior 36 mo	Maintain his or her medical license *and* Meets the MOC requirements of the ABR
Experience (volumes of examination interpreted) Continued education (category 1 CME hours)		Must have performed/interpreted 200 breast ultrasound in the prior 36 mo Meets the MOC requirements for the ABR *or* Completes 150 h (75 h of category 1 CME) pertinent to the physicians' practice patterns in the prior 36 mo *or* Completes 15 h CME (half of which category 1) in the specific imaging modality (*ultrasound*) or organ system (*breast*) in the prior 36 mo

Clinical Images for Accreditation

Similar to MAP, the ACR accreditation application process includes submitting clinical ultrasound images. The clinical images that must be submitted are those for a case of a solid mass and those for a case of a simple cyst.

Requirements of the submitted images are as follows:

- There should be one finding per case.
- These should represent the facilities' best work.
- Ultrasound images should have been acquired without compound imaging.
- Ultrasound images should be labeled per ACR recommendations (Table 8.10).
- Images submitted per case should include:
  - Two orthogonal ultrasound views (transverse and longitudinal) without calipers
  - One ultrasound image with calipers
  - Two orthogonal mammographic views with a single circle on the corresponding mammographic finding

ACCREDITATION PROGRAMS FOR BREAST INTERVENTIONAL PROCEDURES

The accreditation programs for the breast interventions have few requirements in common, and thus are discussed in the same section.

Ultrasound-Guided Breast Biopsy Accreditation Module

The accreditation program for ultrasound-guided procedures is not a stand-alone accreditation program. However, it is a supplemental module to the breast ultrasound accreditation program that is applied for if facilities perform ultrasound-guided breast interventions in addition to their diagnostic ultrasound services.

Timing

A 3-year accreditation cycle, in conjunction with the breast ultrasound accreditation cycle

Components

Personnel Qualifications

- Physicians must meet the requirements for ultrasound accreditation program to be accredited to perform ultrasound-guided biopsies. Table 8.12 lists the additional requirements for initial and continued accreditation for radiologists to perform breast ultrasound-guided interventions.
- Additional information on the accreditation requirements for non-radiologist can be reviewed on the ACR website: www.acr.org/~/media/ACR/Documents/Accreditation/BreastUS/Requirements.pdf

Equipment Specifications and Quality Control

The equipment specifications and QC components of the ultrasound-guided breast biopsy module are typically fulfilled

Table 8.12 ACR BREAST ULTRASOUND-GUIDED BIOPSY ACCREDITATION MODULE: ADDITIONAL REQUIREMENTS FOR INITIAL AND CONTINUED CERTIFICATION FOR INTERPRETING RADIOLOGISTS.

Radiologists	
Initial certification	Qualified to interpret mammograms under MQSA
Continued experience	Must have performed 36 image-guided breast biopsies in the prior 36 mo

through the application process for the breast ultrasound accreditation program.

Quality Assurance

QA in breast biopsy programs is crucial to avoid missing cancers and identify areas of deficiencies that would benefit from quality improvement initiatives. The components of QA in breast procedures are partly addressed through the accreditation requirements for the individual ACR programs, and partly addressed through the ACR practice performance parameters for the individual procedures.

Clinical Images for Accreditation

Clinical images documenting the competency of the physicians performing the ultrasound-guided procedures must be submitted with the accreditation packet.

- Cases selected should be BI-RADS category 4 or 5.
- Cases should be not older than 6 months.
- Cases should represent the facility's best work.
- Mammographic images and biopsy images must be from the same patient.
- The submitted images must include the following:

Images	Core Biopsy Needles— Fire Mode	Core Biopsy Needles— Nonfire Mode	Fine Needle Aspirations
Mammograms	Two orthogonal mammographic views with the corresponding single finding circled and visible in both images		
Pre-biopsy ultrasound	Single mass seen on two orthogonal views (long and trans)		
Pre-fire ultrasound	The needle seen in long axis aiming toward the mass just prior to firing and parallel to chest wall	N/A	N/A
Postbiopsy ultrasound	The needle seen in long axis through the mass (or under if nonfiring) and parallel to chest wall		

Stereotactic Breast Biopsy Accreditation Program

Timing

A 3-year accreditation cycle, starting from the date the unit passed the full evaluation

Components

Personnel Qualifications

The ACR identified two distinct practice settings to perform stereotactic biopsies: a collaborative setting (biopsies performed by radiologist and nonradiologist physicians) and independent setting (biopsies performed by either radiologist or nonradiologist physician) on the same accredited unit.

Similar to the MAP, there are specific qualification requirements for physicians performing stereotactic biopsies; the type of practice setting will dictate the different qualification requirements for radiologists or the nonradiologist physicians (typically surgeons). Table 8.13 displays the requirements for initial and continuing certification for interpreting radiologists in an independent setting.

Additional information and requirements for collaborative setup can be reviewed at www.acr.org/~/media/ACR/Documents/Accreditation/SBB/Requirements.pdf

Equipment Specifications

There are specific equipment types that are approved by the ACR for stereotactic biopsy:

- Dedicated, stand-alone stereotactic units that are exclusively used for biopsy or needle localization
- Mammography equipment with add-on biopsy units specifically designed for breast biopsy or with a lateral arm-support system that allows the biopsy needle to be visualized in relation to the targeted calcifications in two views

Quality Control

Similar to the mammography accreditation process, the stereotactic program accreditation requires specific QC tests to be conducted on a daily, weekly, monthly, quarterly, and semiannually basis by the lead technologist.

Medical physicist's survey is also required after the initial installation, and then at least annually or after major hardware or software repair or upgrade. Written reports from the lead physicist should be provided after each survey

PM is also a requirement for biopsy equipment and performed by qualified service engineers. Any deficiencies identified and corrected should be recorded and a final detailed report kept for records.

Quality Assurance

QA in breast biopsy programs is crucial to avoid missing cancers and identify areas of deficiencies that would benefit from quality improvement initiatives. The components of QA in breast procedures are partly addressed through the accreditation requirements for the individual ACR programs and partly addressed through the ACR practice performance parameters for the individual procedures.

Clinical Images for Accreditation

Clinical images documenting the competency of the physicians performing the stereotactic-guided procedures must be submitted with the accreditation packet.

Requirements for the submitted images are as follows:

- Case selected should be BI-RADS category 4 or 5.
- Case should not be older than 6 months.
- Case should represent the facility's best work.
- Mammographic images and biopsy images must be from the same patient.
- Case submitted should be for calcifications.

Quality and Safety in Breast Imaging

Table 8.13 ACR BREAST STEREOTACTIC BREAST BIOPSY ACCREDITATION PROGRAM: REQUIREMENTS FOR INITIAL AND CONTINUED CERTIFICATION FOR PERFORMING RADIOLOGISTS IN AN INDEPENDENT SETTING.

	Initial Certification	Maintenance of Certification
Licensure	Qualified as an interpreting physician under MQSA	Maintain his or her medical license *and* Meets the MOC requirements of the ABR
Experience (volumes of biopsies performed)	Performed 12 stereotactic breast biopsies or 3 hands-on stereotactic breast biopsies under direct supervision of qualified physician	Upon renewal, must have performed 36 image-guided breast biopsies (at least 9 of them must be stereotactic biopsies) in the prior 36 mo
Continued education (category 1 CME hours)	3 h of category 1 CME in stereotactic breast biopsy *and* 15 h of category 1 CME in breast imaging pathophysiology of benign and malignant breast diseases and clinical breast examination	Meets the MOC requirements for the ABR *or* Completes 150 h (75 h of category 1 CME) pertinent to the physicians' practice patterns in the prior 36 mo *or* Completes 15 h CME (half of which category 1) in the specific imaging modality (*stereotactic breast biopsy*) or organ system (*breast*) in the prior 36 mo

- The images should document accurate positioning of the needle in relation to the targeted calcifications (the calcifications should be clearly seen on all submitted images and not obscured by the needle).
- The submitted images must include:
  - Two orthogonal mammographic views with the corresponding single finding circled and visible in both images
  - Post-fire stereotactic pair (preferred) with the sampling chamber at the level of the calcifications or the pre-fire stereotactic pair with the needle pointing toward the calcifications. The scout image should not be submitted.
  - The specimen radiograph
  - Postbiopsy scout or stereo pair image with the clip in place

Quality Assurance for Percutaneous Image-Guided Breast Interventions

QA in breast biopsy programs applies to stereotactic-, ultrasound-, and MRI-guided interventions. It entails two key components:

a. Quality assessment of procedures performed through radiologic–pathologic correlation of each biopsy. Success of this component is multifactorial, although depends primarily on individual radiologist's performance. It requires wide knowledge base of the various differential diagnoses for imaging findings and good understanding of the appropriate follow-up recommendations for various pathologies.

Radiologic pathologic correlation: The ACR in its practice parameters for performance of stereotactic biopsies and ultrasound-guided core biopsies and fine needle aspirations (FNAs) strongly recommends that a radiologic–pathologic correlation process is in place for every percutaneous image-guided biopsy performed. This is preferably conducted by the physician who performed the procedure.[41,42]

The process of radiologic–pathologic correlation entails:

1. Confirming that the intended lesion was correctly targeted
2. Confirming that the targeted lesion was adequately sampled
3. Confirming that the pathology results explain the imaging finding (concordance)
4. Deciding on follow-up recommendation

b. Quality assessment of the biopsy program in its entirety, through the medical outcomes audit data and tracking complications. This allows assessment of the collective performance of the practice and identification of systems' errors.

Each facility should routinely collect data on every image-guided breast biopsy performed for the evaluation of performance and identification of areas for improvement.

The ACR requires separate outcomes data for each biopsy program for their individual accreditation.

For each guidance modality, data collected should include:

1. Total number of biopsies
2. Total number of malignant biopsies
3. Total number of benign biopsies
4. Total number of biopsies requiring repeat sampling and broken down by: reason for repeat sampling (insufficient, discordant, atypia/radial scar); mode of repeat sampling (core needle biopsy versus surgical excision); and final pathology outcome (benign versus malignant).
5. Total number of complications, classified by type of complication:
   a. Total number of procedures with infection requiring treatment
   b. Total number of procedures with hematoma requiring intervention
   c. Total number of procedures with other complications

There should be a process in place for routine follow-up on biopsy patients and possibly chart review to identify early or delayed complications of image-guided biopsies. This can be performed by radiology nursing or medical assistants.

Breast MRI Accreditation Program

Special Considerations

Medicare Billing

Breast MRI accreditation is not mandatory by MQSA. However, under Medicare Improvement for Patients and Providers Act of 2008 (MIPPA), all outpatient imaging facilities providing advanced imaging services (breast MRI) for Medicare patients who are billing under technical component of part B of the Medicare Physician Fee Schedule must pass accreditation by a CMS-approved accrediting body to qualify for reimbursement.

Mandatory QA processes for passing CMS and ACR accreditation include:

- Process for notifying and allowing patients to obtain HIPAA compliant copies of their medical records and imaging studies, if needed
- Process for documenting qualifications of facility's personnel and providing copies from their original source
- Process for verification that facility personnel are not included on the Office of Inspector General's exclusion list
- Process for informing consumers (patients and families) that they can file a written complaint with the ACR for any event

Facility Requirements for Imaging Correlation and Imaging-Guided Biopsies

Facilities applying for accreditation of their breast MRI program must have the capability to perform mammographic correlation, as well as imaging-guided biopsies (targeted ultrasound and ultrasound-guided biopsies as well as MRI-guided biopsies) of the suspicious findings identified on MRI. If this is not available, then a referral agreement with facilities that have these interventional capabilities must be in place.

Timing

A 3-year accreditation cycle, starting from the date the unit passed the full evaluation

Components

The ACR breast MRI accreditation program is unit specific, and each magnet used for patient care needs to be certified before the facility acquires its accreditation.

Personnel Qualifications

There are specific requirements for initial and continued certification for interpreting physicians, MRI technologists, and medical physicists or MRI scientists working in the breast MRI program. All requirements are based on the previous full calendar year.

Requirements for licensure, continued experience, and continued education for certification of radiologist interpreting breast MRI are listed in Table 8.14. The lead interpreting

Table 8.14 **ACR BREAST MRI ACCREDITATION PROGRAM: REQUIREMENTS FOR INITIAL AND CONTINUED CERTIFICATION FOR INTERPRETING RADIOLOGISTS.**

	Radiologists
Initial certification	**Board Certified** Certified in radiology by: • ABR or • American Osteopathic Board of Radiology (AOBR) or • Royal College of Physicians and Surgeons of Canada or • Le Collège des Médecins du Québec or • Radiologists graduating from residency after June 30, 2014, must be board eligible as defined by the ABR and **If Board certified before 2008**, must also meet one of the following: • Oversight, interpretation, and reporting of 150 breast MRI examinations in the last 36 months or • Interpretation and reporting of 100 breast MRI examinations in the last 36 mo in a supervised situation and • 15 h of category 1 CME in MRI (including clinical applications of MRI in breast imaging, MRI artifacts, safety, and instrumentation) or **Not Board Certified** • Completion of an American College of Graduate Medical Education (ACGME)– or American Osteopathic Association (AOA)–approved resident program and • Interpretation and reporting of 100 breast MRI examinations in the last 36 mo in a supervised situation and • 15 h of category 1 CME in MRI (including clinical applications of MRI in breast imaging, MRI artifacts, safety, and instrumentation)
Continuing experience	Upon renewal, 75 breast MRI examinations in the prior 36 mo
Continuing education	Upon renewal, must meet one of the following: • Meets MOC or • Completes 150 h (that includes 75 h of category 1 CME) in the prior 36 mo pertinent to the physicians' practice patterns or • Completes 15 h CME (half of which must be category 1) in the prior 36 mo specific to imaging modality (MRI) or organ system (breast)

physician of the accreditation program should be the primary physician in charge of creating imaging protocols that adhere to the ACR accreditation requirements. However, individual interpreting radiologists should also approve examination indication, oversee implementation of appropriate imaging protocols, and be available at time of contrast injection for examinations that they interpret.

The accreditation requirements for breast MRI technologists ensure that they have a general understanding of the principles of MRI technology and equipment, clinical imaging protocols, and their optimization as well as MRI safety. More detailed MRI knowledge of acquisition parameters and MRI equipment is mandatory for the medical physicists/MRI scientists. This knowledge and how to optimize it for breast MRI in specific is further reinforced through continuing clinical experience and continuing education programs.

Given the possible adverse effects and allergic reactions with contrast injection, the ACR recommends that technologists performing breast MRI hold the Basic Life Support certification and are capable of using automatic external defibrillator.[43]

Detailed requirements for initial and continued certification for MRI technologists and physicists are available through the ACR website: www.acr.org/~/media/ACR/Documents/Accreditation/BreastMRI/Requirements.pdf

Equipment Specifications

No specific requirements for maximum field strength. However, to perform breast MRI, the equipment must have the following requirements:

- Have dedicated bilateral breast coil
- Be capable of simultaneous, bilateral imaging
- Meet all state and federal performance requirements, which includes those for:
  - Maximum static magnetic field strength
  - Maximum rate of change of magnetic field strength (dB/dt)
  - Maximum radiofrequency power deposition (specific absorption rate)
  - Maximum auditory noise levels

Quality Control

The QC tests for MRI should be conducted by qualified medical physicist or MRI scientist. Trained personnel can be present for assistance; however, all data collection, review, and interpretation of surveys must be conducted under direct supervision of the qualified medical physicist.

The tests conducted should follow instructions provided in the *2015 ACR Magnetic Resonance Imaging Quality Control Manual*.[44]

Part of the application paperwork includes providing documentation of compliance with the ACR QC requirements (Annual MRI System Performance Evaluation report, including performance of the bilateral breast coil).

Acceptance testing should be performed by the medical physicist/MRI scientist after the initial installation of the MRI equipment. It is a comprehensive systems checklist that includes all of the technologist's QC tests and the annual medical physicist's survey tests per the ACR MRI control manual.

Annual medical physicist's survey is part of the acceptance testing at installation and done annually thereafter with appropriate documentation. This includes testing the magnetic field homogeneity, slice position accuracy, slice thickness accuracy, radiofrequency coil checks, soft copy displays (monitors), as well as overall evaluation of the QC program and MRI safety program.

Technologist's QC tests are part of the acceptance testing at installation and done weekly thereafter with appropriate documentation. These are done by the MRI technologists under the supervision of the medical physicist. These include table position, setup and scanning, center frequency, transmitter gain or attenuation, geometric accuracy, high contrast (spatial) resolution, low contrast resolution (detectability), artifact analysis, film (hardcopy) display, and visual checklist.

Some of the tests listed in the QC manual may not be applicable on the ACR MRI accreditation phantom and can be performed on the small-parts MRI phantom.

PM must be performed and documented by the qualified service engineer at the recommended intervals per manufacturer guidelines.

Quality Assurance

Similar to other ACR accreditation programs, a lead interpreting physician and lead technologist for the MRI program must be assigned. The lead interpreting physician and the lead technologist will be responsible for submitting all accreditation paperwork and correspondence with the ACR and will ensure that the program fulfills all the ACR requirements for accreditation, which include the following:

- Participating in a peer-review process (similar to the one described in the ultrasound accreditation program section)
- Ensuring all personnel (interpreting radiologists, technologists, and medical physicists) meet the certification requirements
- Developing and maintaining medical outcomes audit program that tracks MRI examinations by indication as well as follow-up on the final pathology for positive examinations
- Implementing and documenting QC tests, PM, physicist's surveys by a qualified medical physicist
- Developing and implementing policies and procedures that are similar to ones addressed in the mammography program in addition to policies that specifically pertain to the MRI program. The MRI-specific policies include:
  - Procedures addressing MRI safety, in accordance with ACR white paper on Magnetic Resonance Safety[45]
  - Procedures for infection control, contrast injection, and management of contrast allergic reactions
  - Procedures to identify pregnant or potentially pregnant patients
  - Procedures that govern physician presence at time of contrast injection and sedation administration

Clinical Images for Accreditation

In addition to the equipment specifications provided earlier, the ACR aims to standardize the quality of the MRI examinations performed across practices through providing minimal requirements for type/number of sequences as well as some of the scan parameters for breast MRI examinations. Examples of the facility's breast MRI protocol must be submitted for accreditation and will be reviewed by two ACR radiologists.

The requirements for the clinical images submitted for review include the following:

- Examinations must not be older than 6 months.
- They should be actual clinical images of a patient (not volunteer) and should belong to the same patient.
- The patient must not have had mastectomy.
- The submitted sequences should be of adequate signal-to-noise ratio (SNR), not too grainy, and, if artifacts are present, should not interfere with diagnostic quality and image interpretation.
- The patient must be adequately positioned to include the entire breast and axillary tail.

- Specifications for type and parameters of examinations submitted should be easily reviewed through the Digital Imaging and Communications in Medicine (DICOM) header. These specifications include the following:

Sequence	Specification
Localizer or scout	
Fluid-sensitive sequence (T2-weighted or other bright fluid series)	• Sufficient bright fluid contrast • Can be a single series of both breasts, or two separate series (one of each breast)

Multiphase–dynamic T1-weighted series	• Acquired simultaneously of both breast (parallel imaging)
	• Should include one precontrast T1WI sequence, and at least two postcontrast sequences (a total of at least 3 sequences)
	• The first (early) postcontrast sequence must be completed within 4 min of completion of contrast injection
	• Can be submitted as two separate series (one precontrast and the rest of the postcontrast series), or all as one series (pre- and postcontrast all in one series)
	• If fat saturation is not used or failed, then the pre- and postcontrast series as well as the subtraction series of every time point should be included
	• The technical parameters for the pre- and postcontrast series should be identical to allow for postprocessing and subtraction
	• The technical parameters (spatial resolution) specifications include the following:
	  ○ *Plane of acquisition*: sagittal, axial, coronal, or slightly oblique
	  ○ *Slice thickness*: ≤3 mm
	  ○ *Gap*: 0
	  ○ *Maximum in plane pixel dimension for phase and frequency*: ≤1 mm

The submitted images will be reviewed and scored based on:
1. Pulse sequences and image contrast
2. Positioning
3. Artifacts
4. Spatial and temporal resolution
5. Exam identification, which will follow specific requirements as listed in Table 8.10

APPROPRIATE REPORTING AND COMMUNICATION OF RESULTS

The 5th edition of the *Breast Imaging Reporting and Data System* (BI-RADS) atlas, the most recent, was published in February 2014. This atlas provides an evidence-based standardized breast imaging terminology, report organization, assessment structure, and guidance on the performance of mammography and other breast imaging modalities' audits.[46] Following this structured reporting framework allows radiologists to clearly convey their level of concern based on imaging features to referring physicians and minimizes misconception.[47] Each study is given a BI-RADS assessment category that implies a range of probability of malignancy. In the majority of cases, there is concordance between the BI-RADS assessment categories and the accompanying management recommendations, with very few exceptions (Fig. 8.5). The FDA regulations state that for each mammographic study, an overall BI-RADS assessment category should be rendered and should be based on the most suspicious imaging finding in both breasts. The FDA mandates that a signed report should be provided to the referring primary care provider and a summary letter in lay terms provided to the patient in a timely fashion (no longer than 30 days). If the examination is given a suspicious of malignancy (BI-RADS category 4) or highly suggestive of malignancy (BI-RADS category 5), then every attempt should be made to communicate these results to the referring primary care provider as soon as possible, no longer than three business days, and communicated to the patient as soon as possible, no longer than 5 days. This reporting and follow-up of results framework is not mandated by MQSA for breast imaging examinations—other than mammography. However, it is mandated to pass accreditation by the ACR in their accreditation programs for breast ultrasound and MRI.

The ACR accreditation programs for each breast imaging modality provide an example of the acceptable framework for imaging reports, which should include:

- Patient name and additional personal identifiers
- Date of examination
- Name of interpreting physician
- Body of the report containing imaging findings of each examination
- An overall final assessment and follow-up recommendation

Structured reporting systems are a valuable IT resource in a breast imaging practice. There are multiple commercially available vendors, all with similar capabilities. The majority of these systems offer a point-and-click report generation platform that follows the report organization framework and imaging descriptors consistent with the BI-RADS atlas. These systems have the capability of integrating with the various EMR systems, hence directly forwarding the final reports to the patient's permanent records within few minutes of the radiologist dictating and signing of reports. Copies of the reports to the referring clinicians and summary letters in lay language to the patients can be automatically printed for mailing, or directly e-mailed to their final destination.

These systems also facilitate the process of medical outcomes audits by allowing prospective, automatic tracking of volumes and types of examinations, individual BI-RADS assessment categories, final recommendations, and final disposition of biopsy results that can be directly linked to the triggering examination and the corresponding interpreting physician. The majority of these systems have the computing ability of generating medical outcomes audits based on the prospectively collected data and adhering to the ACR-recommended methods of calculations.

TIMELINESS AND EFFICIENCY

Timeliness and efficiency are two closely related quality measures and should be an overarching goal in each step of patient care in a breast imaging department.

Assessment Categories	Impression	Follow-up Recommendation	Likelihood of Malignancy
BI-RADS 0	Needs additional imaging and/or prior comparison	Immediate follow-up	N/A
BI-RADS 1	Negative	Routine screening	Essentially 0
BI-RADS 2	Benign	Routine screening	Essentially 0
BI-RADS 3	Probably benign	Short-term follow-up (6, 12, and 24 months)	>0% but ≤2%
BI-RADS 4	Suspicious for malignancy (low, moderate, high)	Tissue diagnosis—biopsy	>2% but <95%
BI-RADS 5	Highly suggestive of malignancy	Tissue diagnosis—biopsy	≥95%
BI-RADS 6	Biopsy-proven malignancy	Follow-up with surgeon or oncologist	

FIG. 8.5 • Follow-up recommendations and likelihood of malignancy for each of the BI-RADS assessment categories.

Timeliness in Scheduling

This is one of the quality indicators for radiology practices and directly contributes to patient satisfaction with mammography services.[48] Electronic scheduling templates or scheduling through the EMR can significantly facilitate scheduling of examinations.

Timeliness in Imaging Acquisition

Adoption of well-acknowledged quality improvement programs that promote successful workflow habits, which value time and efficiency, should be a top priority. The LEAN program is a great example of these initiatives and has been increasingly utilized in health care, specifically in radiology departments.[49] This program typically engages representatives from the entire health-care team that go through a systematic approach of workflow analysis, intervention, and reanalysis. Adoption of such programs as well as embracing technological solutions, as electronic workflow lists, can streamline patient navigation in an imaging center and improve technologist workflow and efficiency, hence increasing patient volumes while maintaining quality services.[50]

Timeliness in Image Interpretation, Reporting, and Communication of Results

The Mammography Quality Assurance Act requires that mammography facilities send or give directly to all women a written summary of the results of the mammography in lay terms no later than 30 days from the date of the examination. However, given the psychosocial stress experienced by patients and often associated with waiting for the results of the breast imaging examinations,[51,52] prompt communication of results is greatly appreciated and often demanded by patients. The transition to digital mammography over the past 15 years and review of images on picture archive and reviewing systems (PACS), in addition to its clinical benefits, has revolutionized workflow in breast imaging practices and significantly improved efficiency in image interpretation.[53] Structured reporting systems are also one of the greatly valuable IT resources that promote efficiency in reporting, as described in earlier section. These systems promote efficiency of radiologists by facilitating report dictation, and promote efficiency of radiology department staff and file room personnel by facilitating prompt communication of results to referring clinicians and patients. And as described in earlier section, they also promote efficiency of technologists by facilitating medical outcomes audit.

In conclusion, a clinical environment that promotes quality and safety at each step of patient care in a breast imaging practice is crucial in achieving the outset goal of identifying breast cancers early and improving patient outcomes and satisfaction.

References

1. Kohn LT, Corrigan JM, Donaldson M, et al. *To Err Is Human–Building a Safer Health System*. Washington, DC: National Academy Press; 2000.
2. Allen B Jr. Five reasons radiologists should embrace clinical decision support for diagnostic imaging. *J Am Coll Radiol*. 2014;11:533–534.
3. Redberg RF. Getting to best care at lower cost. *JAMA Intern Med*. 2013;173:91–92.
4. Hunt DL, Haynes R, Hanna SE, et al. Effects of computer-based clinical decision support systems on physician performance and patient outcomes: a systematic review. *JAMA*. 1998; 280:1339–1346.
5. Boland GW, Weilburg J, Duszak R Jr. Imaging appropriateness and implementation of clinical decision support. *J Am Coll Radiol*. 2015;12:601–603.
6. Khorasani R, Hentel K, Darer J, et al. Ten commandments for effective clinical decision support for imaging: enabling evidence-based practice to improve quality and reduce waste. *Am J Roentgenol*. 2014;203:945–951.
7. Blackmore CC, Mecklenburg RS, Kaplan GS. Effectiveness of clinical decision support in controlling inappropriate imaging. *J Am Coll Radiol*. 2011;8:19–25.
8. Raja AS, Ip IK, Prevedello LM, et al. Effect of computerized clinical decision support on the use and yield of CT pulmonary angiography in the emergency department. *Radiology*. 2012;262:468–474.
9. Ip IK, Raja AS, Gupta A, et al. Impact of clinical decision support on head computed tomography use in patients with mild traumatic brain injury in the ED. *Am J Emerg Med*. 2015;33:320–325.
10. Ip IK, Schneider LI, Hanson R, et al. Adoption and meaningful use of computerized physician order entry with an integrated clinical decision support system for radiology: ten-year analysis in an Urban Teaching Hospital. *J Am Coll Radiol*. 2012;9:129–136.

11. Moriarity AK, Klochko C, O'Brien M, et al. The effect of clinical decision support for advanced inpatient imaging. *J Am Coll Radiol.* 2015;12:358–363.
12. Saadatmand S, Bretveld R, Siesling S, et al. Influence of tumour stage at breast cancer detection on survival in modern times: population based study in 173,797 patients. *BMJ.* 2015; 351:h4901.
13. Greif JM. Mammographic screening for breast cancer: an invited review of the benefits and costs. *Breast.* 2010;19:268–272.
14. McLelland R, Hendrick RE, Zinninger MD, et al. The American College of Radiology Mammography Accreditation Program. *Am J Roentgenol.* 1991;157:473–479.
15. Bassett LW. The regulation of mammography. *Semin Ultrasound CT MRI.* 1996;17:415–423.
16. U.S.Food and Drug Administration. Mammography Quality Standards Act Regulations. [October 14, 2015]; Available from: http://www.fda.gov/Radiation-EmittingProducts/MammographyQualityStandardsActandProgram/Regulations/ucm110906.htm.
17. Reynolds A. Quality assurance and ergonomics in the mammography department. *Radiol Technol.* 2014;86:61M–79M.
18. Elmore JG, Aiello Bowles EJ, Geller B, et al. Radiologists' attitudes and use of mammography audit reports. *Acad Radiol.* 2010;17:752–760
19. Sickles EA. Auditing your breast imaging practice: an evidence-based approach. *Semin Roentgenol.* 2007;42:211–217.
20. Carney PA, Sickles EA, Monsees BS, et al. Identifying minimally acceptable interpretive performance criteria for screening mammography. *Radiology.* 2010;255:354–361.
21. Linver MN, Osuch JR, Brenner RJ, et al. The mammography audit: a primer for the mammography quality standards act (MQSA). *Am J Roentgenol.* 1995;165:19–25.
22. Sickles E, D'Orsi CJ, Bassett LW, et al. ACR BI-RADS® follow-up and outcome monitoring. In *ACR BI-RADS® Atlas, Breast Imaging Reporting and Data System.* Reston, VA, American College of Radiology; 2013.
23. American College of Radiology. *Breast Imaging Reporting and Data System (BI-RADS),* 3rd ed. Reston, VA: American College of Radiology, 1998.
24. Carney PA, Abraham L, Cook A, et al. Impact of an educational intervention designed to reduce unnecessary recall during screening mammography. *Acad Radiol.* 2012;19:1114–1120.
25. Sickles EA. Successful methods to reduce false-positive mammography interpretations. *Radiol Clin N Am.* 2000;38:693–700.
26. Linver MN, Paster SB, Rosenberg RD, et al. Improvement in mammography interpretation skills in a community radiology practice after dedicated teaching courses: 2-year medical audit of 38,633 cases. *Radiology.* 1992;184:39–43.
27. Burnside ES, Park JM, Fine JP, et al. The use of batch reading to improve the performance of screening mammography. *Am J Roentgenol.* 2005;185:790–796.
28. Burnside ES, Sickles EA, Sohlich RE, et al. Differential value of comparison with previous examinations in diagnostic versus screening mammography. *Am J Roentgenol.* 2002;179:1173–1177.
29. Kerlikowske K, Grady D, Barclay J, et al. Variability and accuracy in mammographic interpretation using the American College of Radiology Breast Imaging Reporting and Data System. *J Natl Cancer Inst.* 1998;90:1801–1809.
30. Sickles EA, Wolverton DE, Dee KE. Performance parameters for screening and diagnostic mammography: specialist and general radiologists. *Radiology.* 2002;224:861–869.
31. Elmore JG, Jackson SL, Abraham L, et al. Variability in interpretive performance at screening mammography and radiologists' characteristics associated with accuracy. *Radiology.* 2009;253:641–651.
32. Elmore JG, Nakano CY, Koepsell TD, et al. International variation in screening mammography interpretations in community-based programs. *J Natl Cancer Inst.* 2003;95:1384–1393.
33. Leung JW, Margolin FR, Dee KE, et al. Performance parameters for screening and diagnostic mammography in a community practice: are there differences between specialists and general radiologists? *Am J of Roentgenol.* 2007;188:236–241.
34. Esserman L, Cowley H, Eberle C, et al. Improving the accuracy of mammography: volume and outcome relationships. *J Natl Cancer Inst.* 2002;94:369–375.
35. Rosenberg RD, Yankaskas BC, Abraham LA, et al. Performance benchmarks for screening mammography. *Radiology.* 2006; 241:55–66.
36. Sickles EA, Miglioretti DL, Ballard-Barbash R, et al. Performance benchmarks for diagnostic mammography. *Radiology.* 2005;235:775–790.
37. Carney PA, Parikh J, Sickles EA, et al. Diagnostic mammography: identifying minimally acceptable interpretive performance criteria. *Radiology.* 2013;267:359–367.
38. Cook AJ, Elmore JG, Zhu W, et al. Mammographic interpretation: radiologists' ability to accurately estimate their performance and compare it with that of their peers. *Am J Roentgenol.* 2012;199:695–702.
39. American College of Radiology. National Mammography Database. www.acr.org/Quality-Safety/National-Radiology-Data-Registry/National-Mammography-DB. Accessed October 24, 2015.
40. American College of Radiology. National Mammography Database ABR PQI Project Description. www.acr.org/~/media/ACR/Documents/PDF/QualitySafety/NRDR/NMD/NmdAbrPqiProject.pdf. Updated December 12, 2013. Accessed October 24, 2015
41. ACR Practice Parameter for the Performance of Stereotactic-Guided Percutaneous Breast Interventional Procedures. www.acr.org/~/media/ACR/Documents/PGTS/guidelines/Stereotactically_Guided_Breast.pdf Updated 2014. Accessed November 2, 2015.
42. ACR Practice Parameter for the Performance of Ultrasound-Guided Percutaneous Breast Interventional Procedures. www.acr.org/~/media/ACR/Documents/PGTS/guidelines/US_Guided_Breast.pdf. Updated 2014. Accessed November 2, 2015.
43. The American College of Radiology Breast Magnetic Resonance Imaging (MRI) Accreditation Program Requirements. [May 19, 2016]; Available from: http://www.acraccreditation.org/~/media/ACRAccreditation/Documents/Breast-MRI/Requirements.pdf?la=en
44. American College of Radiology. *ACR Magnetic Resonance Imaging (MRI) Quality Control Manual 2015.* Reston, VA: American College of Radiology; 2015
45. Kanal E, Borgstede JP, Barkovich AJ, et al. American College of Radiology white paper on MR safety: 2004 update and revisions. *Am J Roentgenol.* 2004;182:1111–1114
46. D'Orsi CJ, Sickles EA, Mendelson EB, et al. *ACR BI-RADS® Atlas, Breast Imaging Reporting and Data System.* Reston, VA: American College of Radiology; 2013.
47. D'Orsi CJ. The American College of Radiology mammography lexicon: an initial attempt to standardize terminology. *Am J Roentgenol.* 1996;166:779–780.
48. Engelman KK, Cizik AM, Ellerbeck EF. Women's satisfaction with their mammography experience: results of a qualitative study. *Women Health.* 2006;42:17–35.
49. Shah CJ, Sullivan JR, Gonyo MB, et al. Practice policy and quality initiatives: using lean principles to improve screening mammography workflow. *Radiographics.* 2013;33:1505–1517.
50. Johnston S, Johnston J. Managing a mammography center: a model to thrive. *Radiol Technol.* 2010;82:22–32.
51. Solbjør M, Forsmo S, Skolbekken J-A, Sætnan AR. Experiences of recall after mammography screening—a qualitative study. *Health Care Women Int.* 2011;32:1009–1027.
52. Schou Bredal I, Kåresen R, Skaane P, et al. Recall mammography and psychological distress. *Eur J Cancer.* 2013;49:805–811.
53. Mansoori B, Erhard KK, Sunshine JL. Picture Archiving and Communication System (PACS) implementation, integration & benefits in an integrated health system. *Acad Radiol.* 2012;19:229–235.

SELF-ASSESSMENT QUESTIONS

1. The Mammography Quality Standards Act (MQSA) regulates which of the following breast imaging modalities?
   A. Mammography
   B. Breast ultrasound
   C. Breast MRI
   D. All of the above

2. From what source can benchmarks for physician performance in mammography be obtained?
   A. Food and Drug Administration
   B. State Medical Boards
   C. ACR National Mammography Database
   D. Centers for Medicare and Medicaid Services

Answers To Chapter Self-Assessment Questions

1. A. MQSA requirements apply only to mammography. Accreditation programs for other breast imaging modalities have been developed by the American College of Radiology and are voluntary.

2. C. The ACR's National Mammography Database (NMD) contains data from numerous breast imaging facilities and practicing radiologists. It not only allows comparison to national published benchmarks, but also allows facilities to compare their performance to peers with similar practice type and regional location. The FDA, state medical boards, and CMS do not directly collect mammography results' data.

Quality and Safety in Nuclear Medicine

9

Saima Muzahir

LEARNING OBJECTIVES

1. Know the importance of quality control in nuclear medicine
2. Gain understanding about quality control procedures performed in nuclear medicine
3. Know the frequency and timing of different quality control procedures
4. To recognize various types of artifacts that can occur in gamma camera and PET systems and their potential impact on clinical studies

QUALITY CONTROL IN NUCLEAR MEDICINE

Quality control (QC) is important to ensure the dependable performance of equipment used in nuclear medicine. QC requires performing a routine series of tests on each device used in nuclear medicine. Routine QC testing starts after installation of the instrument, after acceptance testing, and continues on a regular basis throughout its lifetime.

The most common devices used in nuclear medicine include imaging and nonimaging devices. Nonimaging devices include dose calibrator, survey meters, and scintillation detectors. Imaging devices include planar gamma camera, single photon emission computed tomography (SPECT), and PET-CT.

NONIMAGING DEVICES

Dose Calibrator

Dose calibrator is an essential piece of instrument in any nuclear medicine department. It is a well-type ionization chamber capable of measuring quantities in the millicurie (mCi). Dose calibrators are checked for accuracy, constancy, linearity, and geometry (Fig. 9.1).

Accuracy

Accuracy should be checked at installation, annually, and after repair or when the instrument is moved to a new location within the clinic. Accuracy is a measure of the readings of the dose calibrator in comparison with the well-accepted standards. Long-lived radionuclides such as ^{57}Co (half-life 270 days) and ^{137}Cs (half-life 30 years) are measured repeatedly in the dose calibrator, and average readings are compared with the values issued by National institute of Standards and Technology (NIST). If the reading differs by more than 10% of standards, the instrument should not be used.[1]

Constancy

Constancy should be checked daily. For the constancy test, a reference source such as (^{57}Co, ^{133}Ba, ^{68}Ge, or ^{137}Cs) is placed in the

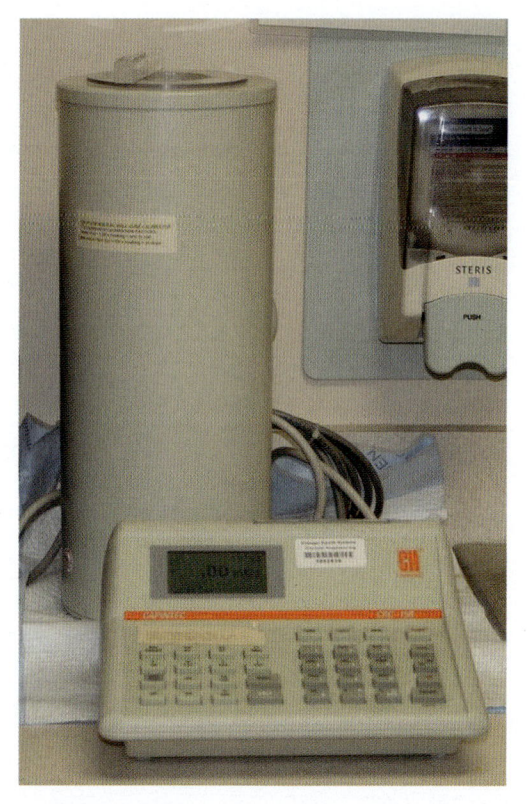

FIG. 9.1 • **Dose calibrator.** It is a gas-filled ionization chamber used to measure radioactivity. The sample to be measured is placed in the shielded ionization chamber.

dose calibrator, and the activity reading on each scale is recorded; day-to-day readings should agree within 10%. The readings at each predefined setting for different radionuclides used in the nuclear medicine department (^{99m}Tc, ^{131}I, ^{123}I, ^{111}In, etc.) are recorded and compared with previous readings.

Linearity

Linearity should be checked at the installation of the device, quarterly, when the instrument is moved from one place to another, and after repairs. For the quarterly check of linearity by the decay method, a high activity (~37 GBq) of Tc-99m is independently calibrated and then the measurements are repeated at 12-hour intervals over three consecutive days. Over that time, which is equivalent to 12 half-lives of ^{99m}Tc, the activity decays to about 11 MBq. The measured activities are then plotted versus time on a semilogarithmic graph, and the best-fit straight line drawn through the data points is plotted. For each data point, the difference between the measured activity and the activity on the best-fit straight line at that point should be less than 10%. To save time, a more rapid technique known as the *shield method* is used. In this technique, lead sleeves of increasing thickness are placed in the dose calibrator with a ^{99m}Tc source (Fig. 9.2). The thickness of sleeves is such that when used both individually and in combination they effectively reproduce the decline in the activity of Tc-99m over 96 hours.

Geometry

The effect of sample geometry should be checked at installation and after repairs. The apparent activity of a dose will vary with the volume and shape of the container, as well as the position of the dose placed within the chamber of a dose calibrator. Dose measurements should not vary by more than 10% when the sample is measured in different types of containers such as vials, syringes, or bottles. The sample geometry can also be checked by placing a small amount of activity at the bottom of the container and then progressively adding a diluent such as water.

Survey Meters

Survey meters are an important component of any nuclear medicine department. They are portable, battery-operated, gas-filled ionization chambers or solid-state scintillation detectors used to measure exposure rates (e.g., in mR/h) or counting rates (e.g., in counts per minute [CPM]). The most familiar ones are Geiger counter and pocket dosimeters. Geiger counters are of high sensitivity and are well suited for low-level surveys, for example, for checking radioactive contamination (Fig. 9.3A, B). Cutie-pies are another type of survey meter that have relatively low-sensitivity ionization chambers and are designed for use where high fluxes of X- and γ-rays are encountered. Generally, cutie-pies are calibrated in exposure rates (mR/h) and Geiger counters in counting rates (cpm). QC of survey meters include a battery check, background check, constancy, and calibration.[1,2]

FIG. 9.2 • Lead sleeves. A set of lead-lined plastic sleeves for evaluation of dose-calibrator linearity by shield method.

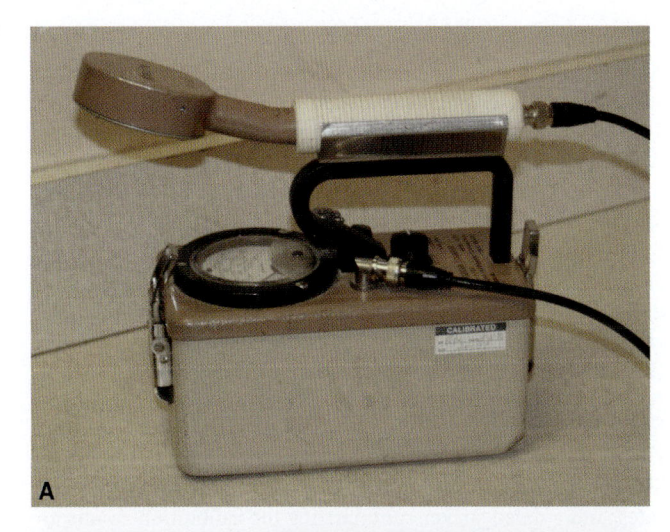

FIG. 9.3 • Geiger–Mueller survey meter. A: This is used to measure low levels of radiation. A pancake detector is located at the end of the detector. A calibration sticker is attached. **B:** The dial reads in either counts per minute (CPM) or milliroentgens per hour (mR/hr).

Battery Check

The battery should be checked daily, with a display indicating whether the voltage supplied by the battery is within the acceptable operating range.

Background Check

Background check should be performed daily to ensure that the survey meter has not been contaminated, and the background exposure or counting rate is performed daily in an area well away from the radioactive sources within the department.

Constancy

A long-live radionuclide should be checked daily to ensure that the survey meter reading of the source remains constant, that is, within 10% of its original value. The survey meter should be recalibrated if the reading differs by more than 10% of original value.

Calibration

Calibration should be performed at installation, after repairs, and annually. All survey meters should be checked for accuracy using long-lived radionuclides. The readings are taken from two long-lived radionuclide sources at incremental distances from the sources (such as every 10th of a meter up to 1 m). The readings must be within 20% of their expected measurement. Many nuclear medicine facilities have their survey meters calibrated by the institutional radiation safety office or by a commercial calibration laboratory. The measurement procedure, the measured and expected exposure rates, and a dated sticker summarizing the calibration results are affixed to the meter itself.

Scintillation Detectors

Scintillation detectors include well counters and organ uptake probes. Well counters are of high sensitivity and are used for counting of radioactive specimens such as blood or urine samples or wipe tests for survey of removable contamination (Fig. 9.4). Counting results are expressed in activity (e.g., µCi), using the appropriate isotope-specific calibration factor (µCi/cpm). Routine QC includes energy peaking and background check, constancy, energy resolution, calibration, and efficiency.[3]

Energy Peaking and Background Check

Routine checks of the photopeak energy window (i.e., energy peaking) are performed if the counter is equipped with a multi-channel analyzer (MCA) and a background check. Before counting samples containing a particular radionuclide, the energy spectrum is checked to verify that the counter is properly peaked so that the photopeak of the radionuclide coincides with the preset photopeak energy window. Isotope-specific radionuclide counting or imaging with a scintillation detector is commonly done using a 20% photopeak energy window, equivalent to an energy range of $E\gamma \pm 10\%$ (i.e., 0.9 to 1.1 $E\gamma$), where $E\gamma$ is the X- or γ-ray energy of the radionuclide. This is performed daily.

Energy Resolution

Energy resolution (percentage full width at half-maximum) should be checked at least quarterly using a reference-source radionuclide such as ^{57}Co. Energy resolution is the ability of a counter to discriminate between light pulses caused by gamma rays of different energies. The full width half-maximum (FWHM) of the photopeak should be less than 10% of the energy of the photopeak.

Calibration

Calibration is performed on a daily basis using a long-lived radionuclide source (such as ^{137}Cs), which is placed in the well counter or in front of the probe.

Efficiency

Efficiency check is performed annually. Efficiency check is performed using reference standard sources with emission sources with similar energy emissions to the radionuclides measured routinely in the counter or in front of the thyroid/organ probe. The efficiency of the thyroid probe or well counter can be calculated using the following equation:

$$\text{Efficiency} = [(\text{counts per minute of standard}) - (\text{counts per minute of background})] \times [(\text{activity of standard in microcurie})]^{-1}.$$

Intraoperative Probes

Intraoperative probes are solid or semisolid state detectors. They are highly collimated handheld devices that are commonly used in surgical practice for sentinel node localization in different types of cancer (e.g., breast cancer, melanoma, etc.). The different QC tests include daily battery check, bias check, and background check. A daily bias check should be performed for both the primary and

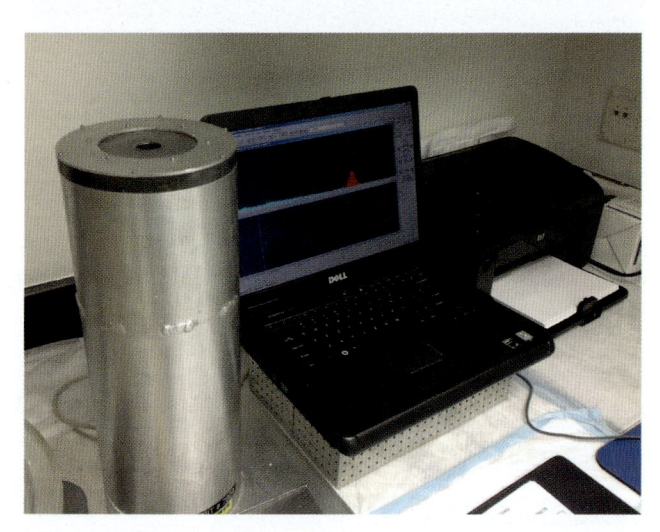

FIG. 9.4 • **Well counter.** Well counters are high-sensitivity heavily shielded scintillation crystals used for counting of radioactive specimens such as blood or urine samples or wipe tests for survey of removable contamination.

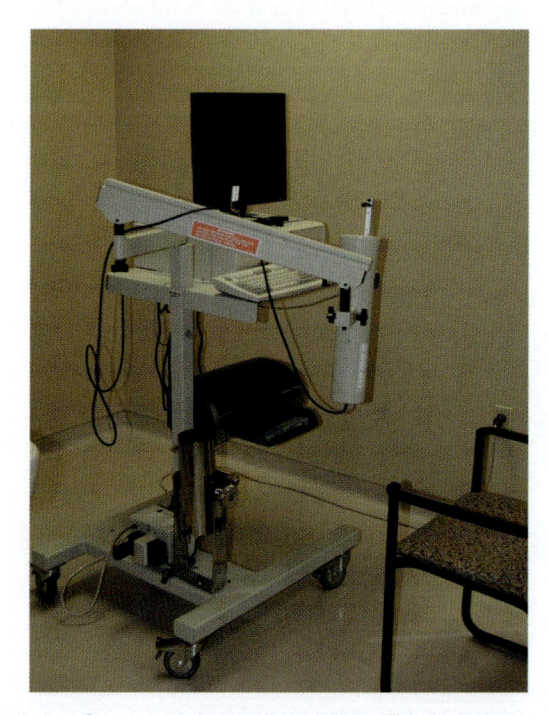

FIG. 9.5 • **Organ uptake probe system.** This includes a single crystal, thyroid/organ probe for measuring radionuclide uptake.

Table 9.1 **SUMMARY OF QC TESTS FOR NONIMAGING DETECTORS.**

Nonimaging Detectors	Quality Control Parameter	Frequency
Dose calibrator	Battery check	Daily
	Constancy	Daily
	Linearity	At installation, quarterly, and after repairs
	Accuracy	At installation, annually, and after repairs
	Geometry	At installation and after repairs
Survey meter	Battery check	Daily
	Background check	Daily
	Constancy	Daily
	Calibration	Annually and after repairs
Well counter	Energy peaking and background check	Daily
	Energy resolution	Quarterly
	Calibration	Daily
	Efficiency	Annually
Organ uptake probe	Battery check	Before each use
	Background check	Before each use
	Constancy	Before each use

any back-up battery to verify that bias voltage is within acceptable limits. Other tests include daily counting rate constancy using long-lived reference sources such as ^{157}Co and ^{133}Ba. A change of ±10% in the net counting rate from one day to the next indicates an inappropriate window setting.[3]

Organ Uptake Probes

Organ uptake probes have been commonly used to measure thyroid uptake and are commonly known as thyroid uptake probes (Fig. 9.5). Most of the QC tests for uptake probes are similar to well counter, and these include checks of the photopeak energy window, background, constancy, and efficiency. Efficiency of uptake probe should be checked more frequently so that net counting rate can be reliably converted to thyroid uptake for each individual patient. Table 9.1 summarizes the commonly performed QC procedures for nonimaging detectors.

PLANAR GAMMA CAMERA

The QC for planar gamma camera includes photopeak, uniformity floods, spatial resolution and linearity, and energy resolution. Daily tests include field uniformity and window setting. Weekly tests include spatial resolution and linearity check. Periodic tests include collimator performance, energy resolution, count-rate performance and count-rate linearity, energy resolution, and sensitivity.[4-7]

Field Uniformity

Field uniformity should be checked daily to ensure uniform image. Imperfections in the collimators, variations in crystal response and within photomultiplier tubes, as well as minor fluctuations in the electrical circuitry lead to image nonuniformities. Uniformity response of gamma camera is performed by imaging a flood source. Measurements made with the collimator in place are called extrinsic flood and those without the collimator are referred to as intrinsic flood. A solid-state plastic disc manufactured with 5 to 20 mCi of CO-57 uniformly distributed throughout its extent or a fluid-filled sheet of radioactivity containing a dilute solution of radioactivity is used. For extrinsic uniformity, the radioactive source is placed at or on the surface of a gamma camera collimator. For intrinsic uniformity, a point source of radioactivity is positioned at the center of the crystal at a certain distance from the uncollimated crystal surface. The rule of thumb is to place the source at a distance at least five times the size of the field of view to acquire a uniform image. In the case of dual-detector fixed SPECT systems, it is not possible to place the source at a necessary distance from the camera so the acquired image has higher counts in the center than on the edges. Typically 1,000 to 5,000 K counts are obtained to evaluate planar uniformity. For extrinsic flood uniformity, a phantom filled with the uniform solution of ^{99m}Tc or a disc source of ^{57}Co is used. The standard practice is to obtain a flood image with each camera before use. Most of the nuclear medicine department acquire flood image with a collimator on daily basis and acquire intrinsic flood images weekly. Images of the flood source should be evaluated daily both visually and quantitatively for nonuniformities. A uniform flood image is show in Figure 9.6. Defects in the crystal such as cracked crystal (Fig. 9.7) and even damage to a collimator can be detected on the flood image. Photomultiplier tube drift or even failure of a photomultiplier tube can also be readily detected (Fig. 9.8). However, visual inspection will not be able to detect nonuniformities with count difference less than 5% variation from the average. Integral uniformity (IU) and differential uniformity (DU) are used to quantify variation in a flood acquisition.

IU is expressed as

$$IU = \frac{\text{Maximum counts per pixel} - \text{Minimum counts per pixel}}{\text{Maximum counts per pixel} + \text{Minimum counts per pixel}} \times 100\%$$

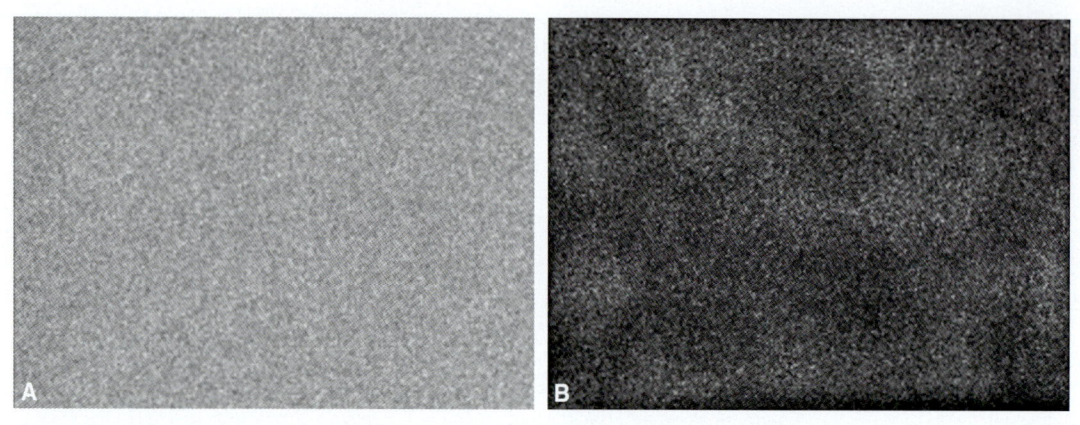

FIG. 9.6 • **Uniformity Flood. A:** Routine intrinsic uniformity image, ^{99m}Tc, 3 million counts, 20% energy window set symmetrically over the 140-keV photopeak of ^{99m}Tc. It is a good-quality image. **B:** A nonuniform flood image caused by wrong energy window setting.

IU searches the entire flood to look for maximum and minimum counts per pixel values. The IU has typical values of 2% to 4% or 4% to 7%.[6,7] DU looks at changes in counts per pixel over short segments of flood. DU is expressed as

$$DU = \frac{High - Low}{High + Low} \times 100\%$$

The high and low refer to highest and lowest counts per pixel, respectively, within a five-pixel segment. DUs are in the range of 1.0% to 2.5%.[6,7]

If gamma camera uniformity for any radionuclide is out of tolerance (i.e., IU or DU > 5%), the uniformity correction table of that radionuclide should be updated.[4–6]

Spatial Resolution and Linearity

Spatial resolution is the ability to display discrete but contiguous sources of radioactivity. The spatial resolution of gamma cameras is termed as inherent or overall resolution. Modern-day gamma cameras have an inherent spatial resolution of about 3 mm. Spatial resolution and linearity is semiquantitatively assessed using bar phantoms. A weekly assessment of spatial resolution and linearity is sufficient. A four-quadrant bar phantom allows a semiquantitative, that is, visual assessment, which is faster and more convenient than actual measurement of spatial resolution of the FWHM of the line-spread function. Resolution is defined as the ability to discriminate between two distinct points. A four-quadrant bar phantom consists of four sectors of radio-opaque lead bars and intervening radio-lucent plastic strips 2, 2.5, 3, and 4 mm in width. A point source of ^{99m}Tc is placed about five crystal dimensions from and centered over the uncollimated detector, with the phantom placed directly over the detector. A 5- to 10-million-count transmission image is then acquired and visually inspected. The lead bars in at least the two coarsest quadrants (i.e., with the 3- and 4-mm-wide bars) should be visually resolvable (Fig. 9.9). Nowadays, at least a portion of the lead bars in the third coarsest quadrant (i.e., with the 2.5-mm-wide bars) should be visible as well. All bars should appear straight.

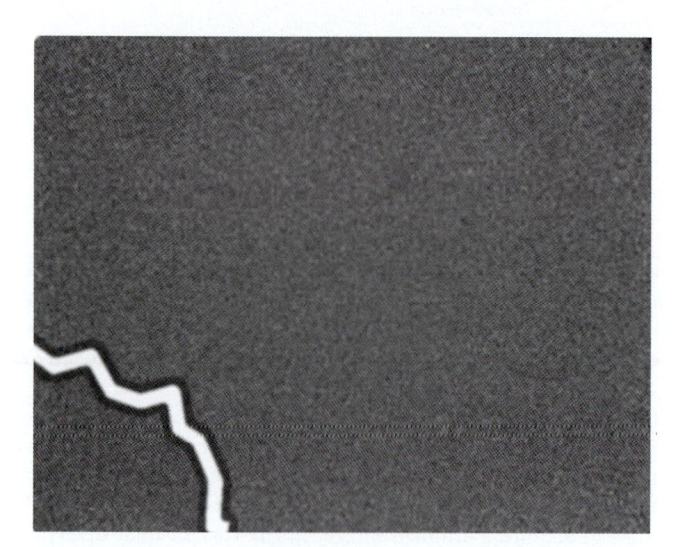

FIG. 9.7 • **Cracked Crystal.** Abnormal flood image from a camera with a cracked crystal. Note that the edge of the cold area is lined by a hot border due to light reflection at the crack in the crystal.

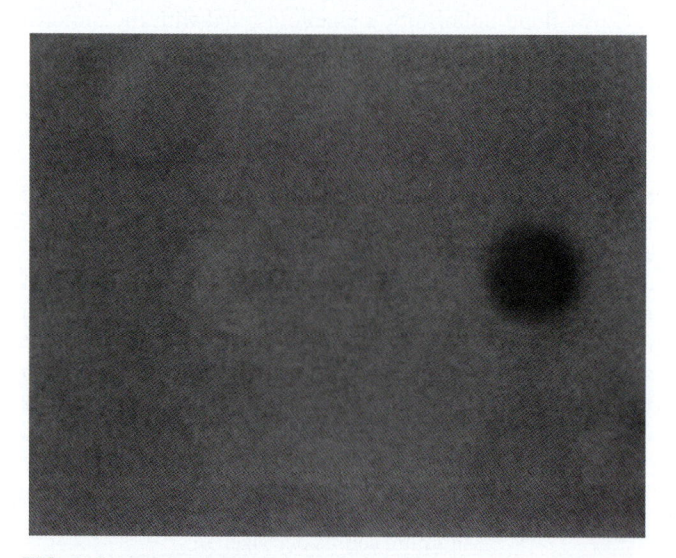

FIG. 9.8 • **Photomultiplier Tube Defect.** Photomultiplier tube defect seen on a uniformity image. The defect appears as a hot spot on the flood uniformity image.

Energy Resolution

Energy resolution is the ability to discriminate between light sources caused by gamma rays of different energies. Energy resolution of a gamma camera may be evaluated by the percentage

Quality and Safety in Nuclear Medicine

SPECT: TOMOGRAPHIC IMAGE RECONSTRUCTION

Additional QC procedures are necessary for SPECT gamma camera. These include tomographic uniformity and center of rotation (COR) alignment. These QC tests apply to both SPECT-only and SPECT-CT gamma cameras.

Center of Rotation

Accurate COR is an important measure for high-quality tomography. It is assumed that the camera heads will rotate in a near-perfect circle and that heads will remain almost precisely aligned in their opposing directions. In rotating gamma camera SPECT, the rotating gamma camera matrix location of the projection of the COR on the projection-image matrix should be independent of the projection-image angle. If the mechanical and electronic CORs are aligned, the pixel location of the projection of the COR onto the projection-image matrix will be the same for all projection images, and for all such images, the counts in each pixel will then be projected across the appropriate row of pixels in the tomographic image matrix. However, if the mechanical and electronic CORs are not aligned, the pixel location of the COR will vary among the projection images and the counts in each projection pixel will be projected across different locations in the tomographic image matrix, resulting in blurred images. The misalignment of COR may result from improper shifting in camera tuning, mechanics of the rotating gantry and misaligned attachment of collimator to the detector. The COR off by more than one pixel may cause image degradation. Proper alignment of the mechanical and electronic CORs is therefore critical in rotating gamma camera SPECT and should be checked routinely.[6,7] In current SPECT systems, COR misalignment may be easily measured and corrections created and automatically applied using the integrated software of the system. Currently, manufacturers include the COR alignment in their maintenance services.

Tomographic Uniformity

Uniformity of gamma camera is critical in SPECT imaging. Detector nonuniformity results in bull's eye or ring artifact. The usual 1 to 5 million counts obtained for planar imaging is inadequate for uniformity correction in SPECT imaging. For

FIG. 9.9 ● **Four-quadrant bar phantom image from a well-tuned camera.** The smallest bars are partially discernible on the bar phantom image. They have a spacing of 3 mm. The bar images show good linearity and spatial resolution.

of the FWHM of the photopeak. The energy spectrum for each radionuclide to be used should be checked at least once a day to verify that the photopeak is centered in the photopeak energy windows currently set.

Collimator Performance

Collimators are manufactured by one of two methods, either in a mold or by gluing together corrugated strips of lead. Collimators are fragile and easily damaged. A dent in the collimator will result in a cold spot on uniformity image. Routine inspection of collimator surface was performed on older gamma cameras. New modern gamma cameras make visual inspection of collimators difficult because of the presence of patient crush pad protection in front of the collimator. In a modern camera, collimator check is performed by obtaining high-count flood with different collimators.

Table 9.2 briefly summarizes various commonly performed QC procedures for planar gamma camera.

Table 9.2 **SUMMARY OF QC TESTS FOR PLANAR GAMMA CAMERA.**

Performance Parameter	Frequency
Uniformity: intrinsic or extrinsic	Daily
Window setting: to confirm energy window setting relative to photopeak for each radionuclide used	Daily for each patient
Energy spectrum: radionuclide photopeak peaking	Daily, automatic on new gamma cameras
Spatial resolution and linearity: using bar phantom	Weekly
Collimator performance: high-count flood with different collimator	Quarterly
Collimator integrity	Quarterly or when damage is suspected
Energy resolution: FWHM of Tc-99m photopeak expressed as % age	Annually
Count-rate performance: maximum count rate for 20% window	Annually
Sensitivity: count-rate performance per unit of radioactivity	Annually or when problem is suspected

large-field-of-view gamma cameras and a 64 × 64 matrix, a 30-million count is acquired in the image to achieve the desired relative standard deviation of 1%. Tomographic uniformity should therefore be evaluated by high-count imaging of a ^{99m}Tc-filled cylinder source (at least 20 cm in diameter by 20 cm in length) and visually inspecting the resulting reconstructed images for the absence of perceptible nonuniformity artifacts; this should be done monthly.[7]

Tomographic Resolution

An overall assessment of system performance can be obtained by imaging a suitable tomographic phantom. These are usually circular phantoms containing a variety of rods or spheres that can be filled with a mixture of water and ^{99m}Tc. The usual purpose of this phantom is to determine optimum system performance (Fig. 9.10). The phantom is imaged under ideal conditions, that is, minimum radius of rotation, high-resolution collimation, 128 × 128 matrix with at least 120 views, and high total counts (30 to 50 Mcts). The phantom should be placed on the headrest of the imaging table. Transaxial images of the phantom are reconstructed with minimum smoothing. Single-pixel thick slices through the uniform section of the phantom can be used to evaluate uniformity. Thicker slices through the resolution elements can be used to determine tomographic resolution. Tomographic resolution and uniformity tests should be performed every 6 months.[4–8]

Gantry Head Alignment

Alignment should be checked once or twice a year and after any major upgrade or modification to the gantry. In a single-headed SPECT system, the gantry is usually set to 0° and the detector head is leveled before acquisition. The detector head level is set on the basis of the assumption that the axis of rotation of the detector head is horizontal. This axis of rotation is determined by the alignment of the gantry. Variations in gantry alignment will be detected in the analysis of the weekly COR measurement as variations in the Y-position of the point source. Gantry alignment and its stability with rotation can also be checked using a small bubble level. The gantry must be leveled at 0°, and then rotating the gantry through 180° it should be checked that the gantry is still level.

Table 9.3 SUMMARY OF QC TESTS FOR SPECT GAMMA CAMERA.

Performance Parameter	Frequency
Uniformity: using high-count flood, at least 30 million counts are acquired	Monthly
Center of rotation: COR should match center of image matrix in the computer	Weekly
System performance: using SPECT phantom	Quarterly
Spatial resolution in air: point or line source reconstructed	6–12 months
Detector head alignment: camera face parallel to axis of rotation	6–12 months

Collimator Hole Alignment

Parallel-hole collimators have holes oriented perpendicular to the surface of the crystal. There can be considerable variation in collimator hole angle both locally and globally. These variations directly affect the center of rotation, and a poorly manufactured collimator may have considerable variations in COR across its surface. These variations cannot be corrected for by the standard COR correction method, and their presence cannot be determined by inspection of planar image quality.[8,9]

Table 9.3 summarizes various QC procedures routinely performed for SPECT.

PET SCANNERS

The routine QC tests for PET scanners are ambient temperature, blank scan, and tomographic uniformity. These tests are intended to monitor the system and ensure consistency and accuracy of PET scanner performance.[10]

Ambient Temperature

Daily checking of scanning room temperature should be performed because PET scanners are extremely sensitive to temperature fluctuations. With the rise in temperature in the scanning room, fewer visible photons are produced by the crystal. The pulse-height analyzer spectrum in the BGO crystals also changes with temperature.

Blank Transmission Scan

This is a common daily QC procedure. The blank scan is examined to look for evidence of defective detectors. The scan is performed by using internal transmission source or a separate low activity without a patient in the field of view. Blanks scans are an excellent method to monitor system. In some respects, the blank scan is analogous to the daily uniformity flood image acquired for gamma cameras, providing an overall assessment of detector response.[10] The data acquired from the blank scan could be displayed as a sinogram (Fig. 9.11). A defective detector appears as a new thin diagonal line across the sonogram.[10]

FIG. 9.10 • SPECT phantom. SPECT phantom used for evaluation of overall performance of tomographic imaging systems.

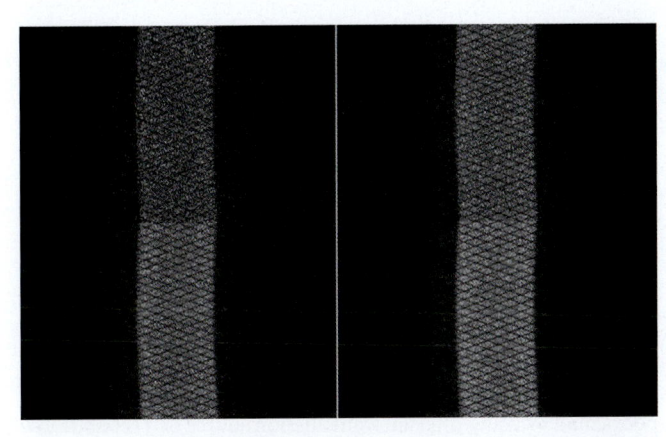

FIG. 9.11 • PET sinograms. PET sinograms of uniform-cylinder source without any visually perceptible discontinuities or other artifacts.

Table 9.5 SUMMARY OF QC TESTS FOR CT.

CT Performance Parameter	Frequency
Tube warm-up	Daily
Air calibration	Daily
Constancy (water, noise, uniformity, CT number, and artifacts)	Daily
Dose check	Annually or after repairs or tube placement
CT/NM 3-D vector alignment	Annually
Dose check	According to industry and regulatory standards

PMT Gain Test

The light output from each PMT tube can vary due to changes in temperature and humidity. The output from each PMT tube is checked daily or weekly to ensure uniform response across the photomultiplier tubes.

Normalization

Most modern PET scanners have 10,000 to 20,000 detectors arranged in blocks and are coupled to multiple photomultiplier (PM) tubes. The detection efficiency varies from detector pair to detector pair due to variation in the gain of PM tubes and location of the detector in the block, which results in nonuniformity of the PET data. In normalization of PET data, all detectors are exposed uniformly to a 511-keV photon source such as Ge-68 without an object in the field of view, and the data are collected in the 2D or 3D mode. This procedure is performed quarterly to adjust PMT gains.

Calibration

This is a quarterly procedure used to calculate the system response to a known amount of radioactivity in a known volume. Calibration is important for quantitative measurements such as standard uptake value.

Table 9.4 gives a brief summary of various QC procedures routinely performed in PET scanners.

Table 9.4 SUMMARY OF QC TESTS FOR PET SCANNER.

Performance Parameter	Frequency
Ambient temperature	Daily
Blank transmission scan	Daily
PMT gain test	Daily or weekly
Normalization	Quarterly
Calibration	Quarterly

CT SCANNERS

The CT scanners have been in use long before their incorporation into SPECT and PET scanners. Although detailed protocols and CT performance procedures are well established, with SPECT and PET scanners, less vigorous and extensive QC procedures are performed for routine QC of CT. Daily QC begins with manufacturer's x-ray tube warm-up and automatic monitoring program including tube coolant temperature, kVp, and mA settings. To ensure accuracy of CT number of water and air, a water-filled phantom is used to check that water measures 0 Hounsefield units (HU) and air measures −1,000 HU with a standard deviation of 2 to 3 units. The water image is evaluated for standard deviation to assess for image noise. Most of these procedures are automated; however, if the images are evaluated visually, they should be inspected to see that that there are no ring or arc artifacts. Table 9.4 briefly summarizes different QC tests routinely performed for CT. A brief summary of different CT QC performance parameters is detailed in Table 9.5.

References

1. Cherry SR, Sorenson JA, Phelps ME. *Physics in Nuclear Medicine*. 3rd ed. Philadelphia: W.B. Saunders; 2003.
2. Rollo FD. *Nuclear Medicine Physics, Instrumentation and Agents*. St. Louise: Mosby; 1977.
3. Zanzonico P. Routine quality control of clinical nuclear medicine instrumentation: a brief review. *J Nucl Med*. 2008;49(7):1114–1131.
4. Paras P, Hine GJ, Adams R. BRH test pattern for the evaluation of gamma camera performance. *J Nucl Med*. 1981;22(5):468–470.
5. Rogers WL, Clinthorne NH, Harkness BA, et al. Field flood requirements for emission computed tomography with an Anger camera. *J Nucl Med* 1982;23(2);162–168.
6. National Electrical Manufacturers Association (NEMA). *Performance Measurements of Scintillation Cameras*. Rosslyn, VA: NEMA; 2001.
7. Gullberg GT: An analytical approach to quantify uniformity artifacts for circular and noncircular detector motion in single photon emission computed tomographic imaging. *Med Phys*. 1987; 14(1):105–114.
8. Greer K, Jaszczak R, Harris C, et al. Quality control in SPECT. *J Nucl Med Technol*. 1985;13:76–85.
9. Cerquira MD, Matsuoka D, Ritchie JL, et al. The influence of collimators on SPECT Center of Rotation measurements: artifact generation and acceptance testing. *J Nucl Med*. 1988;29(8):1393–1397.
10. Zanzonico P. Positron emission tomography: a review of basic principles, scanner design and performance, and current systems. *Semin Nucl Med*. 2004;34(2):87–111.

SELF-ASSESSMENT QUESTIONS

1. How many counts are acquired in a daily flood uniformity image for SPECT imaging?

    A. 5 million
    B. 30 to 100 million
    C. 4 million
    D. 2.5 million

2. The blank transmission scan in PET scanners is performed to look for evidence of defective detectors. This QC scan is performed:

    A. Weekly
    B. Quarterly
    C. Daily
    D. Yearly

Answers to Chapter Self-Assessment Questions

1. B. The usual 1-to-5-million counts obtained for planar imaging is inadequate for uniformity correction in SPECT imaging. A minimum of 30-million count is required for large-field-of-view gamma cameras and a 64 × 64 matrix, to achieve the desired relative standard deviation of 1%.

2. C. This is a common daily QC procedure. The blank scan is examined to look for evidence of defective detectors. The scan is performed by using internal transmission source or a separate low activity, without a patient in the field of view.

Evidence-Based Radiology

10

Jeffrey P. Kanne

LEARNING OBJECTIVES

1. Define evidence-based health care and its principles
2. List agencies involved in evidence-based health care
3. Describe the American College of Radiology Appropriateness Criteria

---

Evidence-based health care (EBHC), also termed evidence-based medicine (EBM), has become a central component to health-care reform. Radiology has lagged behind other medical specialties with respect to EBHC, primarily as a result of the rapid growth in imaging technology.

WHAT IS EBHC?

EBHC can be defined as "the systematic application of the best evidence to evaluate the available options and decision making in clinical management and policy settings."[1] EBHC can be used in any clinical situation where uncertainty exists with diagnosis, intervention, or management. While the philosophies of EBHC predate the era of "modern medicine," the creation of EBHC as a discipline comes from work done by a group at McMaster University (Hamilton, Ontario, Canada) led by Dr. Gordon Guyatt.[2,3]

PRINCIPLES OF EBHC

In contrast to traditional guidelines and recommendations, which were based primarily on "expert" opinion, EBHC follows a strict, transparent, reproducible methodology.[1] Publications are classified by type (e.g., diagnosis, treatment, guidelines). Objective assessment of published literature relies on explicit criteria, and standardized questions are used to assess study methodology and determine validity of reported data. Standard calculations are then used to determine the strength of the results.[4]

In addition to the rigorous process of evaluating published data, EBHC also aims to provide health-care practitioners with the skills and tools needed to perform their own assessments of published data and guidelines and integrate these assessments into the care of individual patients in a given practice.[1]

TERMINOLOGY

Efficacy is defined as "the probability of benefit to individuals in a defined population from a medical technology applied for a given problem under ideal conditions." In contrast, *effectiveness* is defined as the "performance of a medical technology under ordinary, rather than ideal conditions."[5] *Efficiency* focuses on the cost-effectiveness of the medical technology.[1]

EVIDENCE-BASED RADIOLOGY

Evidence-based radiology (EBR) is simply the use of EBHC principles in both interventional and diagnostic radiology. One strong feature of EBR is that it can be used by radiologists in their own practices where imaging and image-guided procedures are performed under ordinary conditions rather than the more regimented conditions often associated with clinical trials,[1] reflecting the effectiveness level.[5]

AGENCIES

Agency for Healthcare Research and Quality

The U.S. Agency for Healthcare Research and Quality (AHRQ), part of the Department of Health and Human Services, defines its mission "to produce evidence to make health care safer, higher quality, more accessible, equitable, and affordable, and to work within the U.S. Department of Health and Human Services and with other partners to make sure that the evidence is understood and used."[6] AHRQ provides data and funding to aid centers across North America to generate evidence reports and assessments of technology and to support guideline development by other groups and organizations.

The United States Preventive Services Task Force

The U.S. Preventive Services Task Force (USPSTF) was formed in 1994 as an independent group of experts in EBM and prevention who volunteer their time and expertise to make evidence-based recommendations to primary care providers about preventive health-care services. Members come from the primary care fields, and most have clinical practices. Recently, the USPSTF gave a grade B recommendation to screening for lung cancer with low-dose computed tomography.[7] A grade B recommendation is defined as "The USPSTF recommends the service. There is high certainty that the net benefit is moderate or there is moderate certainty that the net benefit is moderate to substantial."[8]

PRACTICING EBHC

The steps required to engage in EBHC are well defined. The four major steps include defining the question, finding the evidence, critical appraisal, and developing solutions for individual patients.

Defining the Question

After evaluating patient data and developing a succinct hypothesis, the practitioner must formulate a well-defined, answerable question. This question can focus on diagnosis, treatment, or prognosis and include factors such as benefit and harm.[9] The PICO framework has been proposed as a method to formulate an effective question for EBHC. The components of PICO include **p**atient or group of patients, **i**ntervention, **c**omparison intervention, and **o**utcome. In radiology, the comparison component may not be relevant or there may be more than one comparison.[10]

Finding the Evidence

With the advent of the Internet, searching and obtaining medical literature can be performed at the point of care on a workstation or handheld device. However, because of the large volume of information available, efficient searching requires development of refined searching strategies.

A practitioner must identify his own knowledge gaps, as an effective search strategy depends on the type of knowledge gap in a given scenario. A background knowledge gap is one where the practitioner lacks knowledge of a well-defined clinical scenario because of lack of experience or the relative rarity of the clinical scenario. In contrast, a foreground knowledge gap is one where the practitioner questions the effectiveness of a new technology or treatment as compared with current practices. Background knowledge gaps can be addressed through reading textbooks or review articles and completing continuing medical education activities. A review of recent literature is often required to close address a foreground knowledge gap.

The evidence pyramid described by Haynes[11] (Fig. 10.1) provides a visual paradigm for understanding available scientific evidence for a specific problem. For the most efficient and effective evidence search, practitioners should begin at the highest possible level resource available for the question at hand.

Detailed methods for searching online databases have been described.[10]

AMERICAN COLLEGE OF RADIOLOGY APPROPRIATENESS CRITERIA

ACR Appropriateness Criteria (ACR AC) are designed to aid health-care providers in choosing the most appropriate imaging or therapeutic procedure for a given specific clinical scenario (Fig. 10.2).[12] A multidisciplinary panel of experts develops ACR AC using published data and, when needed, expert opinion. In addition to radiologists, physicians from other medical specialties participate in expert panels to provide appropriate clinical perspectives. ACR AC are developed following the guidelines issued by the Agency for Healthcare Research and Quality as designed by the Institute of Medicine. More than 200 ACR AC have been published, covering nearly 1,000 clinical variants. ACR AC are available for scientific, research, and informational purposes. Additionally, ACR licenses ACR AC for use in commercial products including electronic health record and decision support system software packages. ACR AC criteria are also published on the ACR's website[13] as well as in various radiology journals.

Each ACR AC includes a narrative summary of the evidence, a ratings table (Fig. 10.2), and an evidence table (Fig. 10.3). The evidence tables include the citation, the type of study, the number of patients or events studies, the study objective, the results, and a rating of the study quality. The ratings table includes the variant of the clinical condition, a rating for each radiologic procedure, comments provided by the panel, and a relative radiation level (Fig. 10.4).

References

1. Evidence-Based Radiology Working Group. Evidence-based radiology: a new approach to the practice of radiology. *Radiology.* 2001;220(3):566–575.
2. Guyatt GH. Evidence-based medicine (editorial). *Ann Intern Med.* 1991;114(suppl 2):A16.
3. Straus SE, Glasziou P, Richardson WS, et al. *Evidence-Based Medicine: How to Practice it.* 4 ed. Edinburgh, Scotland: Churchill Livingstone Elsevier; 2010 December 17, 2010.
4. Centre for Evidence-Based Medicine. Critical Appraisal tools. Oxford, UK: Centre for Evidence-Based Medicine. http://www.cebm.net/critical-appraisal/. Accessed June 3, 2016.
5. Brook RH, Lohr KN. Efficacy, effectiveness, variations, and quality. Boundary-crossing research. *Med care.* 1985;23(5):710–722.
6. Agency for Healthcare Research and Quality. http://www.ahrq.gov/cpi/about/mission/index.html. Accessed June 3, 2016.
7. Moyer VA, Force USPST. Screening for lung cancer: U.S. Preventive Services Task Force recommendation statement. *Ann Intern Med.* 2014;160(5):330–338.
8. Force USPST. Grade Definitions. http://www.uspreventiveservicestaskforce.org/Page/Name/grade-definitions. Accessed June 3, 2016.
9. Sackett DL, Rosenberg WM. The need for evidence-based medicine. *J R Soc Med.* 1995;88(11):620–624.
10. Staunton M. Evidence-based radiology: steps 1 and 2--asking answerable questions and searching for evidence. *Radiology.* 2007;242(1):23–31.
11. Haynes RB. Of studies, summaries, synopses, and systems: the "4S" evolution of services for finding current best evidence. *Evid-Based Ment Health.* 2001;4(2):37–39.
12. Cascade PN. The American College of Radiology. ACR Appropriateness Criteria project. *Radiology.* 2000;214(suppl):3–46.
13. American College of Radiology. http://www.acr.org/Quality-Safety/Appropriateness-Criteria. Accessed June 3, 2016.

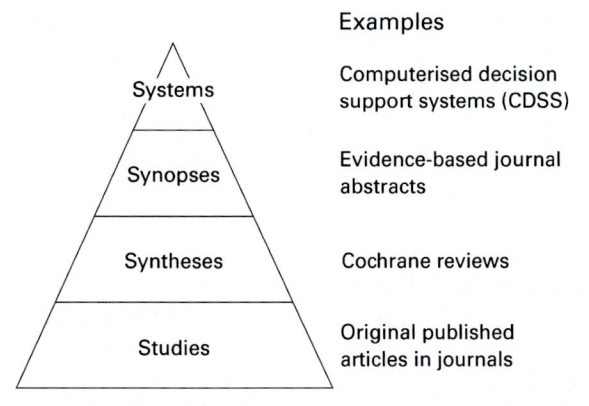

FIG. 10.1 • "4S" level of organization of evidence from research. (Adapted from Haynes RB. Of studies, summaries, synopses, and systems: the "4S" evolution of services for finding current best evidence. *Evid-Based Ment Health.* 2001;4(2):37–39 with permission from BMJ Publishing Group Limited.)

Evidence-Based Radiology 81

American College of Radiology
ACR Appropriateness Criteria®

Date of origin: 1998
Last review date: 2013

Clinical Condition: Dysphagia
Variant 1: Oropharyngeal dysphagia with an attributable cause.

Radiologic Procedure	Rating	Comments	RRL*
X-ray barium swallow modified	8		☢☢☢
X-ray pharynx dynamic and static imaging	6		☢☢☢
X-ray biphasic esophagram	4	Perform this procedure with double contrast and single contrast.	☢☢☢
X-ray barium swallow single contrast	4		☢☢☢
Tc-99m transit scintigraphy esophagus	2		☢☢☢

Rating Scale: 1,2,3 Usually not appropriate; 4,5,6 May be appropriate; 7,8,9 Usually appropriate
*Relative Radiation Level

Variant 2: Unexplained oropharyngeal dysphagia.

Radiologic Procedure	Rating	Comments	RRL*
X-ray pharynx dynamic and static imaging	8	In this procedure both pharyngeal and esophageal examinations are needed since the patient may have referred dysphagia.	☢☢☢
X-ray biphasic esophagram	8	In this procedure both pharyngeal and esophageal examinations are needed since the patient may have referred dysphagia. Perform this procedure with double contrast and single contrast.	☢☢☢
X-ray barium swallow modified	6		☢☢☢
X-ray barium swallow single contrast	6		☢☢☢
Tc-99m transit scintigraphy esophagus	4		☢☢☢

Rating Scale: 1,2,3 Usually not appropriate; 4,5,6 May be appropriate; 7,8,9 Usually appropriate
*Relative Radiation Level

Variant 3: Retrosternal dysphagia in immunocompetent patients.

Radiologic Procedure	Rating	Comments	RRL*
X-ray biphasic esophagram	8	Endoscopy and biphasic esophagram are both excellent diagnostic tests in this setting.	☢☢☢
X-ray barium swallow single contrast	6	This procedure is probably indicated if the patient is not capable of doing anything except swallowing.	☢☢☢
X-ray barium swallow modified	4		☢☢☢
X-ray pharynx dynamic and static imaging	4	Esophageal examination is also necessary.	☢☢☢
Tc-99m transit scintigraphy esophagus	4		☢☢☢

Rating Scale: 1,2,3 Usually not appropriate; 4,5,6 May be appropriate; 7,8,9 Usually appropriate
*Relative Radiation Level

ACR Appropriateness Criteria®   1   Dysphagia

FIG. 10.2 • **Example from ACR Appropriateness Criteria for dysphagia.** The AC includes radiologic procedures, rating, comments, and a relative radiation level.

ACR Appropriateness Criteria®

Dysphagia
EVIDENCE TABLE

	Reference	Study Type	Patients/ Events	Study Objective (Purpose of Study)	Study Results	Study Quality
1.	Kuo P, Holloway RH, Nguyen NQ. Current and future techniques in the evaluation of dysphagia. *J Gastroenterol Hepatol* 2012; 27(5):873-881.	Review/Other-Dx	N/A	To review the current clinical and laboratory assessments of dysphagia and the emerging techniques that have been developed recently that allows better understanding of esophageal motor function.	No results stated in abstract.	4
2.	Wilkins T, Gillies RA, Thomas AM, Wagner PJ. The prevalence of dysphagia in primary care patients: a HamesNet Research Network study. *J Am Board Fam Med* 2007; 20(2):144-150.	Review/Other-Dx	947 patients	To determine the prevalence of dysphagia in primary care patients.	Of the 947 study participants, 214 (22.6%) reported dysphagia occurring several times per month or more frequently. Those reporting dysphagia were more likely to be women (80.8% women vs 19.2% men, P=.002) and older (mean age of 48.1 in patients with dysphagia vs mean age of 45.7 in patients without dysphagia, P=.001). 64% of patients with dysphagia indicated that they were concerned about their symptoms, but 46.3% had not spoken with their doctor about their symptoms. Logistic regression analyses showed that increased frequency (OR = 2.15, 95% CI, 1.41-3.30), duration (OR = 1.91, CI 1.24-2.94), and concern (OR = 2.64, CI 1.36-5.12) of swallowing problems as well as increased problems eating out (OR = 1.72, CI 1.19-2.49) were associated with increased odds of having talked to a physician.	4
3.	Cook IJ. Oropharyngeal dysphagia. *Gastroenterol Clin North Am* 2009; 38(3):411-431.	Review/Other-Dx	N/A	To review oropharyngeal dysphagia.	No results stated in abstract.	4
4.	Garon BR, Sierzant T, Ormiston C. Silent aspiration: results of 2,000 video fluoroscopic evaluations. *J Neurosci Nurs* 2009; 41(4):178-185; quiz 186-177.	Review/Other-Dx	2,000 patients	Retrospectively study aspiration and silent aspiration to increase the awareness of nursing staffs of the diagnostic pathology groups associated with silent aspiration.	51% of patients aspirated on the video fluoroscopic evaluation. Of the patients who aspirated, 55% had no protective cough reflex (silent aspiration). The diagnostic pathology groups with the highest rates of silent aspiration were brain cancer, brainstem stroke, head-neck cancer, pneumonia, dementia/Alzheimer, chronic obstructive lung disease, seizures, myocardial infarcts, neurodegenerative pathologies, right hemisphere stroke, closed head injury, and left hemisphere stroke.	4
5.	Wilcox CM, Alexander LN, Clark WS. Localization of an obstructing esophageal lesion. Is the patient accurate? *Dig Dis Sci* 1995; 40(10):2192-2196.	Observational-Dx	139 patients	To determine if patient's sensation of dysphagia can accurately localize obstructing esophageal lesions.	Patients more accurate in localizing proximal rather than distal lesions, as distal lesions often cause referred dysphagia.	2

* See Last Page for Key   2013 Review   Carucci/Lalani
Page 1

FIG. 10.3 • Example from evidence table for ACR Appropriateness Criteria for dysphagia listing references, study types, patients or events, study objectives, study results, and study quality.

Relative Radiation Level*	Adult Effective Dose Estimate Range	Pediatric Effective Dose Estimate Range	Example Examinations
O	0	0 mSv	Ultrasound; MRI
☢	<0.1 mSv	<0.03 mSv	Chest radiographs; Hand radiographs
☢☢	0.1-1 mSv	0.03-0.3 mSv	Pelvis radiographs; Mammography
☢☢☢	1-10 mSv	0.3-3 mSv	Abdomen CT, Nuclear medicine bone scan
☢☢☢☢	10-30 mSv	3-10 mSv	Abdomen CT without and with contrast; Whole body PET
☢☢☢☢☢	30-100 mSv	10-30 mSv	CTA chest abdomen and pelvis with contrast; Transjugular intrahepatic portosystemic shunt placement

*The RRL assignments for some of the examinations cannot be made, because the actual patient doses in these procedures vary as a function of a number of factors (eg, the region of the body exposed to ionizing radiation, the imaging guidance that is used, etc). The RRLs for these examinations are designated as "Varies."

FIG. 10.4 • Table from ACR Appropriateness Criteria defining the relative radiation levels (RRLs).

SELF-ASSESSMENT QUESTIONS

1. Which of the following best describes effectiveness?
   A. Benefit of a specific treatment in randomized controlled trial
   B. Performance of a specific treatment in a community practice
   C. Probability that a positive test result indicates presence of disease
   D. Financial impact of medical imaging on cost per hospital day

2. Which of the following best defines evidence-based radiology?
   A. Efficacy of imaging tests and procedures
   B. Costs of imaging tests and procedures
   C. Precision of imaging tests and procedures
   D. Effectiveness of imaging tests and procedures

Answers to Chapter Self-Assessment Questions

1. B. Effectiveness is defined as the performance of a medical technology under ordinary, rather than ideal conditions, which would include a specific treatment in a community practice. Efficacy is similar except that the conditions are defined as ideal, such as in a randomized controlled trial. True-positive rate is the probability that a positive test indicates the presence of disease. Cost-effectiveness would describe the financial impact of medical imaging on a hospitalization.

2. D. The practice of evidence-based radiology (EBR) focuses on the effectiveness of imaging tests and procedures, or how well diagnostic imaging and image-guided procedures perform in real-world conditions. Efficacy is a measurement of performance under ideal conditions. EBR does not address cost. Precision is a measurement of test performance but is not a primary focus of EBR.

Peer Review

11

Jeffrey P. Kanne

LEARNING OBJECTIVES

1. List the various methods of peer review used in the practice of radiology
2. Describe the pros and cons of each method of peer review used in the practice of radiology
3. State approaches to using data gathered during the peer-review process

---

In 2000, the Institute of Medicine (IOM) published its report *To Err Is Human*, drawing attention to widespread errors in the practice of medicine.[1] Subsequent increased regulatory and public scrutiny of physician performance lead to the practice of peer review as a method to monitor physician performance. Peer review became more integrated into the practice of medicine through requirements published by The Joint Commission (TJC), the primary accreditation body for hospitals. TJC published new guidelines in 2004 mandating collection and use of provider-specific performance data in the credentialing and recredentialing processes, including clinical judgment, technical skills, communication, professionalism, and continued education and improvement.[2] In 2007, TJC revised these guidelines to emphasize the alignment of provider-specific data with the six core competencies developed jointly by the Accreditation Council for Graduate Medical Education (ACGME) and the American Board of Medical Subspecialties (ABMS).[3] These core competencies include patient care, medical and clinical knowledge, practice-based learning and improvement, interpersonal and communication skills, professionalism, and system-based practice.

As with other medical specialties, radiology as a profession needed to develop a peer-review model that satisfied both public and regulatory pressures driving monitoring of physician performance. The American College of Radiology's (ACR) RADPEER program, which was developed as direct response to the IOM's *To Err Is Human* report and made available in 2005, became the stimulus for radiologists to become regularly engaged in peer review.[4] RADPEER enables participating radiologists and practices to compile individual and practice peer-review data stratified by modality and practice site and compare with other national performance data. Currently, the ACR reports that more than 17,000 radiologists actively participate in the program.[5] However, RADPEER, while popular among practicing radiologists, is only one part of the bigger peer-review process. Other methods of peer review include double reads, consensus-oriented group review, focus practice review, practice audit, and correlation with operative and pathologic findings (Table 11.1).

The central goal of peer review in radiology is to improve patient outcomes by reducing interpretative and procedural errors.

Deciding how to institute a peer-review program can be challenging because each model of peer review has its own advantages and disadvantages. Radiologists may object to this new "intrusion" into their practices because of real or perceived bias among reviewers, unclear policies, lack or perceived lack of transparency, absence of evidence-based reference standards for many cases, additional time pressures on an already busy practice, belief that peer review will not lead to improved patient care, and even legal concerns.

MEASURING PERFORMANCE IN RADIOLOGY

To effectively measure radiologists' performance, metrics must be relevant to individual radiologists, practice leadership, credentialing bodies, and society as a whole. Metrics should be readily reproducible and chosen on the basis of published evidence or established standards or guidelines and should be applicable to each radiologist's respective practice.[3] Furthermore, a sufficient number of data points should be obtained to ensure that data are meaningful (Figs. 11.1, 11.2, 11.3). For example, some authors recommend that 3% to 5% of interpreted examinations undergo peer review,[6] arguing that reviewing only 0.1% of a radiologist's reports may not fully demonstrate a radiologist's true performance level. However, this recommendation is arbitrary and is not supported by any published scientific evidence.[7]

Diagnostic accuracy is the most appropriate and ostensibly the most important performance metric in diagnostic radiology because of its direct relationship to patient outcome.[8] However, medical imaging is typically only one part of the diagnostic workup, and patient outcome is usually the result of many factors, including natural history of disease and patient's response to therapy. Additionally, errors made on diagnostic imaging studies can have variable impact on patient management or ultimate outcome. For example, failing to detect a 2-cm colon carcinoma on an abdominal computed tomography (CT) scan will likely significantly adversely affect patient outcome whereas inaccurately characterizing the pattern of advanced fibrosing diffuse lung disease on a chest CT scan may have little impact on patient outcome.

Table 11.1 **RESPECTIVE ADVANTAGES AND DISADVANTAGES OF PEER-REVIEW METHODS IN RADIOLOGY.**

Method of Peer Review	Advantages	Disadvantages
Retrospective	Data easily accessible	Loss of anonymity
	Can be performed on-the-fly	Potential for bias
		Significant errors may not be identified in a timely manner
Practice audit	Uses reference standards	Labor intensive
	Encourages use of electronic health record and outcomes	Limited scope of studies that can be reviewed
		Validity of reference standard may be in question
Double read	Real-time peer review	Labor and time intensive
	Potential to promptly detect clinically significant errors	Requires large number of studies to be meaningful
Structured feedback	Assesses entire radiology report	Labor intensive
	Encourages focus on communication	May miss clinically significant findings when focus is too much on report verbiage
	Solicits input from referring physicians	
Focused practice review	Highly structured process	Labor intensive
	Robust appeals process	May incite animosity from potential "punitive" nature
	Directly involves departmental leadership	
Comprehensive professional review	Evaluates all facets of professional practice in radiology	Labor intensive
	Aligned with regulatory requirements	Obtaining data may be difficult
		Can be more challenging for smaller practices

Adherence to agreed-upon practice guidelines is another performance indicator that can be measured for each radiologist. For example, a radiology practice can agree to use the Fleischner Society's published guidelines for management of incidentally detected small lung nodules,[9] and adherence to and appropriate use of these guideline can be measured for each radiologist as a component of peer review. Variability in recommendations for managing imaging findings can be confusing to referring physicians and patients.

Radiologist performance can also be evaluated by soliciting feedback from colleagues, trainees, staff, and patients. Specific attributes such as communication skills, professionalism, and "good citizenship" within a department can be assessed. A summary of personal evaluation and review of patient or staff complaints or commendations can be included as a component of a professional practice evaluation in addition to clinical skills.

For a peer-review process to be effective, it should be fair, transparent, consistent, and objective. Conclusions should be defensible, and various opinions should be included. Peer-review activities should be timely, result in useful action, and provide feedback through auditing[6,10].

Date and Time	Accession Number	Exam Type	Score	Comments
2014.09.07 23:42	U24838450	CT abdomen & pelvis w/ contrast	2a	Left L5 pars defect
2014.09.10 08:33	U24840501	Wrist, 2-views	3b	Triquetral fracture
2014.09.14 12:21	U24853207	Chest, 2-views	1	Right apical nodule turned out to be real – nice call!
2014.09.18	U24858415	MRI brain w/ and w/o contrast	1	

FIG. 11.1 • A sample report of peer-review reporting system showing the type of examination, score given, and reviewer's comments.

METHODS OF PEER REVIEW IN RADIOLOGY

Retrospective Peer Review

Peer review in radiology is primarily conducted in a retrospective manner because digital archiving of diagnostic imaging tests and accompanying interpretative reports makes retrospective peer review easy to perform and available to nearly all practicing radiologists. In retrospective peer review, the radiologist interpreting the current study reviews a previously interpreted comparison examination of the same patient with its accompanying report and assigns a score that typically reflects agreement or various levels of disagreement. Some scoring systems also flag disagreements or subdivide scores into those that are clinically relevant and those that are not (Table 11.2).[4] When a disagreement in interpretation occurs, the reviewer can provide feedback to the original interpreting radiologist through various processes. Examinations can be identified for peer review randomly or during review for multidisciplinary conferences or consultation.

Although relatively easy to implement and perform, the retrospective case review model of peer review has received the most scrutiny for its inherent limitations.[6,11,12] One significant weakness is the lack or potential lack of randomness. For example, one radiologist may opt to review less complex studies or apparently normal studies to minimize time and energy spent on peer review. One approach to improving randomness of peer review is to assign for review the first case encountered with a relevant comparison on any given day. Additionally, specific numbers of peer reviews by modality or body part can be required. Optimally, integrating software applications into the radiologist workflow can reduce the time demands on radiologists as well as improve random sampling. Cases can be randomly selected for review from the picture archiving and communication system (PACS), radiology information system (RIS), or the voice recognition (VR)

86 QUALITY AND SAFETY IN MEDICAL IMAGING

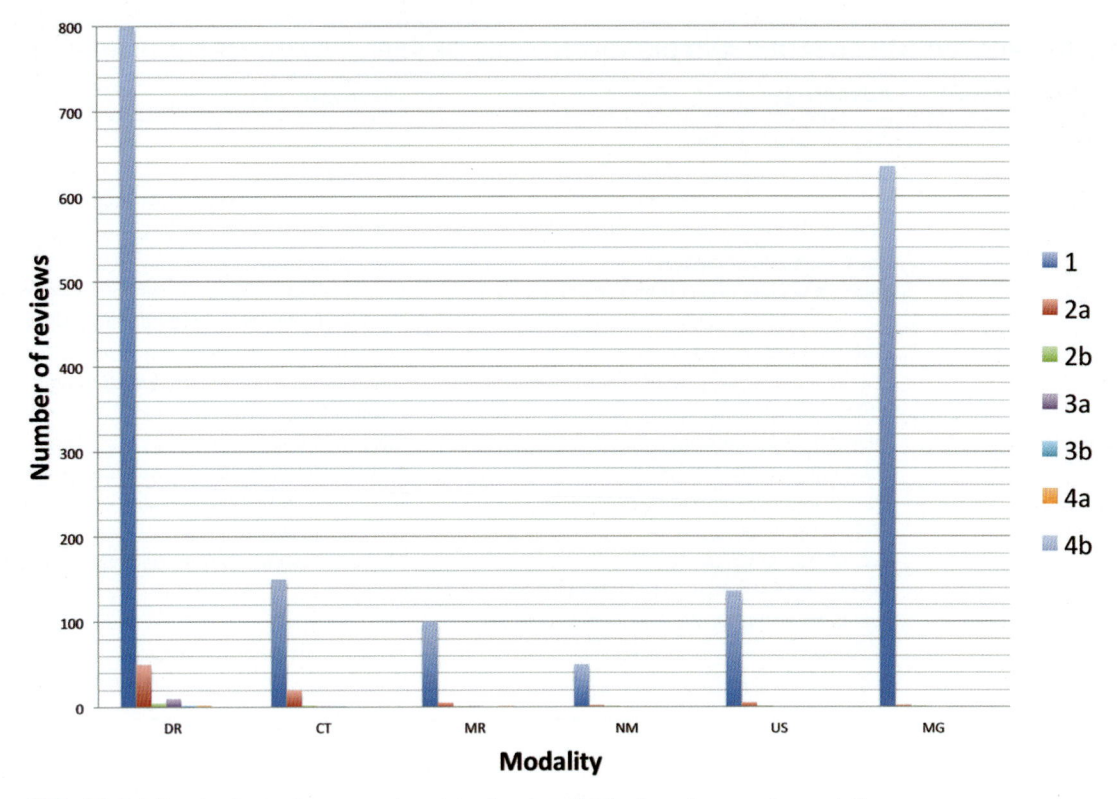

FIG. 11.2 • Graph of sample peer-review data showing distribution of scores by modality.

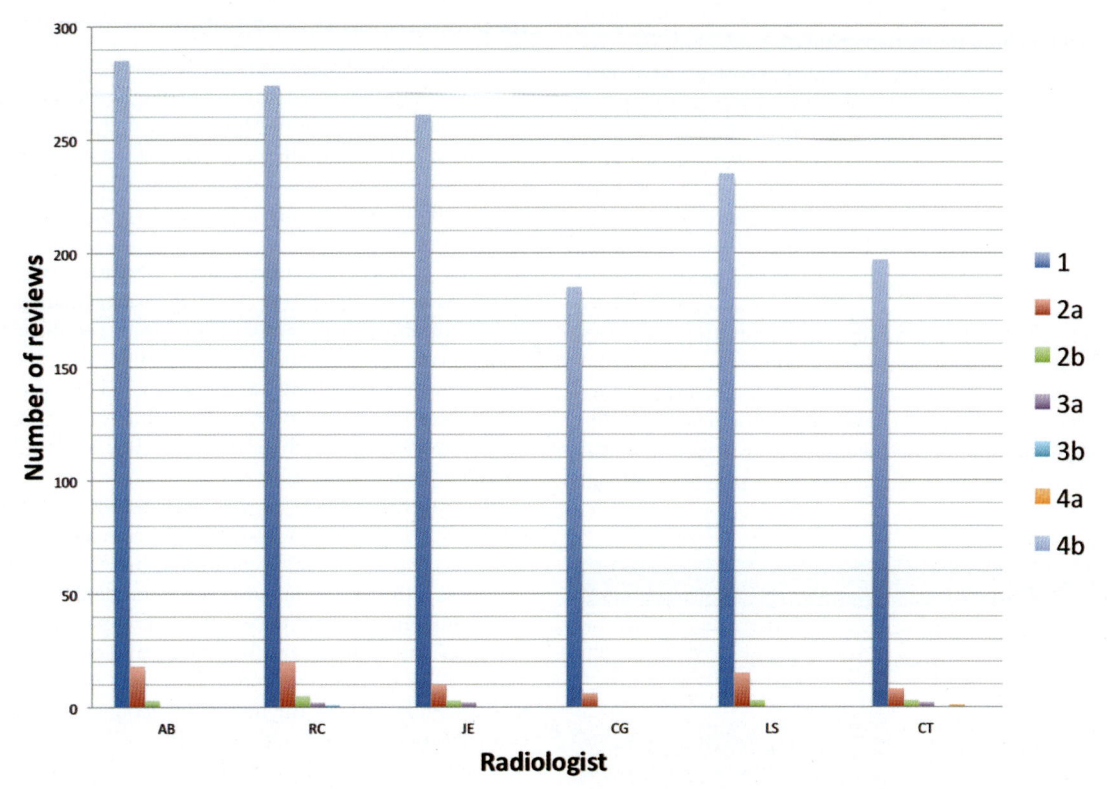

FIG. 11.3 • Graph of sample peer-review data showing distribution of scores by radiologist.

Table 11.2 ACR RADPEER SCORING SYSTEM.		
Score	Definition	Optional
1	Concur with interpretation	
2	Discrepancy in interpretation/not ordinarily expected to be made (understandable miss)	a. Unlikely to be clinically significant b. Likely to be clinically significant
3	Discrepancy in interpretation/should be made most of the time	a. Unlikely to be clinically significant b. Likely to be clinically significant
4	Discrepancy in interpretation/should be made almost every time—misinterpretation of finding	a. Unlikely to be clinically significant b. Likely to be clinically significant

From Jackson VP, Cushing T, Abujudeh HH, et al. RADPEER scoring white paper. *J Am Coll Radiol*. 2009;6(1):21–25.

software database and assigned to an appropriate radiologist for review. Progress of reviews can be tracked, and results can be recorded in a dedicated peer-review database (protected by local peer-review statutes, if applicable). Finally, notifications can be sent to radiologists whose cases were reviewed with the results of those reviews.

Another major criticism of retrospective case review is that anonymity of reviewer and reviewee is frequently compromised. For some practices, this may become an obstacle for objective peer review. For others, a transparent peer review may be a cultural norm. Because reviewers can easily identify the interpreting radiologist of the case under review, conscious or unconscious biases may affect the choice to review as well as the score assigned. Likewise, reviewees can usually identify the radiologist performing peer review simply by finding out who interpreted the subsequent relevant study. For example, a junior faculty member reviewing an abdominal ultrasound interpreted by the division chief or department chair may be inclined to assign a score of "agree," assuming the more experienced radiologist in a leadership role is correct or for fear of potential retribution.

A third significant criticism of retrospective peer review is that the time between when the original interpretation was made and when peer review was performed may be sufficiently long that harm from a misinterpretation could result in an adverse outcome for the patient. A simple solution to this problem is to establish a maximum time period between the current examination and the comparison examination being used for peer review.[13] However, adding this criterion across the board will likely narrow the pool of eligible studies for peer review and has the potential to overemphasize inpatient examinations and radiography. A more prudent approach is to define different maximum time frames for each modality on the basis of their respective relative frequencies across a practice to provide a larger-enough pool of exams for review while maintaining meaningful value in peer review.

Practice Auditing

Practice auditing is another method to retrospectively perform peer review in radiology. In this method, image interpretation is compared with a reference standard such as pathologic data, operative findings, or clinical follow-up. The growth of electronic health records (EHR) has made access to comparative data easier, thus facilitating this type of case review. Advantages of professional auditing include incorporating some objective data into the peer-review process and improving performance through correlation of imaging findings with outcomes or operative or pathologic findings. Furthermore, radiologists are encouraged to increasingly use the EHR as part of professional practice. Upfront agreement on types of imaging studies, disease categories, and subspecialties to target is essential to successfully implement professional auditing. Moreover, reliable comparative data such as pathology reports and operative notes must be easily accessible.

One major deficiency of practice auditing is the limited scope of cases that can be reviewed. For example, the overwhelming majority of small lung nodules are benign, and so failure to detect a small nodule on chest CT may go unnoticed if the patient does not undergo any further evaluation. Additionally, an overlooked subsegmental pulmonary embolism could result in no adverse clinical outcome and would not be identified by peer review. A second deficiency of practice auditing is that the defined "reference standard" is assumed to be accurate. Comparing neck CT angiography results with conventional angiography would seem to be a useful benchmark for a practice audit. However, subtle abnormalities can be overlooked on conventional angiography and, because of the two-dimensional nature of conventional angiographic images, lesion severity can be over- or underestimated. A third example is distinguishing between restrictive and constrictive cardiac physiology. Echocardiography, angiography, or clinical evaluation may diagnose restrictive cardiomyopathy whereas cardiac magnetic resonance imaging (MRI) clearly shows constrictive pericarditis.[14]

Furthermore, problems may even arise when the pathologic diagnosis is used as the reference standard. For example, a radiologist with experience in diffuse lung disease may give a diagnosis of nonspecific interstitial pneumonia on a high-resolution computed tomography (HRCT) of a patient with basal predominant ground-glass opacity, reticulation, and traction bronchiectasis with subtle subpleural sparing. However, the expert pulmonary pathologist interpreting the surgical biopsy specimen reports a final pathologic diagnosis of usual interstitial pneumonia. An experienced thoracic radiologist will immediately recognize that this type of discordance between HRCT and histopathologic findings is not at all that uncommon in the setting of diffuse lung disease and does not necessary reflect an interpretative error on the part of both the radiologist and the pathologist but rather illustrates the significant overlap of HRCT and pathologic features of diffuse lung disease. In contrast, a general radiologist with less experience with diffuse lung disease may consider the radiologist's initial diagnosis as an interpretative error, believing the surgical biopsy to be the reference standard.

To reconcile discrepancies like this, the individual performing peer review must comprehend the accuracy of each examination being reviewed and the accuracy of the test or observation being used as the reference standard, both of which may be difficult for those whose practice covers a broad spectrum of modalities and diseases.

Double Reading

The goal of prospective double reading is to promptly identify interpretative errors that could adversely affect patient outcome.[15,16] Most commonly a second radiologist is assigned to review a recently performed imaging study, usually one performed on the same day. Ideally, the second reviewer is provided with the same clinical information and comparison studies and is blinded to the interpretation of the first radiologist. After the second interpretation is rendered, the two involved radiologists are given the opportunity to reconcile any differences. A third radiologist can provide consultation if disagreement persists. This model is often used in screening mammography and can easily be applied to other high-volume studies such as chest, spine, or extremity radiography given the relatively brief amount of time required for interpretation and reporting of these studies. Implementation of double reads for advanced imaging such as positron emission tomography (PET) and MRI may prove more challenging given the longer time required to interpret these studies.

While double reading provides the advantage of near real-time peer review, major drawbacks still exist. Most importantly, double reading requires additional radiologist time. Furthermore, to make this type of peer review meaningful, a reasonable number of cases need to be double read to achieve statistical usefulness. This increased burden of work has the potential to incite animosity toward the peer-review process and reduce compliance.

Consensus-Oriented Group Review

Consensus-oriented group review (COGR) is a novel approach to peer review that enables a group of radiologists to discuss current cases and reach consensus regarding the appropriateness of dictated reports.[17] The intent of this method of peer review is to focus on education, peer coaching, and systems improvement. Furthermore, data on radiology discrepancy rates can be collected and analyzed. Cases are randomly selected from a pool of eligible exams and reviewed by a group of radiologists. After review, the group comes to one of three conclusions: consensus agreement with the original report, consensus agreement that the original report should change, or no consensus. In cases where the group agrees that the report should be changed, the interpreting radiologists is notified so that the case can be re-reviewed and appropriate changes and notifications can be made (Fig. 11.4).

The advantages of COGR include review of more recent cases, random selection, anonymization of cases, group review and discussion, documentation of both good and poor performance, and recognition that consensus cannot always be achieved. Disadvantages of COGR include greater radiologist time per case, fewer cases reviewed, requirement to assemble group of radiologists at a regularly scheduled time, and information technology requirements.

Referring Physician Feedback

Using direct feedback from referring physicians is also a relatively novel approach to peer review in radiology.[18] Structured commentary on components of the radiology report aside from accurate identification and interpretation of findings can also be used to assess radiologist performance. Referring physicians can offer feedback on report features such as language, internal consistencies, length, whether or not the clinical question is addressed, and inclusion of appropriate or relevant recommendations (Fig. 11.5). For example, retrospective peer review of a complex liver transplant Doppler ultrasound examination by a radiologist may result in agreement

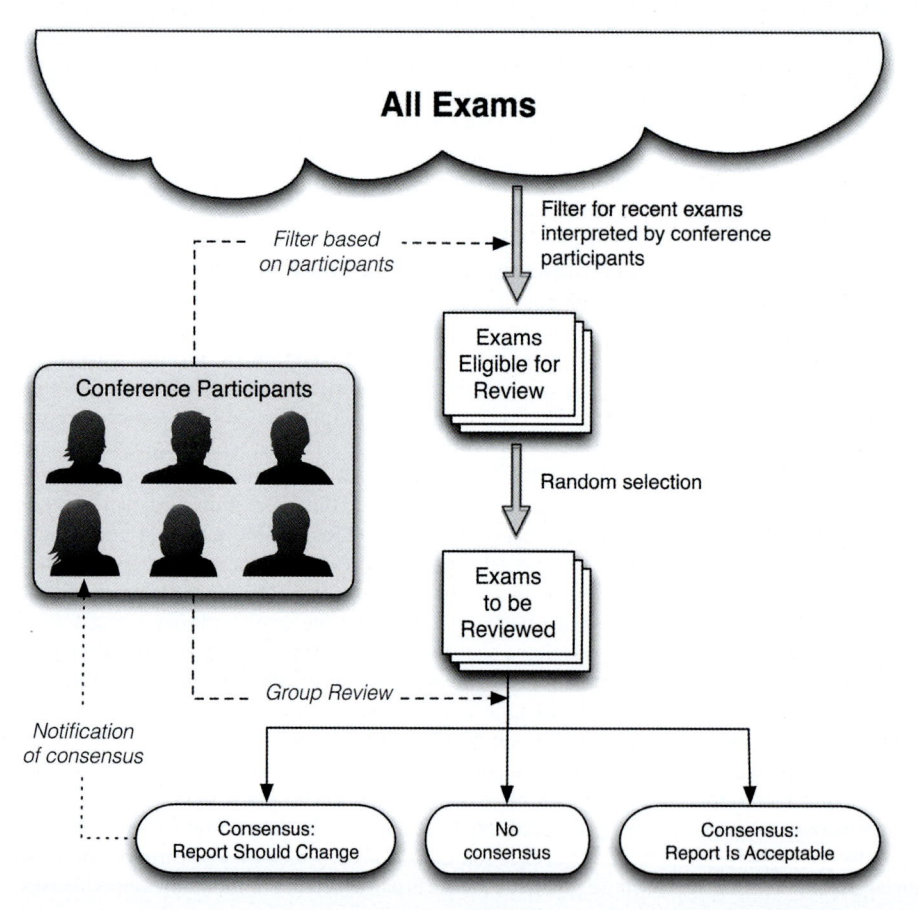

FIG. 11.4 • **Schematic representation of the consensus-oriented group review (COGR) process.** A random sample is selected from all examinations reported on the basis of parameters, including the interpreting radiologist, the study modality, and the time when the study was interpreted. The selected examinations are reviewed by a group of radiologists. Together the group arrives at one of three conclusions: a consensus that the report as issued is acceptable, a consensus that the report should be changed, or a determination that no consensus can be reached. If the group consensus for a case is that the report should change, the interpreting radiologist receives an e-mail indicating the consensus review so that he can determine whether to issue an addendum to the report and notify the ordering provider. (Reproduced with permission from Alkasab TK, Harvey HB, Gowda V, et al. Consensus-oriented group peer review: a new process to review radiologist work output. J Am Coll Radiol. 2014;11(2):131–138.)

Department of Radiology
Referring Provider Survey

Please rate the utility of the radiology report on a scale of 1-5 based on the clinical information provide:

1	2	3	4	5
Not useful				Useful

Please indicate any problems with the radiology report:

Content:
- ☐ Clinical question not answered
- ☐ Too much extraneous information
- ☐ Important detail omitted
- ☐ Internal discrepancies in the report (e.g. left and right mixed up)
- ☐ Relevant or appropriate recommendations omitted
- ☐ Available comparison examination(s) not referenced

Language:
- ☐ Typographical errors
- ☐ Language unclear
- ☐ Non-standard terminology used

Other (please specify): ____________________

If a recommendation was made in the report, was it appropriate? ☐ Yes ☐ No

If no recommendation was made, would one have been useful? ☐ Yes ☐ No

In your opinion, should the findings documented in the report have been directly communicated to the ordering provider? ☐ Yes ☐ No

Accession number: A14558745

FIG. 11.5 • Sample survey for referring providers regarding diagnostic radiology report. (Adapted from Gunn AJ, Alabre CI, Bennett SE, et al. Structured feedback from referring physicians: a novel approach to quality improvement in radiology reporting. *Am J Roentgenol.* 2013;201(4):853–857.)

with the highly detailed and accurate yet verbose and disorganized report but can easily overlook that the referring physician failed to understand the implications of the examination results. Prime advantages of this method of peer review include directing the radiologist toward the needs of the referring physician, aspiring to improve communication between radiologists and referring physicians, and working to improved patient care by increasing the accuracy of communication among health-care team members.

Referring physician feedback as a sole method of peer review can fail to reveal deficiencies in actual image interpretation. For example, a referring physician may be pleased with the quality of one radiologist's report of a knee MRI examination but does not convey the fact that subtle medial meniscal tear was overlooked. Another scenario to consider is one in which HRCT shows scattered foci of patchy ground-glass opacity and the differential diagnosis is appropriately broad given limited clinical information yet the referring physician is frustrated because a specific diagnosis or more limited differential diagnosis is not provided. To make this component of peer review useful, an easy mechanism should be implemented for referring physicians to provide comments and request review of clinically reported diagnostic errors.[7]

Focused Practice Review

Focused practice review (FPR) is a more vigorous method of radiology peer review that delves deeper than retrospective radiologist review by including misdiagnoses or misinterpretations reported by referring physicians.[7] This system of peer review includes a clearly defined sequence of review and, most importantly, a robust appeals process. Senior leadership such as the department quality officer, the division director, and the department chair review cases with significant errors, and, at the conclusion of the FPR, the department chair or a peer-review committee dictates corrective action. This method of peer review is advantageous because it is highly structured and directly involves senior departmental leadership (Fig. 11.6).

Although FPR may enhance the effectiveness of peer review, it has the potential to incite negative feelings toward the process. Specifically, Hussain et al. describe, "Completed FPR cases formed the basis of morbidity and mortality presentations and punitive management decisions."[7] The use of the word "punitive" likely will lead to unintended consequences in the realm of peer review.

Comprehensive Radiologist Performance Assessment

A comprehensive professional peer-review program includes all aspects of radiologic practice. In addition to peer review of case interpretation, performance review can also include other aspects of professional practice such as professional interactions with patients and staff, continuing medical education activities, maintaining appropriate skills and certification such as cardiopulmonary resuscitation, adherence to departmental communication and documentation policies, participation in quality and safety improvement projects, and completion of institutionally or regulatory-mandated training.[3]

Establishing and maintaining a comprehensive performance assessment can be extremely resource intense. Most large community practices and academic departments will have sufficient administrative support to design and track these metrics, but smaller practices may find that acquiring and tracking appropriate data can be challenging.

USING PEER-REVIEW DATA

Once the peer-review process begins, participants expect feedback (Fig. 11.1). With FPR, a predefined structured and tiered review process is used that involves the chief quality officer, division chief, and department chair. At the conclusion of the FPR, the department chair renders a decision as to what further action, if any, is needed.[7] In contrast, some authors argue that for a peer review to be successful and meaningful, auditing should shift away from metrics and error identification toward an overarching culture of improving performance of the entire practice, in a sense moving the bell curve to the right rather than chopping off the lower end.[19] This approach has been successfully used in the aviation industry where learning from the past mistakes of others is stressed so as to avoid repeating the same mistake. Furthermore, this approach establishes a culture in which all participants feel empowered to speak up when they feel an error has been made or, most importantly, is about to be made.[20]

No matter which approach or approaches to peer review a radiology practice selects, using aggregated data for educational purposes is paramount. Some practices may opt for the traditional morbidity and mortality conference. In these conferences, case specifics are discussed in an open forum and the "owner" of the case must defend or justify actions taken or reasons for an interpretation. More preferable is a group presentation of difficult or "missed" cases in a nonpunitive, anonymous forum with the goal to educate attendees. In addition to presenting the cases, participants may be asked to present on a focused topic related to a case or group of cases.

Changes to professional practice may occur as a result of group peer-review activities. Practices may adopt a uniform image

TO: ______________________________

FROM: ______________________________

DATE: ______________________________

MR # ______________________________

ISSUE

Case Overview: ______________________________

Please complete a Focused Peer Review for the case listed above.
Return to Dr. .... before __/__/______. Thank you!

Reviewdate: ___/___/__ ____________________ ____________________

Reviewer Name **Reviewer Signature**

Division Director's or Reviewer's Comments:

Interpreting Radiologists Comments: ______________________________

Quality Review:

Diagnosis	Class	Description of Disagreement	Case Disposal (Circle one)
			A. No further action B. Issue addendum C. Request for skill enhancement D. Reportable event

Class 1 = Concur with the interpret

Class 2 = Difficult diagnosis, not ordinarily expected to be made

Class 3 = Significant discrepancy, no clinical impact

Class 4 = Significant discrepancy, clinical impact

Class 5 = Not applicable

Cause of Error:

( ) Perceptive ( ) Problem Solving ( ) Did not follow protocol
( ) System Related: Old films not provided, labs not checked ( )Technologist Related: Incomplete or poor quality study

Appeal:

Chairman's Decision:

( ) No action
( ) Change in Privilege or Credentials
( ) Policy, Protocol or Guideline Review
( ) Provider Letter / Counseling
( ) Written Warning (1st), (2nd)

Division Director................Vice Chair.......................Chairman........................Date .../...../....

FIG. 11.6 • Template for focused practice review. (Reproduced with permission from Hussain S, Hussain JS, Karam A, Vijayaraghavan G. Focused peer review: the end game of peer review. *J Am Coll Radiol.* 2012;9(6):430–433 e1.)

acquisition protocol, agree to use a defined lexicon of terminology, or adopt practice guidelines. Once a peer-review program is in place, continued participation and support from participating radiologists is a key to ongoing success. Documenting practice improvement or increased standardization may convince skeptics of the value of the peer-review process. Furthermore, radiologists can use peer-review activities to meet part IV (Practice Quality Improvement) requirements for the American Board of Radiology's (ABR) Maintenance of Certification (MOC) program by using their own peer-review data to design and implement a quality-improvement project.[21] Ultimately, a robust peer-review program will engender a practice culture of collaboration and openness with the goal of improving patient care.

References

1. Kohn LT, Corrigan JM, Donaldson MS, et al. (eds.). *To Err is Human: Building a Safer Health System*. Washington, DC: National Acadamies Press; 2000.
2. Donnelly LF, Strife JL. Performance-based assessment of radiology faculty: a practical plan to promote improvement and meet JCAHO standards. *Am J Roentgenol*. 2005;184(5):1398–1401.
3. Donnelly LF. Performance-based assessment of radiology practitioners: promoting improvement in accordance with the 2007 joint commission standards. *J Am Coll Radiol*. 2007;4(10):699–703.
4. Jackson VP, Cushing T, Abujudeh HH, et al. RADPEER scoring white paper. *J Am Coll Radiol*. 2009;6(1):21–25.
5. American College of Radiology. *RADPEER*. Reston, VA: American College of Radiology; 2013.
6. Mahgerefteh S, Kruskal JB, Yam CS, et al. Peer review in diagnostic radiology: current state and a vision for the future. *Radiographics*. 2009;29(5):1221–1231.
7. Hussain S, Hussain JS, Karam A, et al. Focused peer review: the end game of peer review. *J Am Coll Radiol*. 2012;9(6):430–433.e1.
8. Alpert HR, Hillman BJ. Quality and variability in diagnostic radiology. *J Am Coll Radiol*. 2004;1(2):127–132.
9. MacMahon H, Austin JH, Gamsu G, et al. Guidelines for management of small pulmonary nodules detected on CT scans: a statement from the Fleischner Society. *Radiology*. 2005;237(2):395–400.
10. Edwards MT. The objective impact of clinical peer review on hospital quality and safety. *Am J Med Qual*. 2011;26(2):110–119.
11. Borgstede JP, Lewis RS, Bhargavan M, et al. RADPEER quality assurance program: a multifacility study of interpretive disagreement rates. *J Am Coll Radiol*. 2004;1(1):59–65.
12. Cascade PN. Comment on "RADPEER quality assurance program: a multifacility study of interpretive disagreement rates". *J Am Coll Radiol*. 2004;1(4):295–296; author reply 7.
13. Larson PA, Pyatt RS Jr, Grimes CK, et al. Getting the most out of RADPEER. *J Am Coll Radiol*. 2011;8(8):543–548.
14. Francone M, Dymarkowski S, Kalantzi M, et al. Assessment of ventricular coupling with real-time cine MRI and its value to differentiate constrictive pericarditis from restrictive cardiomyopathy. *Eur Radiol*. 2006;16(4):944–951.
15. Royal College of Radiology. Standards for self-assessment of performance. http://www.rcr.ac.uk/docs/radiology/pdf/Stand_self_assess.pdf. Accessed June 3, 2016.
16. Soffa DJ, Lewis RS, Sunshine JH, et al. Disagreement in interpretation: a method for the development of benchmarks for quality assurance in imaging. *J Am Coll Radiol*. 2004;1(3):212–217.
17. Alkasab TK, Harvey HB, Gowda V, et al. Consensus-oriented group peer review: a new process to review radiologist work output. *J Am Coll Radiol*. 2014;11(2):131–138.
18. Gunn AJ, Alabre CI, Bennett SE, et al. Structured feedback from referring physicians: a novel approach to quality improvement in radiology reporting. *Am J Roentgenol*. 2013;201(4):853–857.
19. Butler GJ, Forghani R. The next level of radiology peer review: enterprise-wide education and improvement. *J Am Coll Radiol*. 2013;10(5):349–353.
20. Larson DB, Nance JJ. Rethinking peer review: what aviation can teach radiology about performance improvement. *Radiology*. 2011;259(3):626–632.
21. American Board of Radiology. PQI Topics 2013. http://www.theabr.org/pqi-topics. Accessed June 3, 2016.

SELF-ASSESSMENT QUESTIONS

1. Which of the following is an advantage of focused practice review?

    A. Robust appeals process
    B. Avoids punitive approach
    C. Empowers junior radiologists
    D. Reviews large number of cases

2. Which of the following is an advantage of double reading peer review?

    A. Increased professional billing
    B. Rapid identification of significant error
    C. Improves radiologist productivity
    D. Only small number of cases need review

Answers to Chapter Self-Assessment Questions

1. A. Focused practice review (FPR) includes a clearly defined sequence of review and, most importantly, a robust appeals process. At the end of the process, the department chair or peer-review committee dictates corrective action. Most decision makers are senior radiologists. Because individual cases have to be reviewed by a single person or group of people, the number of cases reviewed is usually small.

2. B. Double reading peer review is positioned to identify potentially significant errors in a timely manner. Radiologists are not able to bill for a second interpretation and productivity may decrease because of increased workload from double reads. Because significant error rates are generally low, a large number of cases need to be reviewed; however, this is usually not possible with double read peer review.

Credentialing and Certification of Programs and Individuals

12

Jeffrey P. Kanne

LEARNING OBJECTIVES

1. List the credentialing and certifications available for health-care facilities and organizations
2. List the credentialing and certifications available for individual practitioners
3. State the ACGME's six core competencies
4. Describe the American Board of Radiology's certification process

---

A variety of required and optional certifications and accreditations are available for health-care organizations and health-care providers. Some credentials fall under the purview of government agencies, whereas others are granted by independent organizations that aim to improve the overall quality of health-care delivery. Because radiology is central to health-care delivery and has a significant role in both inpatient and outpatient settings, certifying and accrediting organizations directly impact radiologists and radiology departments.

PROGRAMS FOR ORGANIZATIONS
American College of Radiology

Under the Medicare Improvement for Patients and Providers Act of 2008 (MIPPA), providers of advanced diagnostic imaging (CT, MRI, and PET) that bill under the technical component of part B of the Medicare Physician Fee Schedule (i.e., outpatient imaging) must be accredited by a Centers for Medicare and Medicaid Services (CMS)–designated accrediting organization. The American College of Radiology (ACR) offers accreditation to facilities in various advanced imaging modalities (see Chapter 1).[1]

The Joint Commission

The Joint Commission (TJC) accredits and certifies more than 20,000 health-care organizations and programs in the United States. Facilities ranging from office-based surgical suites to large hospitals can apply for TJC accreditation. Organizations can also earn certification from TJC for programs focused on specific chronic diseases such as asthma, diabetes, and heart failure.[2]

Other Accrediting Bodies

In addition to TJC, several smaller organizations have been granted "deeming" status by CMS for accrediting hospitals and other health-care delivery entities. Det Norske Veritas Healthcare, Inc. (DNV), the Healthcare Facilities Accreditation Program (HFAP), and Center for Improvement in Healthcare Quality (CIHQ) also have accrediting programs for health-care organizations.

The Leapfrog Group

The Leapfrog Group (Leapfrog) is an independent, not-for-profit organization founded by a group of large employers in 2000, with the purpose of assessing safety, quality, and efficiency of health-care organizations so that those who use and pay for health care can make informed decisions. Furthermore, Leapfrog promotes high-value health care through various incentives and rewards. Leapfrog members include large corporations and public employers, organizations of purchasers such as business coalitions and alliances, and its liaisons, which include the Centers for Medicare & Medicaid Services (CMS) and the Department of Defense (DOD).

In 2001, Leapfrog launched the Leapfrog Hospital Survey to encourage hospitals to publically report their respective progress in meeting key safety practices. The three initial areas assessed in the survey were computerized physician order entry, intensive care unit physician staffing, and evidence-based hospital referral. The survey has evolved into a balanced assessment of quality and safety that focuses on hospital structure, processes of care, and outcomes.[3] After survey data are received and verified, Leapfrog publically publishes its results, giving each institution a letter Grade (A through F) and reporting measure of specific performance compared with other surveyed hospitals.[4]

INDIVIDUAL CREDENTIALING AND CERTIFICATION
American Board of Radiology

The American Board of Radiology (ABR), founded in 1934, is a not-for-profit organization that is one of the 24 independent national boards belonging to the American Board of Medical Specialties (ABMS). The ABR currently issues primary certification in diagnostic radiology, radiology oncology, and medical physics. The ABR is also planning to offer a combined diagnostic and interventional radiology primary certificate in the near future. Subspecialty certificates currently offered by the ABR include hospice and palliative medicine, neuroradiology, nuclear radiology, pediatric radiology, and vascular and interventional radiology.

Certification in Diagnostic Radiology

ABR certification in diagnostic radiology requires completion of an Accreditation Council for Graduate Medical Education (ACGME) or Royal College of Physicians and Surgeons of Canada (RCPSC)–accredited diagnostic radiology residency training program and passing of the ABR's Core Examination and Certifying Examination in diagnostic radiology (Table 12.1). The ABR also provides an alternative pathway to certification for international medical graduates.[5]

Core Examination

Currently, eligible trainees can sit for the Core Examination following completion of 36 months of residency training. The Core Examination is computer based and image rich and covers 18 subspecialty and modality areas. Examinees must pass all categories to receive a passing result.[6]

Certifying Examination

Radiologists can sit for the Certifying Examination no sooner than 15 months following completion of residency training and only after receiving a passing result on the Core Examination. Unlike the Core Examination, which examines all subspecialties and modalities, the Certifying Examination allows examinees to select the areas in which they wish to be examined on the basis of training, experience, and practice emphasis. Up to three subspecialty areas can be selected. The Certifying Examination also includes a module in noninterpretative skills such as quality and safety, professionalism, and ethics, as well as an "Essentials of Diagnostic Radiology" module that focuses on "basic knowledge that every radiologist should know, such as recognizing child abuse, pneumothorax, shock bowel, and subdural hematoma."[7]

Board Eligible and Board Certified

Upon successful completion of residency training, radiologists are deemed "Board Eligible" by the ABR and have six full calendar years from the end of training to receive certification in diagnostic radiology from the ABR. Upon successful completion of both the Core Examination and the Certifying Examination, diplomates are "Board Certified" by the ABR.[5]

Subspecialty Certificates

The ABR offers subspecialty certificates (formerly certificates of added qualification) in pediatric radiology, neuroradiology, vascular and interventional radiology, nuclear radiology, and hospice and palliative medicine. These certificates are intended for radiologists who have undergone additional training in these areas. Certification and maintenance of certification (MOC) in these subspecialties are integrated into the overall certification and MOC processes.

Maintenance of Certification

The ABMS mandates that all member specialty boards require MOC for their respective diplomates. Up until 2002, the ABR issued lifetime certificates in diagnostic radiology, and holders of these certificates retain their lifetime board certification. Beginning in 2002, all diplomates in diagnostic radiology were issued time-limited (10 years) certificates by the ABR. Holders of time-limited certificates are required to enroll in the ABR's MOC program. In 2012, the ABR transitioned from a 10-year MOC cycle to Continuous Certification, in which new and renewed certificates no longer have "valid-through" dates but rather state, "Ongoing validity of this certificate is contingent upon meeting the requirements of Maintenance of Certification."[8]

MOC consists of four parts, the requirements of which must be met in order for diplomates to maintain their board certified status with the ABR (Table 12.2). These four parts evaluate the six core competencies designated by the ACGME and ABMS (Table 12.3). The ABR uses a three-year look back to determine whether or not a diplomate is meeting MOC requirements.[9] In 2012, ABMS began reporting on its public website whether or not each physician certified by the 24 ABMS member boards is meeting MOC requirements. The ABR reports publically on its own website and includes radiologists with lifetime certificates who are not required to participate in MOC.

Part 1: Professional Standing—Diplomates must maintain active, current, valid, and unrestricted medical licenses relevant to all locations of practice.

Part 2: Lifelong Learning and Self-Assessment—Diplomates must complete 75 AMA PRA Category 1 Credits, of which at least 25 must be self-assessment–continuing medical education (SA-CME) credits, every 3 years.

Part 3: Cognitive Expertise—Diplomates must pass an ABR MOC or initial certification examination within the last 10 years. The MOC exam is computer based and image rich and consists of four modules, one in noninterpretative skills and three in up to three different subspecialty areas based on the diplomate's reported practice profile.

Part 4: Practice Quality Improvement (PQI)—Diplomates must complete at least one PQI project in the previous 3 years. PQI projects can be individual or group projects, but each diplomate must report his own participation to the ABR. Diplomates can design

---

Table 12.1 AMERICAN BOARD OF RADIOLOGY DIAGNOSTIC RADIOLOGY EXAMINATION.

Examination	Eligibility	Features
Core exam	After 36 months of diagnostic radiology residency	18 subspecialty and modality areas examined
Certifying exam	15 months following the end of training	1. Noninterpretative skills 2. Essentials of diagnostic radiology 3. Up to three subspecialty specific areas
Maintenance of certification (MOC) exam	Within 10 years after initial certification or previous MOC exam	1. Noninterpretative skills 2. Up to three subspecialty specific areas[a]

[a]MOC subspecialty certificates require at least two modules be in that subspecialty.

Table 12.2 **AMERICAN BOARD OF RADIOLOGY MAINTENANCE OF CERTIFICATION.**

Part	Requirements
Professional standing	Hold active, current, valid, and unrestricted medical licenses relevant to all practice locations
Lifelong learning and self-assessment	75 AMA Category 1 CME credits per 3 years, 25 of which must be self-assessment CME
Cognitive expertise	Passing score on certifying or MOC exam within the past 10 years
Practice quality improvement	Participate in and complete at least one practice quality improvement project in the past 3 years or regular participation in other quality-related activities

Table 12.3 **ACGME SIX CORE COMPETENCIES.**

Core Competency	Description
Medical knowledge	Demonstrate knowledge about established and evolving biomedical, clinical, and cognate (e.g., epidemiological and social–behavioral) sciences and the application of this knowledge to patient care
Patient care	Provide patient care that is compassionate, appropriate, and effective for the treatment of health problems and the promotion of health
Interpersonal and communication skills	Demonstrate interpersonal and communication skills that result in effective information exchange and teaming with patients, patients' families, and professional associates
Professionalism	Demonstrate a commitment to carrying out professional responsibilities, adherence to ethical principles, and sensitivity to a diverse patient population
Practice-based learning and improvement	Investigate and evaluate patient care practices, appraise and assimilate scientific evidence, and improve patient care practices
Systems-based practice	Demonstrate an awareness of and responsiveness to the larger context and system of health care and the ability to effectively call on system resources to provide care that is of optimal value

their own PQI projects or select from a variety of projects sponsored by professional societies. Alternatively, diplomats can engage in other quality-related activities such as regular participation in multidisciplinary conferences, serving on a quality committee, or participating in a root cause analysis.

Focused Practice Recognition

Focused practice recognition (FPR) is designed for components of clinical practice that neither have ACGME-approved fellowship training nor constitute an integral component of general training. The ABMS currently has a pilot FPR program in cardiac CT (CCT) offered only through the ABR. The FPR-CCT program requires primary certification in diagnostic radiology from the ABR for at least 1 year, current and active participation in ABR MOC, completion of at least 150 ECG-gated cardiac CT scans in the past 3 years (with primary responsibility for protocol and interpretation of at least 75), at least 4 SA-CME and at least 50 AMA PRA Category 1 Credits in cardiac CT, completion of at least 1 PQI project in cardiac CT, and a passing score on a secure exam on cardiac CT. The ACR's Cardiac CT Advanced Proficiency examination, which consists of knowledge-based multiple-choice questions and a practical component focusing on interpretation of cardiac CT, meets this requirement.

State Medical Boards

State medical boards issue licenses for the general practice of medicine. Medical licenses are not limited to specific medical specialties, and physicians are not required to hold certification in a medical specialty. Requirements for licensure, including postgraduate training requirements, number of attempts at licensing examination (United States Medical Licensing Examination), and time limit for completing licensure examination sequence, vary by jurisdiction. Aside from issuing medical licenses, state medical boards are also charged with investigating complaints against practitioners, disciplining practitioners who violate state law, and evaluating and facilitating rehabilitation for impaired physicians.[10]

Credentialing and Medical Staff Appointment

Health-care facilities and organizations require credentialing of physicians and midlevel providers and appointment to the medical staff of that institution or organization. Under TJC guidelines, appointments cannot exceed 2 years. Applicants are granted specific privileges on the basis of training and experience. Core privileges are typically granted *en bloc*, and providers can request additional specific privileges. Requirements for any privilege must be the same for all practitioners regardless of medical specialty. For example, a radiologist can be granted core diagnostic radiology privileges such as supervision and interpretation of radiography, CT, MRI, and ultrasound in addition to specific privileges such as image-guided injection or biopsy. A surgeon wishing to perform image-guided injections would need to meet the same requirements for that privilege as a radiologist granted the same privilege. Members of an institution or organization's medical staff must adhere to institutional bylaws and follow the policies and procedures of that organization.[11]

Ongoing Professional Practice Evaluation

In 2007, TJC mandated that accredited organizations establish a detailed evaluation of practitioners' professional performance as part of the organization's process for granting and maintaining professional privileges in that organization (Table 12.4). Ongoing professional practice evaluation (OPPE) has three main purposes. First, OPPE is a core component of monitoring of professional competency. Second, OPPE is intended to identify areas for possible performance improvement by individual practitioners. Third, OPPE relies on objective data to aid decision making regarding continuance of professional privileges. Because OPPE is intended to be a screening tool, practitioners who are performing at or above acceptable levels

Table 12.4 ONGOING PROFESSIONAL PRACTICE EVALUATION VERSUS FOCUSED PROFESSIONAL PRACTICE EVALUATION.

Ongoing Professional Practice Evaluation (OPPE)	Focused Professional Practice Evaluation (FPPE)
Required of all practitioners	Used when a practitioner is identified by OPPE as possibly performing below the acceptable standard
Performed more often than once year to meet TJC standard of "ongoing"	Performed for a predetermined time limit (or predetermined number of procedures) only when required by OPPE

Table 12.5 PURPOSES OF ACGME MILESTONES.

ACGME	Training Programs	Trainees
Continuous monitoring of training programs	Provide a detailed framework for evaluating clinical competency of trainees	Provide a clearly defined set of expectations of performance
Provide aggregate data for public reporting	Guide curriculum development	Enable better self-evaluation and self-directed learning
Contribute to culture of continuous improvement in graduate medical education	Provide tools for better assessment of trainees	Facilitate better feedback for professional development
	Aid in earlier identification of struggling trainees	

may be identified for further evaluation (false positive). Criteria such as readmission rates, cost per admission, mortality rates, and so forth may be used in OPPE. For radiology, peer-review data, referring physician complaints, and procedure complication rates may be part of OPPE. To be considered ongoing by TJC, evaluations must be performed more frequently than annually.[12]

Focused Professional Practice Evaluation

Focused professional practice evaluation (FPPE) is the process designed to follow up on clinicians identified through OPPE who warrant further evaluation. FPPE is also used when practitioners are first granted privileges and when practitioners request new privileges. TJC does not specify the precise contents or duration of FPPE, but for the process to be effective, its terms must be defined up front. Typically, FPPE is performed for 3 to 6 months but may be extended over a longer period if the services being monitored are performed infrequently. In some disciplines, such as pathology or radiology, a fixed number of cases may be reviewed rather than monitoring over a predefined time period. If the results of FPPE indicate that the practitioner is performing at or above the expected level, that practitioner continues with OPPE. If the FPPE identifies a significant practice deficiency, organizational processes for additional education or supervision can be activated.[13]

Accreditation Council for Graduate Medical Education

The ACGME awards accreditation of residency training programs in diagnostic radiology as well as some fellowship programs (pediatrics, neuroradiology, and interventional radiology). The ACGME is a private professional organization that accredits approximately 9,500 training programs in 140 specialty and subspecialty areas. To ensure that standards are appropriately maintained, the ACGME has 27 specialty-specific residency review committees (RRC), which continually review and revise accreditation standards as well as review specific training programs to ensure that standards are being met.

Just as health-care organizations and certifying organizations such as the ABR have transitioned to continuous certification, the ACGME has also transitioned to a model of continuous resident evaluation incorporating milestones within the six ACGME core competencies. For the ACGME, milestones enable continuous monitoring of training programs, provide data for aggregate reporting to the public, and contribute to a culture of continuous improvement in graduate medical education. For training programs, milestones provide a detailed framework for evaluating clinical competency of trainees, guide curriculum development, provide tools for better assessment of trainees, and aid in earlier identification of struggling trainees. For trainees, milestones provide a clearly defined set of expectations of performance, enable better self-evaluation and self-directed learning, and facilitate better feedback for professional development[14] (Table 12.5).

References

1. American College of Radiology. Accreditation. http://www.acr.org/Quality-Safety/Accreditation. Accessed June 3, 2016.
2. The Joint Commission. About the Joint Commission. http://www.jointcommission.org/about_us/about_the_joint_commission_main.aspx. Accessed June 3, 2016.
3. Austin JM, D'Andrea G, Birkmeyer JD, et al. Safety in numbers: the development of Leapfrog's composite patient safety score for U.S. hospitals. J Patient Saf. 2014;10:64–71.
4. The Leapfrog Group. About Leapfrog. http://www.leapfroggroup.org/about_leapfrog. Accessed June 3, 2016.
5. The American Board of Radiology. Initial certification: diagnostic radiology. http://www.theabr.org/ic-dr-landing. Accessed June 3, 2016.
6. The American Board of Radiology. Initial certification: diagnostic radiology—core exam. http://www.theabr.org/ic-dr-core-exam. Accessed June 3, 2016.
7. The American Board of Radiology. Initial certification: diagnostic radiology—certifying exam. http://www.theabr.org/ic-dr-certifying-exam. Accessed June 3, 2016.
8. The American Board of Radiology. Maintenance of certification. http://www.theabr.org/moc-gen-landing. Accessed June 3, 2016.

9. The American Board of Radiology. Maintenance of certification, Tucson, AZ; 2014 http://wwwtheabrorg/sites/all/themes/abr-media/pdf/4PanelBrochure_DRpdf. Accessed June 3, 2016.
10. Federation of State Medical Boards. 2014. http://www.fsmb.org. Accessed June 3, 2016.
11. The Joint Commission. Standards FAQs. http://www.jointcommission.org/standards_information/jcfaq.aspx?ProgramId=39. Accessed June 3, 2016.
12. The Joint Commission. Ongoing Professional Practice Evaluation (OPPE). March 6, 2013 http://www.jointcommission.org/standards_information/jcfaqdetails.aspx?StandardsFAQId=470&StandardsFAQChapterId=74. Accessed June 3, 2016.
13. The Joint Commission. Focused Professional Practice Evaluation. 2013. January 31, 2013. http://www.jointcommission.org/standards_information/jcfaqdetails.aspx?StandardsFAQId=467&StandardsFAQChapterId=74. Accessed June 3, 2016.
14. Accreditation Council for Graduate Medical Education. https://http://www.acgme.org/acgmeweb/tabid/430/ProgramandInstitutionalAccreditation/NextAccreditationSystem/Milestones.aspx. Accessed June 3, 2016.

SELF-ASSESSMENT QUESTIONS

1. Peer-review activities can be used to meet which of the following requirements for the American Board of Radiology's Maintenance of Certification (MOC) program?

   A. Professional standing
   B. Lifelong learning and self-assessment
   C. Cognitive expertise
   D. Practice quality improvement (PQI)

2. Which of the following requires accreditation of providers of advanced imaging (CT, MRI, and PET) in order to bill under the technical component of part B of the Medicare Physician Fee Schedule?

   A. American College of Radiology
   B. US federal law
   C. The Joint Commission
   D. The Leapfrog Group

Answers to Chapter Self-Assessment Questions

1. D. Currently, radiologists enrolled in the American College of Radiology's Maintenance of Certification (MOC) program can use peer-review activities to meet the practice quality improvement (PQI) requirements. Professional standing is focused on unrestricted licensure. Continuing medical education and self-assessment activities fulfill the lifelong learning and self-assessment requirements. Cognitive expertise requirements are based on a computer-based examination.

2. B. The Medicare Improvement for Patients and Providers Act of 2008 (MIPPA) requires accreditation of providers of advanced diagnostic imaging (CT, MRI, and PET) that bill under the technical component of part B of the Medicare Physician Fee Schedule. The American College of Radiology is approved by the Centers for Medicare & Medicaid Services to accredit providers of advanced diagnostic imaging. The Joint Commission accredits hospitals and other health-care facilities but not diagnostic imaging programs. The Leapfrog Group assesses quality, safety, and efficiency of health-care organizations.

Quality Dashboards

13

Jeffrey P. Kanne

LEARNING OBJECTIVES

1. Describe different types of dashboards that might be used in a radiology practice
2. List the steps involved in designing and maintaining a dashboard

Business intelligence or business analytics is a field focused on mining and analyzing raw data from across many sources and presenting them in a useful manner to improve productivity, reduce inefficiencies, and identify new opportunities.[1] Business intelligence has been extremely successful across many industries[2] and is increasingly used in the health-care industry.[3,4]

Managing a radiology department requires detailed knowledge of operational, quality, safety, and fiscal information. Traditional monthly or quarterly reports are rapidly becoming a thing of the past, as the ability to aggregate data for immediate analysis is becoming or already has become a reality for many practices. Digital "dashboards" are tools that display real-time data consisting of key performance indicators (KPIs) in a useful format tailored to an individual's specific needs. A dashboard has been defined as "a concise, context-specific display of KPIs for quick evaluation of multiple subsystems."[5] Dashboards can enable communication of the current state of a practice and can facilitate identifying specific goals for practice improvement.[6]

TYPES OF DASHBOARDS

Three primary types of dashboards have been described: operational, tactical, and strategic (Table 13.1). Operational dashboards provide real-time monitoring of core operational processes. In radiology, these may include radiologist report turnaround time (TAT) and patient wait time. Tactical dashboards look at trends, with data updated less frequently, usually daily or weekly. Tactical dashboards in radiology may include access (e.g., the next available appointment for a specific exam), IV contrast extravasation rates, and patient "no-show" rates. Strategic dashboards focus on KPIs related to the overall enterprise and are used to monitor and reflect on common goals. In a radiology department, a strategic dashboard might present data on patient satisfaction, referring physician satisfaction, and financial health.

GOALS OF DASHBOARDS

The primary reason for developing a dashboard should be focused and defined upfront. Limiting objectives can allow managers to quickly identify critical issues and allocate appropriate resources to key issues. Objectives usually fall into one of three categories: financial, operational, and quality (Table 13.2).[7,8] Common financial

Table 13.1 **TYPES OF QUALITY DASHBOARDS.**

Type of Dashboard	Function	Examples in Radiology
Operational	Real-time monitoring of core operational processes	Report turnaround time Patient wait time
Tactical	Monitor trends in operations	Access IV contrast extravasation Patient "no-show" rate
Strategic	Monitor and reflect on enterprise goals	Patient satisfaction Referring physician satisfaction Financial health

Table 13.2 **TYPES OF KEY PERFORMANCE INDICATORS (KPIs).**

Type of KPI	Examples in Radiology
Financial	Cost per relative value unit Collections by modality Days in accounts receivable Actual expenses Total revenue
Operational	Total examination volume Examination volume by modality Examination volume by location
Quality	Report turnaround time Accuracy of interpretation (peer review) Correct patient imaged Correct exam performed Correct side imaged Patient access Communication of critical tests and critical results

KPIs include cost per relative value unit (RVU), collections by modality, days in accounts receivable, actual expenses, and total revenue. Operational KPIs include total examination volume, examination volume per modality, and examination volume per location. Quality KPIs include TAT, accuracy of interpretation (peer review), correct exam, patient access, and prompt communication of critical tests and critical results.[6,9]

DESIGNING A DASHBOARD

For a dashboard to be useful, it must contain meaningful information that can be acted upon promptly. Thus, a clear mission must be in place when designing a dashboard (Fig. 13.1). First, a team of major stakeholders should be assembled, consisting of key leaders including physicians, nurses, technologists, and information technology (IT), financial, and operations managers.[10] Having representation from all aspects of a practice can ensure that common goals are set and are aligned with the goals of the overarching organization, that appropriate KPIs are included, and that functionality can meet expectations. Furthermore, investing in the initial planning stage can reduce both dashboard development time and need for redesign.[11,12]

After assembling the dashboard design team and defining the goals of the dashboard, specific KPIs need to be selected to include on the dashboard. Chosen KPIs should be aligned to the goals of the dashboard, relevant to the specific practice, and draw from data that can be readily obtained.[13–15] KPIs that are part of regulatory requirements, such as those needed for accreditation and credentialing, should be flagged and included on the dashboard so that these can be actively monitored and reported on (Fig. 13.2).[3,13] Having too few KPIs can lead to a dashboard with little utility, whereas selecting too many KPIs can result in a dashboard that is too "busy" to be useful for review at a glance. A dashboard consisting of 15 to 25 KPIs is optimal.[7]

Once KPIs have been selected, data need to be readily accessible and accurate. Dashboard data are frequently pooled from various sources, including the radiology information system (RIS), hospital information system (HIS), picture archiving and communications system (PACS), and billing and other financial software. External data, such as patient satisfaction data, may also be incorporated into a dashboard. Definitions of selected KPIs should follow accepted standards and definitions across the industry so that KPIs can be compared to local, regional, and national benchmark data.[16] Identifying the data source for each KPI and the individual responsible for each KPI should be established up front.[10]

Data should be archived in standard formats (such as a structured query language [SQL] database or comma-separated values [CSV]) so that they can be easily shared, manipulated, and integrated into the dashboard. Security of dashboard data should be maintained on the basis of institutional IT security policies, and Health Insurance Portability and Accountability Act (HIPAA) standards should be followed at all times to safeguard patient privacy.[17]

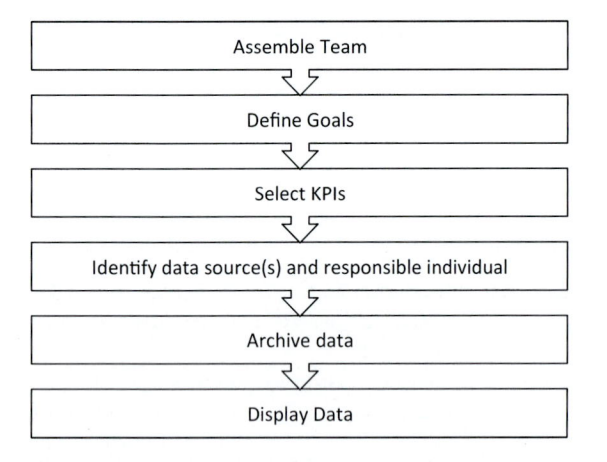

FIG. 13.1 • **Process of creating a quality dashboard.** KPI, key performance indicator.

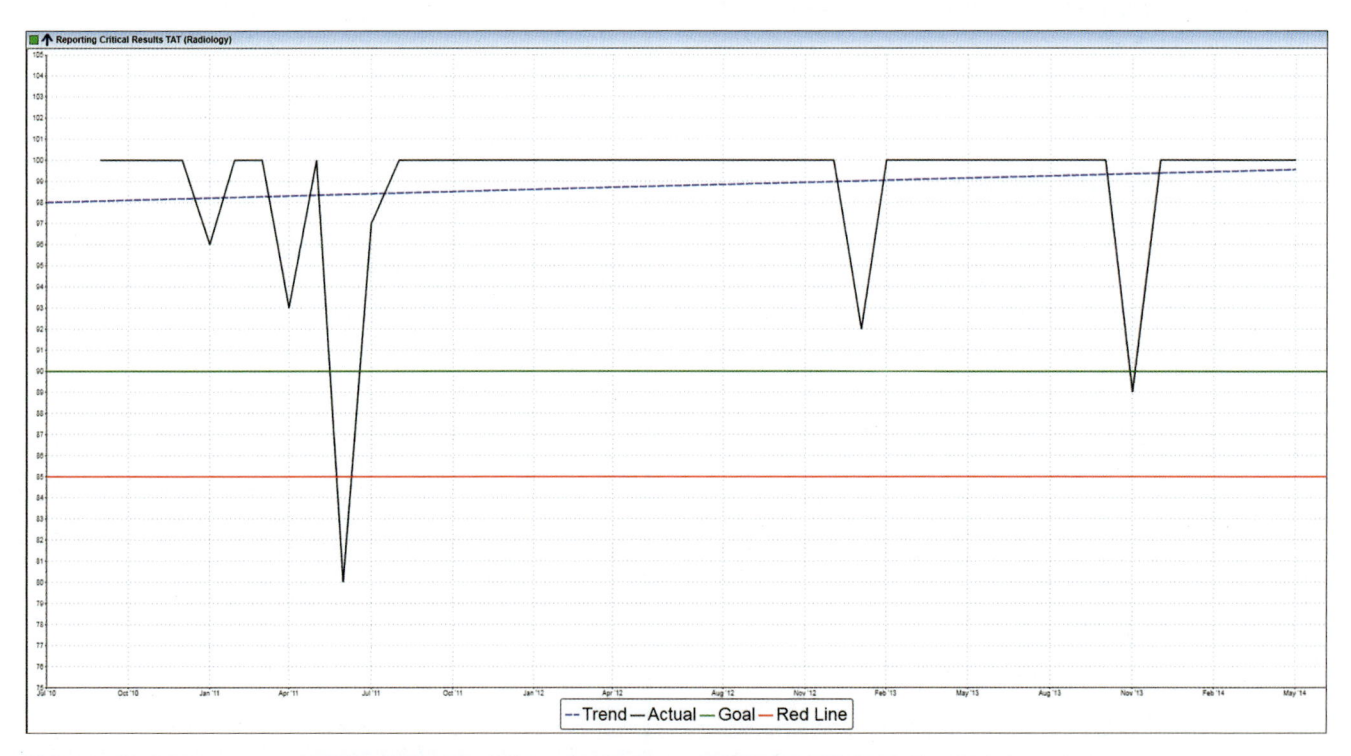

FIG. 13.2 • Example display of critical result reporting, a regulatory requirement put forth by The Joint Commission.

Quality Dashboards   99

To facilitate viewing of a dashboard, data should ideally be organized into sections. A radiology department's dashboard could be organized into three sections: user-level data, sectional- or divisional-level data, and departmental- or health-care system–level data.[18] Alternatively, the dashboard could be aligned with major institutional goals (Fig. 13.3). Using the example of report TAT, individual radiologists could use a dashboard to view their own mean report TAT and compare it with the practice as a whole. Section chiefs could view individual and composite TAT for their respective group and compare with other sections (Fig. 13.4). Department vice chairs or chairs could view report TAT performance for all sections and the department as a whole (Fig. 13.5).

		Actual	Goal	Red Line	Period
	To Improve the Performance of Selected Enterprise and Department Metrics for Radiology				
●	Communication with Doctors: HCAHPS	81.6%	82.0%	n/a	Oct 2013 - May 2014
●	Doctor Explained Illness/Treatment %SA	91.0%	91.5%	n/a	Oct 2013 - Apr 2014
●	Physician Participation in Peer Review (Radiology)	94.4%	95.0%	n/a	Oct 2013 - Jun 2014
■	Physician Report Turnaround Time (Radiology)	97.5%	95.0%	n/a	Oct 2013 - Jul 2014
	1 Patient Satisfaction				
	1.1 Improve Patient Satisfaction within Radiology Imaging Services				
■	Courtesy of X-ray Staff: Inpt %VG (Radiology)	75.0%	74.0%	65.6%	Jun '14
●	Patient Satisfaction: Radiology (ED)	84.9	87.6	86.9	Jun '14
	Communication with Doctors: HCAHPS	83.3%	n/a	n/a	May-Jul 2014
	2 Market Focus				
	2.2 Ensure Timely Access for Radiology Patients				
■	Appointment Availability - Average Days (Radiology)	95.8%	90.0%	80.0%	Jul '14
	2.1 Increase Volume in Selected Patient and Procedure Categories				
■	Procedure Volume (Radiology)	29,764	29,165	27,706	May '14
	3 Clinical Effectiveness, Quality, and Safety				
	3.1 Improve Quality of Patient Services				
●	Hand Hygiene - Radiology Tech	85.2%	90.0%	88.0%	Jun '14
■	Hand Hygiene - Radiology Unit	94.2%	90.0%	88.0%	Jun '14
■	Hand Hygiene - Radiology Medical Staff	100.0%	90.0%	88.0%	Jun '14
■	Hand Hygiene - Radiology Nursing	100.0%	90.0%	88.0%	Jun '14
■	Perf Maint On Time (Radiology)	100.0%	95.0%	90.0%	Oct '13
■	Reporting Critical Results TAT (Radiology)	100.0%	90.0%	85.0%	May '14
▼	Communication of Critical Tests	97.0%	100.0%	80.0%	Jun '14
	QA Participation	n/a	n/a		
	Resident Read Discrepancy Rate (Total)	n/a	n/a	n/a	n/a
	4 Operational Efficiency				
	4.1 Increase Operational Efficiency				
■	Radiology TAT	2.97	12.00	24.00	Jul '14
●	Clinic Missed Calls (Radiology)	10.1%	3.0%	8.0%	Jun '14
●	Wait Time in Queue (Radiology)	72	30	60	Jun '14
■	Patient No-Show (Radiology)	1.22%	3.00%	5.00%	Jun '14
■	Avoidable Days (Radiology)	0	0	1	Jun '14
▼	ED Radiology Interpretation Time	85	90	80	Jul '14
	5 Employee Growth and Management				
	5.1 Maximize Recruitment and Retention of Qualified Staff				
■	Vacancy Rate (Radiology)	3.8%	10.0%	11.0%	Jul '14
▼	Turnover Rate (Radiology)	7.6%	7.0%	8.0%	Jul '14
●	Employee Engagement Score (Radiology)	66.0	75.0	73.5	2014
	6 Financial Health				
	6.1 Deliver Care in a Fiscally Responsible Manner				
■	Gross Margin Ratio (Radiology)	89.3	88.8	84.4	May '14
■	Equipment Maintenance Budget (Radiology)	$332,614	$359,019	$376,970	May '14
▼	Expense per Unit of Service (Radiology)	$97.23	$96.37	$101.19	May '14

FIG. 13.3 • **Example quality dashboard for a hospital-based radiology practice.** Note that key performance indicators are grouped by enterprise-wide values.

Radiologist Median Turn-Around-Time (TAT) in Hours

Signer	Jan	Feb	Mar	Apr	May	Jun	Jul
Radiologist 1	1.74	2.23	1.8	1.72	2.12	2.42	1.90
Radiologist 2	2.16	2.07	1.53	3.79	1.47	1.64	3.48
Radiologist 3	1.07	2.50	2.03	2.87	2.70	1.37	4.17
Radiologist 4	0.57	1.69	2.17	2.00	1.25	1.13	2.80
Radiologist 5	1.7	2.12	2.2	4.73	0.78	2.48	2.38
Radiologist 6	3.24	2.17	2.9	1.80	0.60	2.72	1.62
Radiologist 7	1.43	0.92	0.87	0.85	0.97	1.02	2.43
Radiologist 8	4.65	4.96	4.17	3.85	2.27	2.97	4.25
Radiologist 9	3.93	1.28	1.68	0.82	0.75	1.05	1.77

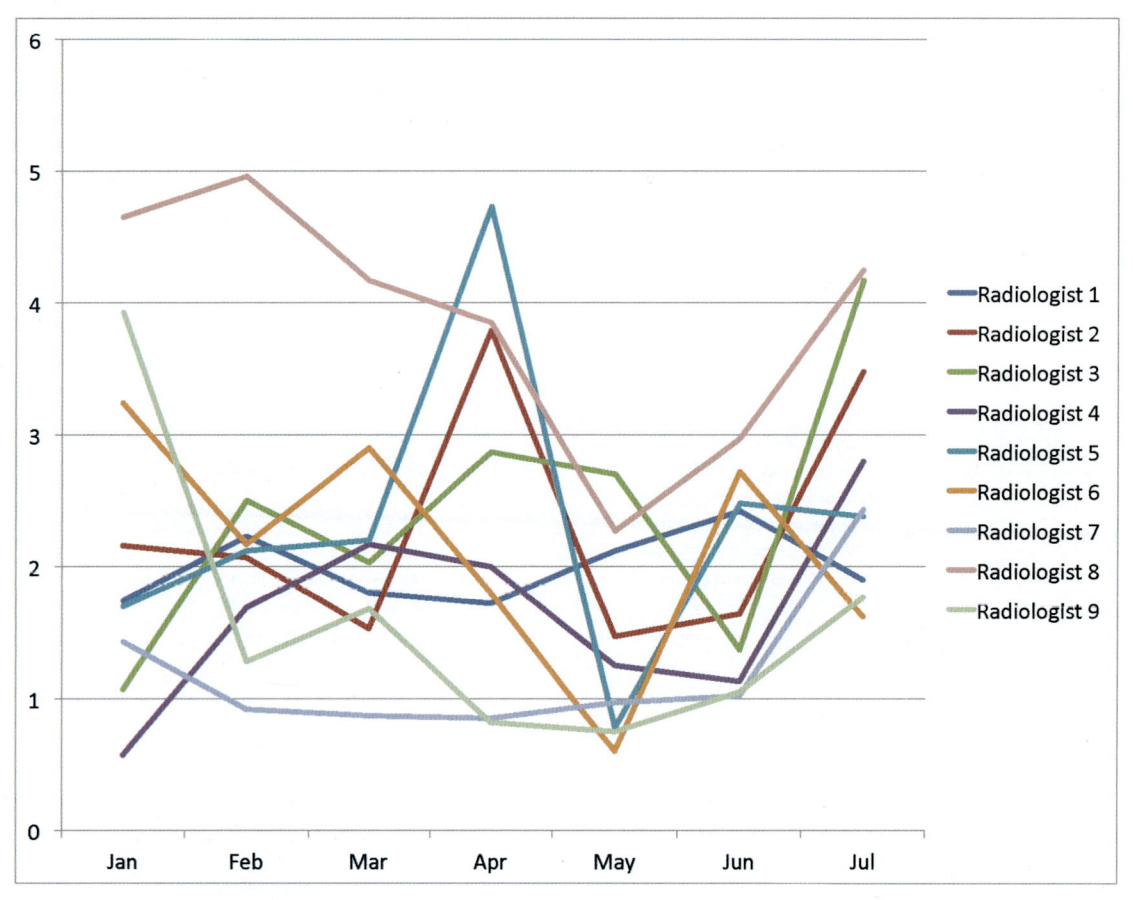

FIG. 13.4 • **Example turnaround time report comparing monthly values by radiologist.** These data could represent a small practice or a subspecialty section in a larger practice.

Visual presentation of aggregated data also affects the utility of a dashboard. For example, graphs depicting trends of each metric as compared with goals can be quite helpful (Figs. 13.6 and 13.7).[10] Depending on the KPI being reviewed, the ability to select which type of graph to display can also help the user better understand the data.[19] One common practice in dashboard design is color-coding data on the basis of current status vis-à-vis predetermined goals, quickly drawing the attention of viewers to problematic or potentially problematic areas. For example, stoplight charts are commonly used to highlight KPIs failing to meet predetermined goals (Fig. 13.8). In a stoplight chart, KPIs meeting or exceeding goals are colored green, KPIs close to falling behind goals are coded yellow, and KPIs falling behind goals are coded red.[14,18,20]

Besides enabling viewer to see "the big picture" at a glance, a useful dashboard provides the ability for the user to drill down to more granular data to understand why performance is what it is. Having access to more specific data can better help identify root causes for underperformance and aid in driving improvement. For example, patient access (Figs. 13.9 and 13.10) is an important quality metric and can impact patient satisfaction. Access to more granular data that roll-up into patient access metrics can help the operations team make good business decisions regarding improving patient access. Decisions such as whether to expand business hours, add imaging equipment, or revisit scheduling practices can be data driven, and results can be measured after implementation of solutions.

Quality Dashboards 101

Radiology Median Turn-Around Time (TAT) in Hours

Diagnostic Section	Jan	Feb	Mar	Apr	May	Jun	Jul
Abdominal	3.10	3.43	2.84	3.42	3.18	3.03	3.64
Cardiothoracic	2.71	2.26	2.17	2.16	2.15	2.05	2.86
Community	0.97	1.11	1.04	1.14	1.05	0.96	1.10
Musculoskeletal	2.28	2.22	2.85	3.78	1.43	1.97	3.01
Neuroradiology	7.70	6.19	7.80	6.48	4.91	6.37	4.42
Nuclear Medicine	2.42	2.30	2.23	2.26	2.17	2.38	2.60
Pediatric	2.33	1.41	1.78	1.57	1.80	1.69	3.26

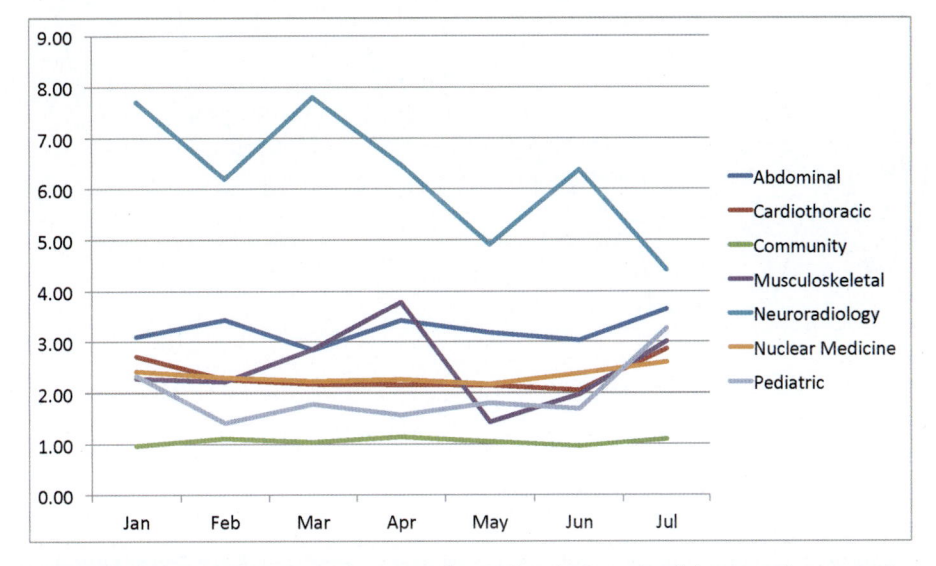

FIG. 13.5 • Example turnaround time report for a university-based radiology practice comparing subspecialty sections.

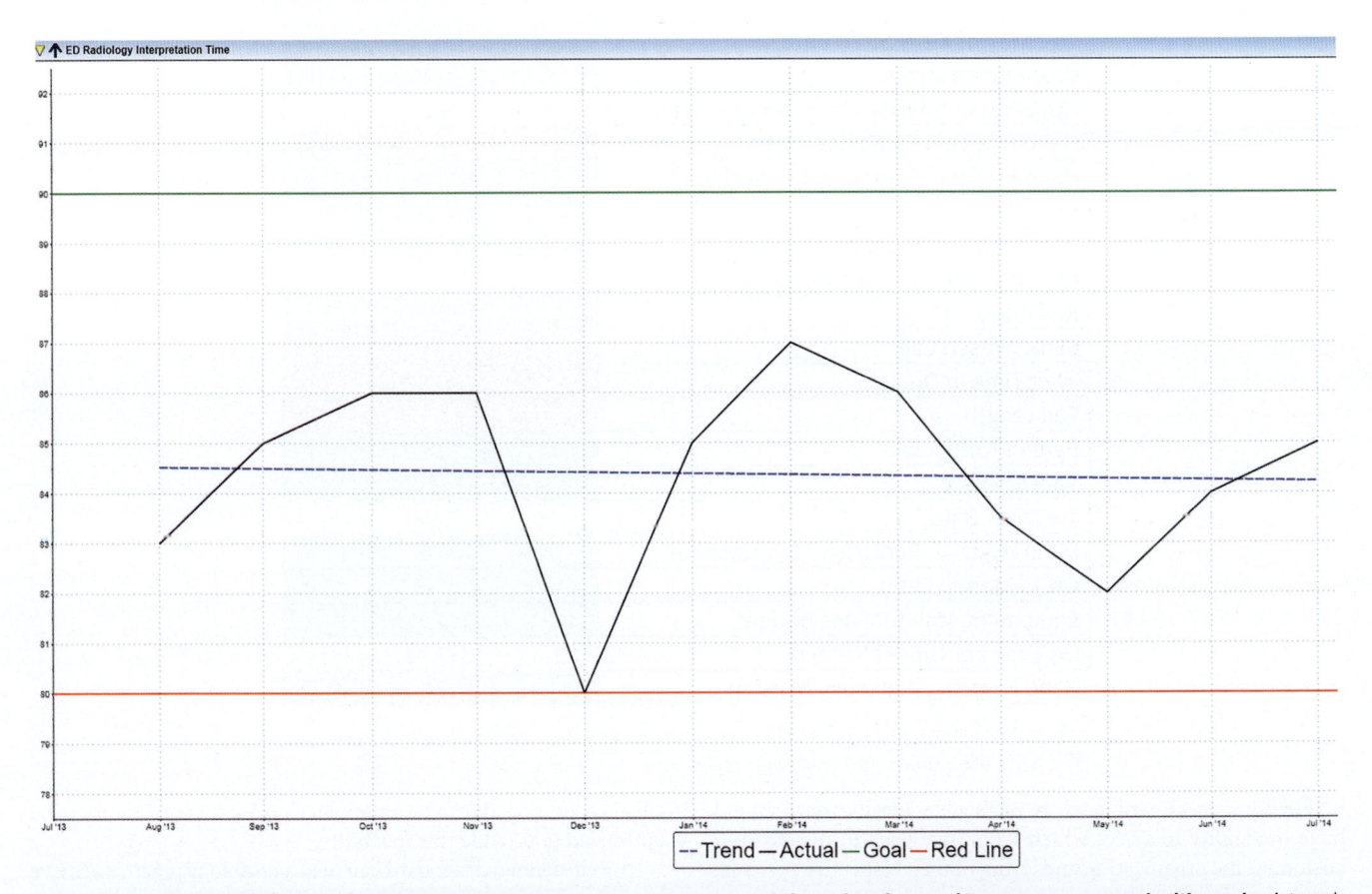

FIG. 13.6 • Example display of emergency department report turnaround time showing performance compared with goals. A trend line (*black line*) is superimposed on actual performance.

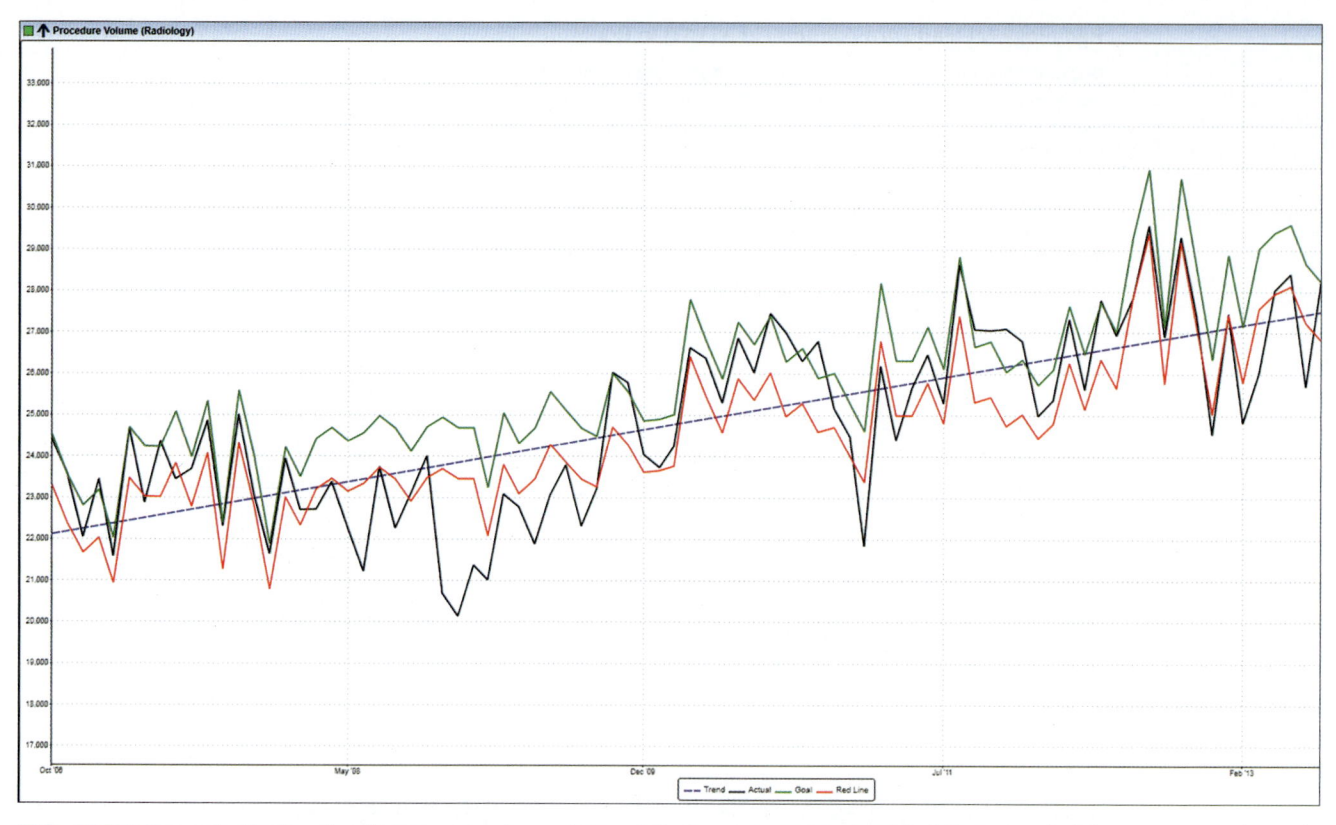

FIG. 13.7 • **Example display of radiology procedure volume plotted over an approximately 6.5-year period.** Long-term trends can be used to assess sufficiency of appointment slots, available equipment, staffing, etc.

Courtesy of X-ray Staff: Inpt %VG	75.0%
Procedure Volume	29,764
Appointment Availability – MRI Hospital	9.3
Hand Hygiene: Radiology Tech	85.2%
Hand Hygiene: Radiology Medical Staff	100.0%
Perf Maint On Time	100.0%
Reporting Critical Results TAT	100.0%
Communication of Critical Tests	97.0%
Radiology TAT	2.97
Clinic Missed Calls	10.1%
Wait Time in Queue	72
Call Length	3.14
Patient No-Show	1.22%
Vacancy Rate	3.8%
Turnover Rate	7.6%
Hand Hygiene: Radiology Unit Hospital	100.0%
Gross Margin Ratio	89.3
Equipment Maintenance Budget	$332,614
Expense per Unit of Service	$97.23
Hand Hygiene: Radiology Nursing	100.0%

FIG. 13.8 • Example stoplight chart easily highlights key performance indicators that are not meeting goals (*red, yellow*).

Finally, a dashboard needs to be flexible. Ideally, users should have the ability to select which KPIs they wish to display and customize the organization and layout of their respective personal dashboard.[7,17] Moreover, adding additional KPIs and making changes to current KPIs should be fairly simple.[3,14] By planning in advance, user needs can be anticipated and software design can be optimized to provide this flexibility.

A well-defined dashboard can help a radiology practice achieve its goals, improve efficiency and quality of care, and make smart, data-supported business decisions. By having the ability to rapidly

FIG. 13.9 • Example chart showing trends of the next available appointment for three commonly performed magnetic resonance cardiovascular examinations over approximately a 1-year-period.

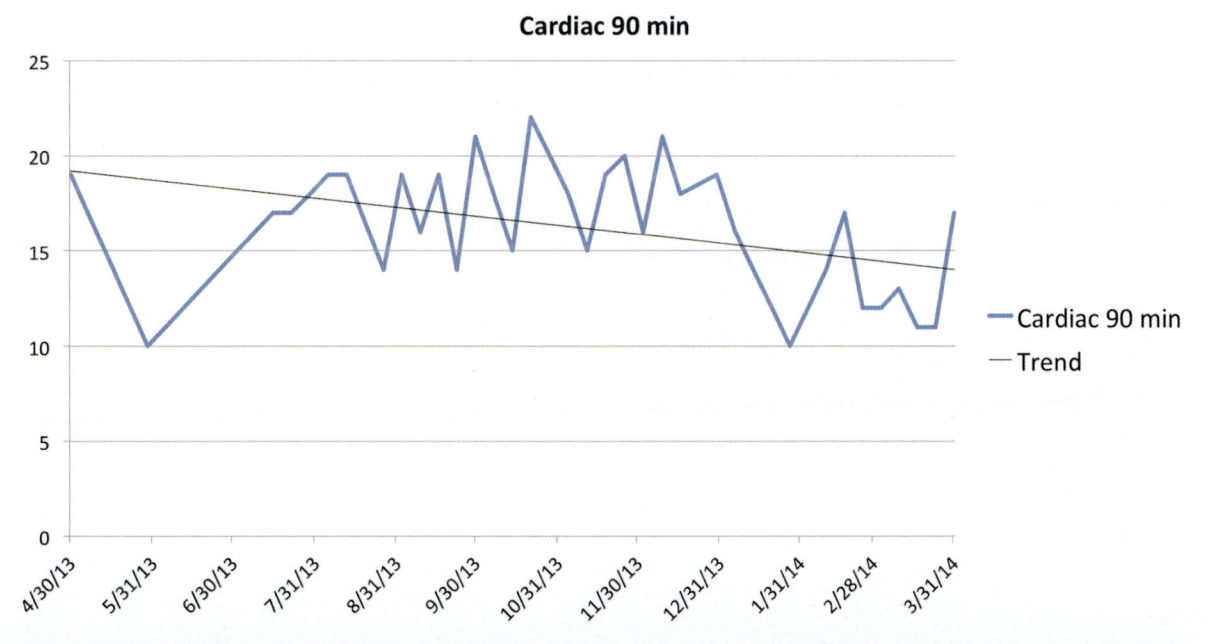

FIG. 13.10 • Example chart showing drill-down on 90-minute cardiac magnetic resonance imaging examinations shows a trend toward increased access. However, trends should be viewed cautiously when displayed over short periods of time. Furthermore, the fluctuation in times in this example suggests that access issues may be multifactorial and deeper investigation is warranted.

identify underperforming areas, practice leaders can efficiently deploy necessary resources to targeted areas to facilitate improvement.

References

1. Rud OP. *Business Intelligence Success Factors: Tools for Aligning your Business in the Global Economy*. Hoboken, NJ: Wiley & Sons, 2009:xix, 283 p.
2. Ayres I. *Super Crunchers: Why Thinking-by-Numbers Is the New Way to be Smart*. New York: Bantam Books, 2007:260 p.
3. Mick J. Data-driven decision making: a nursing research and evidence-based practice dashboard. *J Nurs Admin*. 2011;41:391–393.
4. Wadsworth T, Graves B, Glass S, et al. Using business intelligence to improve performance. *Healthc Financ Manag*. 2009;63:68–72.
5. Morgan MB, Branstetter BFt, Mates J, et al. Flying blind: using a digital dashboard to navigate a complex PACS environment. *J Digit Imaging*. 2006; 19:69–75.
6. Khorasani R. Can metrics obtained from your IT databases help start your practice dashboard? *J Am Coll Radiol*. 2008;5:772–774.
7. Serb C. Effective dashboards. What to measure and how to show it. *Hosp Health Netw*. 2011;85:8 p. following 40, 42
8. Hardee S. Magnet hospitals and benchmarking: the perioperative dashboard. *SSM*. 2003;9:13–17.
9. Mansoori B, Novak RD, Sivit CJ, et al. Utilization of dashboard technology in academic radiology departments: results of a national survey. *J Am Coll Radiol*. 2013;10:283–288.e283.
10. Khorasani R. Setting up a dashboard for your practice. *J Am Coll Radiol*. 2008;5:600.
11. Koopman RJ, Kochendorfer KM, Moore JL, et al. A diabetes dashboard and physician efficiency and accuracy in accessing data needed for high-quality diabetes care. *Ann Fam Med*. 2011;9:398–405.
12. Randell R, Dowding D. Organisational influences on nurses' use of clinical decision support systems. *Int J Med Inform*. 2010;79:412–421.

13. Blais R, Champagne F, Rousseau L. TOCSIN: a proposed dashboard of indicators to control healthcare-associated infections. *Healthc Q.* 2009; 12(Spec No Patient):161–167.
14. Clarke S. Your business dashboard: Knowing when to change the oil. *J Corp Acc Financ.* 2005;16:51–54.
15. Hoekzema G, Abercrombie S, Carr S, et al. Residency "dashboard": family medicine GME's step towards transparency and accountability? *Ann Fam Med.* 2010;8:470.
16. Frith KH, Anderson F, Sewell JP. Assessing and selecting data for a nursing services dashboard. *J Nurs Admin.* 2010;40:10–16.
17. Olsha-Yehiav M, Einbinder JS, Jung E, et al. Quality dashboards: technical and architectural considerations of an actionable reporting tool for population management. *AMIA Annu Symp Proc.* 2006;2006:1052.
18. Morgan MB, Branstetter BFt, Lionetti DM, et al. The radiology digital dashboard: effects on report turnaround time. *J Digit Imaging.* 2008;21:50–58.
19. Baskett L, LeRouge C, Tremblay MC. Using the dashboard technology properly. *Health Prog.* 2008;89:16–23.
20. Nagy PG, Warnock MJ, Daly M, et al. Informatics in radiology: automated Web-based graphical dashboard for radiology operational business intelligence. *Radiographics.* 2009;29:1897–1906.

SELF-ASSESSMENT QUESTIONS

1. Which of the following is **not** a primary goal of business intelligence?
   A. Obtain trade secrets
   B. Improve productivity
   C. Reduce inefficiencies
   D. Identify new opportunities

2. Which of the following are the key components of digital dashboards?
   A. Raw data output from information systems
   B. Key performance indicators
   C. Daily printed reports
   D. Root cause analyses

Answers to Chapter Self-Assessment Questions

1. A. The three primary goals of business intelligence are to improve productivity, reduce inefficiencies, and identify new opportunities. These goals are reached through mining raw data across various sources and presenting them in a useful, understandable manner. Business intelligence is not about obtaining trade secrets or other clandestine activities.

2. B. Digital dashboards comprise selected key performance indicators and present them in a way that is useful to the dashboard user. Dashboards typically do not display raw data but rather an aggregate and often an analysis of these data. Digital dashboards optimally show real-time data, making printed reports less useful. Root cause analyses (RCAs) are a method of investigating causes of an adverse event and are not the key components of digital dashboards.

Departmental and Institutional Quality Committees

14

Jeffrey P. Kanne

LEARNING OBJECTIVES

1. Describe the ideal makeup of a radiology quality committee
2. Define the responsibilities of the radiology quality committee
3. List types of patient safety events
4. Identify key components of an institutional quality committee

DEPARTMENT QUALITY OFFICER

The department quality officer is the designated leader responsible for overseeing quality improvement and patient safety in the radiology department. This individual must possess knowledge of quality improvement methods as well as have full support and a mandate of authority from senior departmental leadership. Furthermore, the quality officer must build relationships in and outside of the department that are based on trust to successfully lead quality improvement. To be successful, the quality officer must acknowledge the value of these trusting relationships, recognize the many boundaries that are intrinsic to a health-care organization, and be able to foster meaningful professional and strategic relationships.[1]

RADIOLOGY QUALITY COMMITTEE

Quality Committee Makeup

The makeup and responsibilities of a radiology quality committee will vary widely across practices. Large practices may include physician and technologist representatives from each imaging modality in addition to representatives from department administration, information technology, and nursing (Fig. 14.1). Quality committees of smaller practices may consist of a few designated radiologists, technologists, nurses, and administrators (Fig. 14.2). The committee should have a designated leader, typically the departmental quality officer. Hospital-based practices might have joint committee leadership shared by the physician quality leader and the hospital administrative department head. Radiology departments associated with residency or fellowship training programs often benefit from including trainee representation on the quality committee, as well.

Responsibilities of the Quality Committee

Defining the mission and responsibilities of the radiology quality committee up front is important for implementing successful and meaningful change. By establishing common team goals, participants can better understand the value of the work they are doing. First, the committee should champion compliance with safety measures in the department. Second, the committee should serve as the main driving force behind continuous quality improvement and provide support to employees engaged in quality improvement projects. Finally and most importantly, the quality committee needs to lead the way in building a culture of safety and quality improvement across the department. Lee and colleagues offer a useful blueprint of responsibilities for the radiology quality committee and provide a foundation on which a strong quality improvement program can be established (Table 14.1).[2]

Patient Safety

Safety Reporting

One of the major responsibilities of the radiology quality committee is to ensure patient safety. Because patient safety is the responsibility of all members of the health-care team, having representatives from multiple disciplines is essential for an effective safety team. Three mutually reinforcing requirements comprise a culture of safety: trust, reporting, and improvement.[3] Trust in one another will enable physicians and staff in a radiology practice to feel safe in reporting adverse events or, more often, "near misses." Furthermore, physicians and staff should trust that the quality management team will work to identify and correct reported problems.[4] When safety improvements are made in response to concerns about potential or actual patient harm, the value of reporting is reinforced, trust is strengthened, and the culture of safety within the organization can flourish.[2]

A process for adverse or "near-miss" event reporting needs to be in place for an organization to successfully address issues of patient safety.[5] This allows safety leaders to understand the scope of the problem and to adjust priorities. Various commercial products as well as services

FIG. 14.1 • Sample organizational chart outlining the makeup of a radiology quality committee in a small practice.

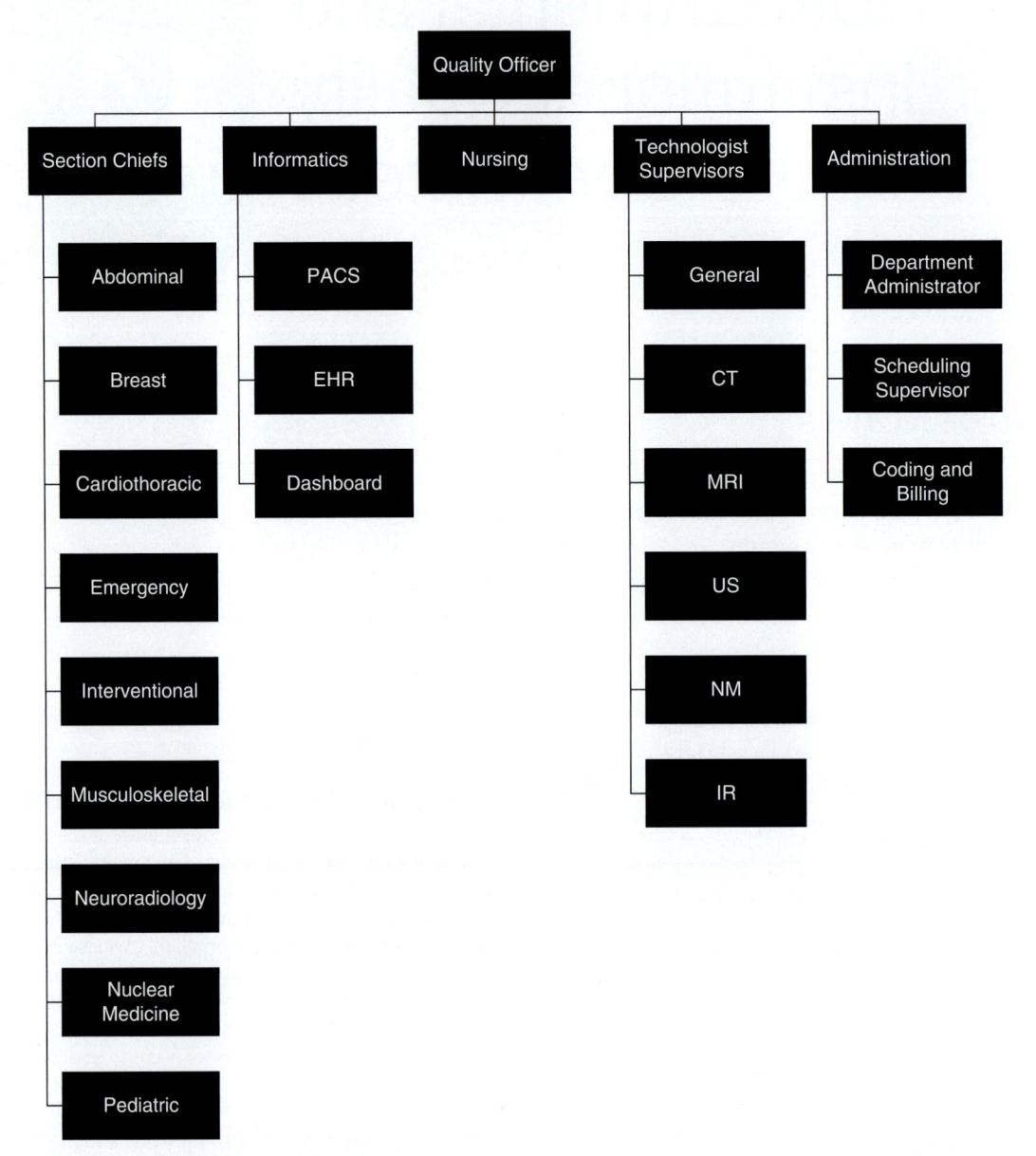

FIG. 14.2 • **Sample organizational chart outlining the makeup of a radiology quality committee in a large practice.** Computed tomography (CT), electronic health record (EHR), interventional radiology (IR), magnetic resonance imaging (MRI), nuclear medicine (NM), picture archiving and communication system (PACS), and ultrasound (US).

Table 14.1 ROLES AND RESPONSIBILITIES OF THE RADIOLOGY QUALITY COMMITTEE.

Patient Safety	Continuous Quality Improvement	Creating a Culture of Quality
Safety reporting	Utilization	Assessing climate of safety
MRI safety	Image quality control	Peer review
Radiation safety	Critical findings	Continuing education
Pharmacy		Patient advocacy and customer service
Regulatory compliance		

Adapted from Lee CS, Paine L, Nagy P. Functions of the quality committee in radiology. *J Am Coll Radiol* 2012;9:586–588.

provided through institutional consortiums are available, the latter of which can also provide benchmark data. Smaller organizations may still use paper-based systems. Regardless of how reports are submitted, providing feedback to reporters and demonstrating improvement initiatives are essential for reinforcing the culture of safety.

Sentinel events, defined by The Joint Commission (TJC) as "an unexpected occurrence involving death or serious physical or psychological injury or risk," require a formal review process.[6] The radiology quality committee should oversee and standardize this process. The components of sentinel event review include the following: confirmation of the sentinel event, timely communication with clinical staff members to ensure information is consistent and accurate, discussion of contributing factors and development of action plan, review of action with all staff members, presentation to the patient safety committee, and identifying challenges and how to overcome them.[2] As of June 2013, 25 states and the District of Columbia require reporting of sentinel events (Table 14.2). TJC's sentinel event reporting policy stipulates a voluntary reporting process be in place. This nonpunitive process is designed to improve action plans through knowledge sharing across organizations.[7]

Specific areas of patient safety may require additional expertise beyond that of the safety committee. Enlisting support from disciplines such as pharmacy and medical physics for addressing specific areas of patient safety can help a department improve its safety.

Magnetic Resonance Imaging

The radiology quality committee should ensure that magnetic resonance imaging (MRI) screening and safety guidelines remain current, working closely with MRI technologists, nursing, and administration. Responsibility for MRI safety can be delegated to a medical director or other physician designee or remain within the quality committee. The majority of reported cases of injury occurring during MRI are related to either failure to follow current safety guidelines or inaccurate information related to biomedical devices or implants.[8] Resources on MRI safety are available from the International Society for Magnetic Resonance in Medicine, the American College of Radiology, the Society of Nuclear Medicine, the Federal Drug Administration, the National Electrical Manufacturers Association, the International Electrotechnical Commission, and the Medical Devices Agency (Table 14.3).[2] A protocol should also be in place for screening patients for nephrogenic systemic fibrosis.[9,10]

Radiation Safety

Each facility that uses ionizing radiation must have a designated radiation safety officer (RSO), who oversees the radiation protection plan for the facility.[11] The RSO may be a physician or physicist in the radiology department, a physician or medical physicist employed by the hospital, or other designated individual. Within the radiology department, the quality committee can implement published guidelines on radiation dose reduction as well as implement improvement projects to optimize imaging protocols.

Pharmacy

Iodinated contrast material is the most common pharmaceutical agent administered in a radiology department. Although agents currently in use are much safer than their predecessors, they are not risk free and complications can still occur. Most contrast reactions are mild, but severe reactions can occur. The radiology quality committee should oversee contrast reaction management protocols and ensure that adequate training and up-to-date education materials are available to physicians and staff.[12,13]

Many radiology departments may provide conscious sedation for image-guided procedures, often administered under the direct supervision of radiologists. The quality committee should ensure proper safety protocols and documentation requirements are in place, radiologists are appropriately trained and credentialed, and necessary support staff are included in the process.[13,14]

Regulatory Compliance

The radiology quality committee should ensure that the practice follows guidelines and meets standards required by external bodies such as TJC and the Centers for Medicare and Medicaid Studies (CMS). The committee should work with practice administrators and staff to ensure that members of the organization are familiar with regulatory requirements, including self-reporting of key performance indicators, and maintain an environment that is always prepared for unannounced site inspections.

Continuous Quality Improvement

Increasingly, as a result of requirements put forth by the American Board of Radiology's Maintenance of Certification program and the Accreditation Council for Graduate Medical Education, radiologists

Table 14.2 STATES THAT HAVE MANDATORY REPORTING OF SENTINEL EVENTS (AS OF JUNE 2013).

California	Nevada
Colorado	New Hampshire
Connecticut	New Jersey
District of Columbia	New York
Florida	Pennsylvania
Georgia	Rhode Island
Illinois	South Carolina
Indiana	South Dakota
Kansas	Tennessee
Maine	Utah
Maryland	Vermont
Massachusetts	Washington
Minnesota	Wyoming

Table 14.3 SAMPLE CRITICAL RESULTS.

Thoracic	Pneumothorax (unexpected)
	Tension pneumothorax
	Acute pulmonary embolism
Cardiovascular	Aortic rupture or dissection or leaking aneurysm
	Acute deep venous thrombosis
Abdominal	Acute ischemic bowel
	Pneumoperitoneum (not postoperative)
	Ectopic pregnancy
	Massive hemoperitoneum
Neuroradiology	Unstable spine fracture
	Acute extra-axial collection
General	Significant misplacement of support device
	Unexpected retained foreign body

and trainees will be increasingly involved in practice quality improvement projects. The radiology quality committee can serve as a coordinating body for these projects and provide guidance and resources to physicians and staff engaged in improvement projects.[2]

Utilization

The American College of Radiology developed the Appropriateness Criteria project to improve quality in diagnostic imaging and reduce unnecessary use of imaging.[15] The quality committee can work with referring physicians to implement these guidelines as appropriate. Additionally, the quality committee can partner with a hospital or medical center to implement decision-support software.[16]

Image Quality Control

Part of the practice of radiology includes assessment of image quality. In order for a practice to maintain high-quality diagnostic imaging examinations, a mechanism needs to be in place for the radiologist to provide feedback to technologists. Ideally, this process should be integrated into the picture archiving and communication (PACS) workflow, allowing feedback to be recorded at the point of care.[17] The quality committee can serve as the liaison between radiologists and supervisors to address recurring issues with image quality.[2]

Critical Findings

TJC, as part of its National Patient Safety Goals, mandates that institutions "report critical results of tests and diagnostic procedures on a timely basis" and that a method to track these results and communications is put in place. However, TJC does not define a critical result nor does it define what constitutes a "timely basis," leaving these designations to individual institutions.[18] The radiology quality committee should be responsible for developing these definitions and working with hospital quality management and safety to formalize a critical results policy and audit procedure (Table 14.3).

Creating a Culture of Quality
Climate of Safety Assessment

To foster a culture of quality improvement, the radiology quality committee first needs to assess the current climate of safety in an organization. The Safety Attitudes Questionnaire (Fig. 14.3), a validated instrument, help leadership detect real or perceived unsafe working conditions as well as areas of low employee morale.[19] Follow-up questionnaires can be distributed to assess impact of change as well as to maintain ongoing engagement with employees. The quality committee can use the results to work with appropriate managers and supervisors and to establish annual quality improvement goals.

Peer Review

TJC mandated in 2007 that physician recredentialing include a component of ongoing professional practice evaluation (OPPE). In radiology, this is usually carried out through peer review (see Chapter 11). The quality committee should be responsible for developing and managing a departmental peer-review process and work with departmental leadership to ensure that physicians meet OPPE requirements to maintain credentials. Furthermore, the quality committee should work with other departments to establish multidisciplinary educational conferences and cross-departmental quality improvement project teams.

Continuing Education

As part of maintaining a quality of culture, the radiology quality committee should organize educational conferences focused on quality improvement.[20] These can include journal club, education in quality improvement, discussion of difficult or "missed" cases, and a venue for project teams to showcase their improvement projects.

Patient Advocacy and Customer Service

In radiology, the "customer" includes both the patient and the referring health-care provider. Five key factors related to customer satisfaction have been described and apply to any particular service, including medical imaging: reliability, responsiveness, assurance, empathy, and tangibles.[21] First, examinations and their respective interpretations should be reliable. Second, the department should be responsive to patients' needs with ready access to imaging studies or procedures and timely communication of results to referring providers. Third, patients should feel assured by the confidence, competence, and courtesy of radiologists and their staff. Fourth, patients should feel that physicians and staff are empathetic. Finally, patients expect a maintained and pleasing appearance of the imaging facility and the use of high-quality equipment. Lee and colleagues recommend that the radiology quality committee provide regular customer service training to all employees, hold periodic open meetings and solicit anonymous written suggestions, and thoroughly define job responsibilities and stress accountability (Table 14.4).[2]

INSTITUTIONAL QUALITY COMMITTEE

Hospitals and medical centers are multifaceted entities with administrative and operational components that are far more elaborate than those within a single department. Thus, the quality and safety structure of an entire institution is far more complex. Hospitals typically have an executive leadership team consisting of the chief executive officer, chief financial officer, chief operations officer, and chief medical officer. Executive-level nursing, information technology, legal, and other personnel may also be part of the executive team.

Because of the complexities of managing a hospital, oversight of operations, quality, and safety may fall under a variety of committees and groups such as ambulatory care, inpatient care, surgical services, pharmacy and therapeutics, nursing, and so forth. The institutional quality committee is positioned to oversee the activities of these committees.

An ideal institutional quality committee will consist of executive leadership; quality and safety administrative staff; department chairs and division chiefs (or their respective designees); nursing leadership; pharmacy support, legal, and risk management representatives; and information technology leadership. For hospitals with graduate medical education programs, trainee representation is also encouraged. Some institutions opt to include members of the public who volunteer as patient and family representatives. The authority of the quality committee should be defined up front, and a charter should be established defining the group's mission.

Just as the departmental quality committee defines quality and safety goals for the department, the institutional quality committee defines similar goals for the entire institution. Besides internal goals, the institutional committee is charged with addressing publically reported key performance indicators as mandated by government and accrediting bodies. How an organization defines and addresses these goals can have a significant impact on defining the culture of an organization.

In contrast to a departmental quality committee, members of the institutional quality committee are often not the closest to operational processes. This can lead to disconnect between the "boots on the ground" and those driving quality improvement. To bridge the gap, creating multidisciplinary teams or clinical service groups structured around a particular service line or clinic has been suggested. These teams should be focused on operations, quality

QualityHealthCare.org

INSTITUTE FOR HEALTHCARE IMPROVEMENT

Date: _____

Safety Climate Survey

Survey Number: _____

Please answer the following items with respect to your specific unit or clinical area. Choose your responses using the scale below:

	A Disagree Strongly	B Disagree Slightly	C Neutral	D Agree Slightly	E Agree Strongly	X Not Applicable
1. The culture of this clinical area makes it easy to learn from the mistakes of others.						
2. Medical errors are handled appropriately in this clinical area.						
3. The senior leaders in my hospital listen to me and care about my concerns.						
4. The physician and nurse leaders in my areas listen to me and care about my concerns.						
5. Leadership is driving us to be a safety-centered institution.						
6. My suggestions about safety would be acted upon if I expressed them to management.						
7. Management/leadership does not knowingly compromise safety concerns for productivity.						
8. I am encouraged by my colleagues to report any safety concerns I may have.						
9. I know the proper channels to direct questions regarding patient safety.						
10. I receive appropriate feedback about my performance.						
11. I would feel safe being treated here as a patient.						
12. Briefing personnel before the start of a shift (i.e., to plan for possible contingencies) is an important part of safety.						
13. Briefings are common here.						
14. I am satisfied with the availability of clinical leadership (please respond to all three): Physician						
Nursing						
Pharmacy						
15. This institution is doing more for patient safety now, than it did one year ago.						
16. I believe that most adverse events occur as a result of multiple system failures, and are not attributable to one individual's actions.						
17. The personnel in this clinical area take responsibility for patient safety.						
18. Personnel frequently disregard rules or guidelines that are established for this clinical area.						
19. Patient safety is constantly reinforced as the priority in this clinical area.						

Have you ever completed this survey before?
- ❑ Yes   ❑ No   ❑ Don't Know

Job Position: (mark only one)
- ❑ Attending/Staff Physician
- ❑ Physician in Training
- ❑ Pharmacist
- ❑ Technician (e.g., EKG, Lab, Radiology)
- ❑ Staff Nurse
- ❑ Nurse Manager/Charge Nurse
- ❑ Respiratory Therapist
- ❑ Physical, Occupational, or Speech Therapist
- ❑ Dietician
- ❑ Support Associate
- ❑ Administrator
- ❑ Other

Experience in Position:
- ❑ < 6 months   ❑ 6 to 11 months   ❑ 1 to 2 yrs   ❑ 3 to 7 yrs
- ❑ 8 to 12 yrs   ❑ 13 to 20 yrs   ❑ 21 yrs or over

Experience in Specialty:
- ❑ < 6 months   ❑ 6 to 11 months   ❑ 1 to 2 yrs   ❑ 3 to 7 yrs
- ❑ 8 to 12 yrs   ❑ 13 to 20 yrs   ❑ 21 yrs or over

Experience in Organization:
- ❑ < 6 months   ❑ 6 to 11 months   ❑ 1 to 2 yrs   ❑ 3 to 7 yrs
- ❑ 8 to 12 yrs   ❑ 13 to 20 yrs   ❑ 21 yrs or over

Age:
- ❑ < 30   ❑ 30 to 34   ❑ 35 to 39   ❑ 40 to 44   ❑ 45 or over

Unit (please write in title and/or location): _____

Thank you for completing the survey. Your time and participation are greatly appreciated.

FIG. 14.3 • Safety Climate Survey. (From Sexton JB, Helmreich RL, Neilands TB, et al. The Safety Attitudes Questionnaire: psychometric properties, benchmarking data, and emerging research. *BMC Health Serv Res.* 2006;6:44.)

Table 14.4 **KEY ASPECTS OF CUSTOMER SATISFACTION.**

Key Factor	Example in Radiology
Reliability	High-quality imaging and accurate interpretation of results
Responsiveness	Availability of imaging examination appointments
	Timely conveyance of results to ordering providers
Assurance	Competent, confident, and courteous staff
Empathy	Concern for patient as human beings, expressed by physicians and staff
Tangibles	Physical appearance of department
	Modern imaging equipment

improvement, utilization management, and financial health.[22] Each clinical service group develops and maintains its own dashboard of key performance indicators. Importantly, data on dashboards must be current and accurate to demonstrate the effects of improvement.

References

1. Hawkins M, Nagy P. The effective quality officer: the role of trust, boundaries, and relationships. *J Am Coll Radiol.* 2013; 10:802–804.
2. Lee CS, Paine L, Nagy P. Functions of the quality committee in radiology. *J Am Coll Radiol.* 2012;9:586–588.
3. Reason JT, Hobbs A. *Managing Maintenance Error: A Practical Guide.* Burlington, VT: Ashgate, 2003:xiv, 183 p.
4. Chassin MR, Loeb JM. The ongoing quality improvement journey: next stop, high reliability. *Health Aff.* 2011;30:559–568.
5. Small SD, Barach P. Patient safety and health policy: a history and review. *Hematol Oncol Clin N Am.* 2002;16:1463–1482.
6. Daly M. The McGill University Health Centre Policy on sentinel events: using a standardized framework to manage sentinel events, facilitate learning and improve patient safety. *Healthc Q.* 2006; 9 Spec No:28–34.
7. Joint Commission Resources. Clarifying misconceptions about sentinel event reporting. *Jt Comm Perspect.* 2013;33:9–10.
8. Shellock FG, Spinazzi A. MRI safety update 2008: part 2, screening patients for MRI. *Am J Roentgenol.* 2008;191:1140–1149.
9. Kaewlai R, Abujudeh H. Nephrogenic systemic fibrosis. *Am J Roentgenol.* 2012;199:W17–W23.
10. Thomsen HS, Morcos SK, Almen T, et al. Nephrogenic systemic fibrosis and gadolinium-based contrast media: updated ESUR Contrast Medium Safety Committee guidelines. *Eur Radiol.* 2013;23:307–318.
11. American Association of Physicists in Medicine. *Radiation Safety Officer Qualificatons for Medical Facilities.* College Park, MD: American Association of Physicists in Medicine; 2010.
12. Iyer RS, Schopp JG, Swanson JO, et al. Safety essentials: acute reactions to iodinated contrast media. *Can Assoc Radiol J.* 2013;64:193–199.
13. Thomsen HS. Contrast media safety-an update. *Eur J Radiol.* 2011;80:77–82.
14. Olsen JW, Barger RL Jr, Doshi SK. Moderate sedation: what radiologists need to know. *Am J Roentgenol.* 2013;201:941–946.
15. Cascade PN. The American College of Radiology. ACR Appropriateness Criteria project. *Radiology.* 2000; 214(suppl):3–46.
16. Blackmore CC, Mecklenburg RS, Kaplan GS. Effectiveness of clinical decision support in controlling inappropriate imaging. *J Am Coll Radiol.* 2011;8:19–25.
17. Nagy PG, Pierce B, Otto M, et al. Quality control management and communication between radiologists and technologists. *J Am Coll Radiol.* 2008;5:759–765.
18. The Joint Commission. National Patient Safety Goals. https://www.jointcommission.org/standards_information/npsgs.aspx. Accessed July 25, 2016
19. Ikusika OM, Joseph L, Nagy P. The safety attitudes questionnaire in radiology: a cornerstone of a successful quality program. *J Am Coll Radiol.* 2012;9:150–151.
20. Meyer JS, Nagy P. Building a community of practice for quality. *J Am Coll Radiol.* 2010;7:808–809.
21. Alderson PO. Customer service and satisfaction in radiology. *Am J Roentgenol.* 2000;175:319–323.
22. Stony Brook University Hospital. Translating institutional goal-setting and benchmarking to the bedside: dashboards, clinical service groups and goal sheets. In: *The Quality Colloquium on the Campus of Harvard University.* Boston, MA: Stony Brook University Hospital; 2006.
23. Sexton JB, Helmreich RL, Neilands TB, et al. The Safety Attitudes Questionnaire: psychometric properties, benchmarking data, and emerging research. *BMC Health Serv Res.* 2006;6:44.

SELF-ASSESSMENT QUESTIONS

1. Which of the following best reflects continuous quality improvement activity for a radiology quality committee?

    A. Patient advocacy and customer service
    B. Radiation safety
    C. Regulatory compliance
    D. Utilization

2. Which body mandates timely reporting of critical test results?

    A. The Joint Commission (TJC)
    B. Centers for Medicare and Medicaid Services (CMS)
    C. US Preventive Services Task Force (USPSTF)
    D. Agency for Healthcare Research and Quality (AHRQ)

Answers to Chapter Self-Assessment Questions

1. D. Roles and responsibilities of the radiology quality committee have been grouped into three categories: patient safety, continuous quality improvement, and creating a culture of quality. Utilization (of imaging resources) is included in continuous quality improvement. Patient advocacy and customer service belongs to creating a culture of quality, and radiation safety and regulatory compliance are part of patient safety.

2. A. The Joint Commission (TJC), as part of its National Patient Safety Goals, mandates that accredited institutions "report critical results of tests and diagnostic procedures on a timely basis" and that a method to track these results and communications is put in place. The Centers for Medicare and Medicaid Services (CMS) does not specifically mandate critical result reporting. The US Preventative Services Task Force (USPSTF) issues recommendations for preventive health services on the basis of published data, and the Agency for Healthcare Research and Quality (AHRQ) works with professional organizations to develop guidelines for diagnosis and management in health care.

Self-Assessment Exam

1. Which of the following requires accreditation under the Medicare Improvements for Patients and Providers Act (MIPPA)?
   A. Outpatient radiography
   B. Inpatient computed tomography (CT)
   C. Outpatient positron emission tomography (PET)
   D. Inpatient ultrasound

2. Which of the following is **true** regarding the American College of Radiology's (ACR) practice guidelines and technical standards?
   A. Review and renewal occur annually
   B. Adherence is required by the Centers for Medicare and Medicaid Services (CMS)
   C. Include radiation oncology
   D. Adherence is required by The Joint Commission (TJC)

3. What is the primary purpose of the American College of Radiology (ACR) Appropriateness Criteria?
   A. Assist health-care providers in selecting the appropriate imaging test
   B. Serve as peer-review tool for diagnostic and interventional radiologists
   C. Provide guidance for the Centers for Medicare and Medicaid Services (CMS) and private insurance coverage of imaging tests and procedures
   D. Meet requirements put forth by The Joint Commission (TJC)

4. What is the primary purpose RadiologyInfo.org?
   A. Continuing medical education for radiologists
   B. Patient-centered information on radiologic test and procedures
   C. Guidance for health-care providers for selecting imaging examinations
   D. Detail insurance coverage of imaging examinations

5. Which of the following has been a driving force for hospitals to improve patient satisfaction?
   A. Requirements put forth by The Joint Commission (TJC)
   B. Mandatory publication of satisfaction scores in local newspapers
   C. Mandates of the American Hospital Association
   D. The Centers for Medicare and Medicaid Services (CMS) Value-Based Purchasing Program

6. Which of the following has been shown to be **true** regarding implementation of voice recognition software for radiology reporting?
   A. Decrease in transcription errors
   B. Decrease in dictation time
   C. Ability to use standardized reports
   D. Increased radiologist efficiency

7. Which is the best method to compare radiologist report turnaround times (TATs)?
   A. Group by workflow
   B. Compare means
   C. Use single benchmark
   D. Include complex procedures

8. Which of the following has **not** been shown to reduce radiologist turnaround time (TAT)?
   A. Pay-for-performance incentives
   B. E-mail reminders
   C. Dissatisfaction of referring providers
   D. Use of reporting templates

9. Which of the following is the biggest impediment to quality management programs in ultrasound?
   A. Increased use of ultrasound equipment outside of radiology
   B. Growing complexity of ultrasound cases
   C. Decline in reimbursements
   D. Introduction of 3-D and 4-D ultrasound units

10. Which of the following is **not** part of a magnetic resonance imaging (MRI) image quality management program?
    A. Phantom testing
    B. Patient prescreening
    C. Addressing artifacts
    D. Coil testing

11. Who is the primary stakeholder in the pre-exam archival phase of Reiner's medical imaging chain?
    A. Radiologist
    B. Scheduler
    C. Radiology technologist
    D. Department administrator

12. Who is the primary stakeholder in the postarchival phase of Reiner's medical imaging chain?
    A. Radiologist
    B. Scheduler
    C. Radiology technologist
    D. Department administrator

13. Which of the following methods will most likely yield the greatest improvement in image quality?
    A. Paper-based quality assurance (QA) form
    B. Standalone web-based QA form
    C. Electronic QA form integrated into picture archiving and communication system (PACS)
    D. Telephone reporting of QA issues to manager

14. In what percentage of hospitalizations are adverse events estimated to occur?
    A. 0.5%
    B. 1.0%
    C. 3.0%
    D. 5.0%

15. Which of the following would be classified as a near miss in radiology?
    A. Intubation from oversedation during a procedure
    B. Documenting the incorrect birthdate
    C. Radiation-induced alopecia
    D. Aspiration of oral contrast requiring intubation

16. Which of the following is the most common cause of error in diagnostic radiology?
    A. Incorrect decision making
    B. Satisfaction of search
    C. Poor lighting
    D. Eye fatigue

17. Which of the following is **true** regarding mandatory error-reporting systems?
    A. The Joint Commission (TJC) requires their use
    B. They are usually overseen by state regulatory agencies
    C. They apply only to outpatient facilities
    D. They are mandated by the American Hospital Association

18. What is the primary focus of voluntary reporting systems?
    A. Meeting requirements put forth by state medical boards
    B. Identifying and penalizing individuals who cause errors
    C. Identifying near misses
    D. Capture all sentinel events

19. Which of the following should be included in an event report?
    A. Determination of negligence
    B. Perceived level of harm
    C. Action plan
    D. Disciplinary action

20. What is the primary goal of a root cause analysis (RCA)?
    A. Avoid litigation or other legal action
    B. Identify and discipline person or persons at fault
    C. Analyze data for publication in peer-reviewed journals
    D. Identify causes of sentinel event and avoid future events

21. Which of the following is **true** regarding disclosure of medical errors to patients?
    A. Disclosure is required by The Joint Commission (TJC)
    B. Patient satisfaction usually decreases
    C. Patient trust usually decreases
    D. Patients are more likely to file malpractice claims

22. Which of the following agencies oversees the Children's Healthcare Insurance Program (CHIP)?
    A. Centers for Disease Control and Prevention (CDC)
    B. Food and Drug Administration (FDA)
    C. State medical boards
    D. Centers for Medicare and Medicaid Services (CMS)

23. Which of the following agencies runs the B reader program for pneumoconiosis?
    A. National Institute for Occupational Safety and Health (NIOSH)
    B. Navy and Marine Corps Public Health Center
    C. Food and Drug Administration (FDA)
    D. Centers for Medicare and Medicaid Services (CMS)

24. Which of the following best reflects the American College of Radiology's (ACR) Imaging 3.0 program?
    A. Promoting practice patterns that increase the radiologist's value in the delivery of health care
    B. Mandatory implementation of digital imaging and reporting
    C. Reducing the number of examinations performed with ionizing radiation
    D. Lobbying for increased reimbursement for radiology examinations

25. Which of the following programs focuses on shared decision making between physician and patient regarding diagnostic testing?
    A. Image Gently
    B. Image Wisely
    C. Choosing Wisely
    D. Accountable Care Organization (ACO)

26. For what part of evidence-based health care was the PICO (**P**atient, **I**ntervention, **C**omparison, **O**utcome) framework designed?
    A. Defining the question
    B. Finding the evidence
    C. Critical appraisal
    D. Developing solutions

27. Which of the following would be an example of a foreground knowledge gap?
    A. A subspecialist breast imager being asked to interpret a liver magnetic resonance imaging (MRI)
    B. A medical student being asked to protocol a knee MRI
    C. A chest radiologist being asked to evaluate image quality on a new computed tomography (CT) scanner
    D. Asking an ultrasonographer to operate a fluoroscopy unit

28. Which of the following defines number needed to treat (NNT)?
    A. Number of subjects enrolled in a double-blind, randomized controlled study
    B. Average number of patients who need to undergo a specific treatment for one patient to benefit
    C. The number of treatments necessary for a patient to benefit from a specific therapy
    D. The number of times a practitioner must perform a procedure in order to be deemed competent

29. Which of the following is **true** regarding the U.S. Preventive Services Task Force (USPSTF)?
    A. Members are employees of the Centers for Disease Control and Prevention (CDC).
    B. Members consist of one representative from each member board of the American Board of Medical Specialties.
    C. Members are volunteers with expertise in evidence-based health care.
    D. Recommendations are targeted primarily to medical specialists.

30. American College of Radiology (ACR) Appropriateness Criteria are developed following guidelines of which agency?
    A. Agency for Healthcare Research and Quality (AHRQ)
    B. U.S. Preventive Services Task Force (USPSTF)
    C. Centers for Medicare and Medicaid Services (CMS)
    D. Centers for Disease Control and Prevention (CDC)

31. Which of the following **is not** a core competency of the Accreditation Council for Graduate Medical Education (ACGME)?
    A. Patient care
    B. Medical and clinical knowledge
    C. Professionalism
    D. Licensure

32. Which of the following peer-review methods uses prospective methodology?
    A. American College of Radiology (ACR) RADPEER
    B. Consensus-oriented peer review
    C. Double reads
    D. Practice audit

33. Which of the following is **true** regarding peer review in radiology?
    A. The department chair should be the final arbiter in contested cases.
    B. The peer-review process should be transparent.
    C. 10% of all examinations should undergo peer review.
    D. Section chiefs and other departmental leaders should be exempted.

34. Which of the following is an advantage of retrospective peer review?
    A. Identifies errors in a timely manner
    B. Effective at preserving anonymity
    C. Easy to perform during daily clinical work
    D. Avoids any underlying bias

35. Which of the following is an advantage of practice auditing?
    A. Incorporation of objective data into peer review
    B. Broad scope of cases reviewed
    C. Highly accurate reference standards
    D. Easily performed at the point of care

36. Which of the following is **not** an advantage of referring physician feedback as a method of peer review?
    A. Identification of issues with organization of radiology report
    B. Shifts burden of peer-review process to referring physician
    C. Improved relationships between radiologists and ordering providers
    D. Better patient care through improved communication

37. Which of the following is a subspecialty certificate issued by the American Board of Radiology?
    A. Neuroradiology
    B. Cardiac radiology
    C. Thoracic radiology
    D. Abdominal radiology

38. Which of the following is **not** a part of the American Board of Radiology's Maintenance of Certification (MOC) program?
    A. Professional standing
    B. Lifelong learning and self-assessment
    C. Peer review
    D. Practice quality improvement (PQI)

39. Which of the following is **not** a primary purpose of ongoing professional practice evaluation (OPPE)?
    A. Monitoring professional competency
    B. Identify areas for performance improvement
    C. Decisions of continuance of professional privileges
    D. Assess practitioners and grant new privileges

40. Which of the following is **not** a primary type of dashboard?
    A. Operational
    B. Tactical
    C. Quality
    D. Strategic

41. Which of the following key performance indicator (KPI) would be considered operational?
    A. Cost per relative value unit (RVU)
    B. Examination volume per location
    C. Accuracy of interpretation
    D. Days in accounts receivable

42. Which of the following will most likely result in an effective radiology dashboard?
    A. Design and management by single designated individual
    B. Including as many key performance indicators (KPIs) as will fit on the screen
    C. Archiving data in proprietary formats to ensure security
    D. Using a mix of graphics and text to present data

43. Which of the following is essential for a departmental quality officer to be an effective leader?
    A. Domineering personality
    B. Advanced degree in business
    C. Mandate of authority from leadership
    D. Formal training in informatics

44. Which of the following is the optimal composition of a radiology quality committee?
    A. Radiologists, technologists, managers, nurses, and information technology
    B. Senior radiologists
    C. Department chair, business administrator, and hospital CEO
    D. Radiologists and technologists

114 QUALITY AND SAFETY IN MEDICAL IMAGING

45. Which of the following is a key factor in patient satisfaction in radiology?
    A. Likeability
    B. Assurance
    C. Structured reports
    D. Cost per relative value unit (RVU)

46. Which of the following is **true** regarding institutional quality committees?
    A. Members tend to be more removed from operational processes
    B. Senior leadership is usually not involved
    C. Focus is on only publically reported key performance indicators (KPIs)
    D. Committee functions best when limited to physicians

47. Which agency regulates the practice of mammography?
    A. Centers for Disease Control and Prevention (CDC)
    B. State Department of Health
    C. Food and Drug Administration (FDA)
    D. Centers for Medicare and Medicaid Services (CMS)

48. Which of the following is a primary responsibility of the lead interpreting physician with respect to quality control (QC) in mammography?
    A. Perform mandated QC tests and checklists
    B. Attend manufacture QC procedure training sessions
    C. Maintain logs of all QC activities
    D. Compare individual radiologist performance against benchmarks

49. For which scenario a mammography equipment evaluation (MEE) must be performed?
    A. A previously accredited unit is moved to a different location
    B. The facility hires a new medical physicist
    C. An interpreting radiologist's callback rate is below benchmark
    D. A minor repair is made the mammography unit

50. For which of the following breast imaging programs does the American College of Radiology (ACR) offer accreditation?
    A. Mammography
    B. Ultrasound
    C. Magnetic resonance imaging (MRI)
    D. All of the above

51. Which of the following is a requirement for the American College of Radiology (ACR) breast magnetic resonance imaging (MRI) accreditation?
    A. Minimum field strength of 3.0 T
    B. Ability to simultaneously image both breasts
    C. Use of body or other general coil
    D. Fellowship training for all interpreting radiologists

52. Which of the following is a component of the radiologic–pathologic correlation process?
    A. Confirming that the intended lesion was correctly targeted
    B. Reviewing the biopsy slides in person with the pathologist
    C. Periodic peer review of biopsy interpretations
    D. Ensuring proper specimen handling

53. Which of the following survey meters is best to assess for contamination of an imaging room?
    A. Geiger counter
    B. Cutie-pie
    C. Pocket dosimeter
    D. Photomultiplier

54. Which of the following tests should be performed daily on a planar gamma camera?
    A. Spatial resolution
    B. Linearity check
    C. Collimator performance
    D. Field uniformity

55. SPECT gamma cameras require which additional quality control (QC) assessment?
    A. Blank transmission scan
    B. Ambient temperature
    C. Center of rotation alignment
    D. Photomultiplier tube gain test

Answers to Chapter Self-Assessment Questions

1. C. The Medicare Improvements for Patients and Providers Act (MIPPA) requires accreditation for all private outpatient facilities that provide computed tomography (CT), magnetic resonance imaging (MRI), breast MRI, nuclear medicine, and positron emission tomography (PET) to bill for technical components of examinations under Part B of the Medicare Physician Fee Schedule (see Chapter 1).

2. C. The American College of Radiology's (ACR) practice parameters and technical standards cover a range of topics from general modality standards to specific body part imaging. Radiation oncology practice guidelines are also published in conjunction with the American Society for Radiation Oncology. Practice parameters on communication and continuing medical education are also published. Technical standards and practice parameters are reviewed or renewed at least every 5 years or earlier if necessary. The Centers for Medicare and Medicaid Services (CMS) and The Joint Commission (TJC) do not mandate adherence to these standards.

3. A. The American College of Radiology (ACR) Appropriateness Criteria are designed to assist physicians and other health-care providers in selecting the most appropriate imaging or therapeutic procedure for a specific clinical scenario. They are not intended to be used for determining insurance coverage of imaging tests or for radiologist peer review. ACR Appropriateness Criteria are not a part of accreditation by The Joint Commission (TJC).

4. B. RadiologyInfo.org is a patient-centered resource published jointly by the American College of Radiology (ACR) and the Radiologic Society of North America (RSNA). It provides information in both English and Spanish for patients regarding diagnostic imaging, radiologic procedures, and radiation therapy. While not targeted primarily to health-care providers, the website may provide important information on patients' perspective about radiology and radiation oncology.

5. D. The Centers for Medicare and Medicaid Services (CMS) Value-Based Purchasing Program is designed to reward hospitals with high-quality scores with financial incentives. Hospitals with poor scores risk losing money. The Joint Commission (TJC) accredits hospitals and other facilities but does not directly assess patient satisfaction. Although hospital quality data are publically reported, there are no mandates for publication of scores in local newspapers. The American Hospital Association does not have patient satisfaction requirements.

6. **C.** VR software has been shown to result in increased transcription errors, as well as radiologist underestimating the number of errors. Additionally, studies have shown VR software to cause increased dictation time and decreased radiologist efficiency. However, most, if not all, VR software packages enable radiologists to design and implement prepopulated templates for specific examinations.

7. **A.** Grouping turnaround time (TAT) by radiologist workflows allows radiologist performance for similar practice patterns. Reporting medians is preferable to mean because mean penalizes radiologists who report routine overnight or weekend studies or studies such as cardiac magnetic resonance imaging (MRI), which may have significant postprocessing times. Using a single benchmark for most practices is not ideal, as it does not take into account differences in workflow, such as batching of screening mammograms or lengthy procedures with detailed coding and reporting.

8. **D.** The use of reporting templates has not been shown to significantly reduce reporting time for examinations, and their use may result in increased report length. Pay-for-performance incentives, e-mail reminders, and dissatisfied referring providers (who might send their referrals elsewhere) can all result in improved report turnaround time (TAT).

9. **A.** Because of increased use of ultrasound equipment outside of radiology (e.g., emergency department, operating room, intensive care unit), maintaining an ultrasound quality management program can be challenging. Regardless of the complexity of ultrasound cases, a quality management program needs to be in place to ensure image quality and patient safety. Declining reimbursements may put financial pressure on an ultrasound practice but do not exempt users from ensuring appropriate image quality and patient safety. Newer technology may require additional testing but is not the biggest impediment to ultrasound quality management programs.

10. **B.** Patient prescreening is part of a magnetic resonance imaging (MRI) safety program but is not part of an image quality management program. Phantom and coil testing is important to ensure proper calibration and functioning of the equipment. Investigating artifacts, especially when they occur across multiple examinations, is important for identifying hardware or software problems.

11. **C.** The radiology technologist is the primary stakeholder in the pre-exam archival phase of Reiner's medical imaging chain. The technologist is responsible for performing the requested imaging procedure and ensuring that it is available for interpretation by a radiologist. Nevertheless, many other individuals including radiologists, scheduling staff, and department administrators are stakeholders in this part of the medical imaging chain.

12. **A.** The radiologist is the primary stakeholder in the postarchival phase of Reiner's medical imaging chain, ensuring an accurate interpretation and transmission of results to the ordering provider. Nevertheless, many other individuals including radiology technologists, scheduling staff, and department administrators are stakeholders in this part of the medical imaging chain.

13. **C.** A QA reporting system that is the least intrusive to a radiologist's workflow is most likely to get the most use. Requiring an image quality score on each exam has been proposed as a method to best identify strengths and weaknesses of image quality and potentially help identify issues with personnel and equipment. Paper-based QA forms and even standalone web-based QA forms are much more likely to disrupt radiologist workflow. Telephone reporting would be disruptive to all involved parties.

14. **C.** Adverse events (those associated with patient harm as a result of health-care administration) are estimated to occur in approximately 3.0% of hospitalizations.

15. **B.** A near miss is a patient safety event that does not reach a patient or results in minimal harm. Documenting the incorrect birthdate could potentially result in mixing up two patients. However, no harm is yet to occur. Radiation-induced injuries or temporary harm requiring life-sustaining intervention (such as endotracheal intubation) are considered sentinel events.

16. **A.** A decision-making error, which is incorrectly interpreting a normal finding as abnormal or an abnormal findings as normal, is the most common cause of error in diagnostic radiology. Satisfaction of search, poor lighting, and eye fatigue can all contribute to perceptual errors. Often, cause of error in diagnostic radiology is multifactorial.

17. **B.** Mandatory reporting systems are usually overseen by state agencies and programs that have the authority to investigate specific cases and issue penalties for wrongdoing. Mandatory reporting systems can apply to any health-care facility, inpatient or outpatient. The Joint Commission (TJC) strongly urges accredited facilities to implement voluntary reporting systems. The American Hospital Association represents hospitals, their patients, and their communities and is not a regulatory body.

18. **C.** The primary focus of voluntary reporting systems is to identify near misses for building a nonpunitive culture of quality and safety and avoid future, potentially injurious errors. State medical boards regulate physician practice and not those of health-care facilities. Voluntary reporting systems are not designed to be punitive. Although sentinel events should be included in a voluntary reporting system, they are not the primary focus of these systems.

19. **B.** An event report should include as much information as possible, including patient demographics, date and time of event, personnel involved, responses taken (if any), and the perceived level of harm. Negligence is a legal term and is not part of an event report. An action plan is the result of review of an event report. Disciplinary action, if any, should only be taken once a complete review of an incident has occurred.

20. **D.** The primary goal of a root cause analysis (RCA) is to identify the primary causes of a sentinel event and suggest changes to avoid such future events. RCAs are usually protected under state peer-review statutes and are not used to avoid legal action. RCAs may identify deficiencies with personnel, but they are designed to improve quality, either through education or changes in practice. RCAs are not designed for data analysis for scientific research.

21. **A.** The Joint Commission (TJC) currently requires that accredited facilities inform patients of unexpected outcomes including whether they are the result of medical error. Some studies have shown that disclosure of medical errors to patients can improve patient satisfaction, increase patient trust, and possibly reduce the likelihood of malpractice litigation.

22. **D.** The Centers for Medicare and Medicaid Services (CMS) administrates the Children's Health Insurance Program along (CHIP) with Medicare and Medicaid. The Centers for Disease Control and Prevention (CDC), the Food and Drug Administration (FDA), and the state medical boards do not administer health insurance plans.

23. **A.** The National Institute for Occupational Safety and Health (NIOSH) runs the B reader program, which is a certification program from the classification of chest radiographs for pneumoconiosis. Although B reader certification is required for the Asbestos Medical Surveillance Program, it is not administered by this program or its overseeing agency, the Navy and Marine Corps Public Health Center. The Food and Drug Administration (FDA) and the Centers for Medicare and Medicaid Services (CMS) do not oversee the B reading program or other occupational health programs.

24. **A.** Imaging 3.0 is a campaign developed by the American College of Radiology (ACR) to increase the radiologist's value in the delivering of health care, focusing on the role of the radiologist beyond imaging interpretation. Imaging 3.0 does not mandate the use of digital imaging nor does it attempt to reduce the number of examinations performed that use ionizing radiation. Finally, Imaging 3.0 is not focused on lobbying for increased reimbursement for diagnostic imaging studies.

25. **C.** The Choosing Wisely campaign was developed by the American Board of Internal Medicine Foundation to promote conversations between patients and providers by helping patients and their providers choose care that is supported by scientific evidence, not duplicative of other care, free of harm, and truly necessary. Image Gently is a campaign developed to raise awareness of potential harm of ionizing radiation for children, and Image Wisely is a campaign developed to raise public and professional awareness about risks and benefits of the use of ionizing radiation in medical imaging with respect to adults. Accountable Care Organizations (ACOs) constitute a voluntary program of the Centers for Medicare and Medicaid Services (CMS) to reduce health-care spending while providing high-quality care to Medicare beneficiaries.

26. **A.** The PICO (**P**atient, **I**ntervention, **C**omparison, **O**utcome) framework was designed to help the practitioner formulate a well-defined, answerable question. It does not address finding evidence, appraising the evidence, or applying the evidence.

27. **C.** A foreground knowledge gap is one where the practitioner questions the effectiveness of a new technology or treatment as compared with current practices. A background knowledge gap is one where the practitioner lacks knowledge of a well-defined clinical scenario because of lack of experience or the relative rarity of the scenario. Being asked to interpret imaging studies, make decisions about how to perform imaging studies, or operate imaging equipment outside of one's training all constitute background knowledge gaps. Background knowledge gaps can be closed through reading, formal didactic education, and hands-on education.

28. **B.** Number needed to treat (NNT) is the average number of patients who need to undergo the therapy to benefit one patient and is calculated from the results of a scientific trial. NNT does not measure cohort size, number of treatments, or competency.

29. **C.** The U.S. Preventive Services Task Force (USPSTF) consists of volunteers with expertise in evidence-based health care. The USPSTF issues guidelines directed toward primary care providers regarding the value of a range of preventive care services. USPSTF members are not employed by the Centers for Disease Control and Prevention (CDC), they are not designated representatives from member boards of the American Board of Medical Specialties, and the target audience is primary care providers.

30. **A.** The American College of Radiology (ACR) Appropriateness Criteria are developed following guidelines issued by the Agency for Healthcare Research and Quality (AHRQ) as designed by the Institute of Medicine. They are independent of the U.S. Preventive Services Task Force (USPSFT), Centers for Medicare and Medicaid Services (CMS), and Centers for Disease Control and Prevention (CDC).

31. **D.** The six core competencies of the Accreditation Council for Graduate Medical Education (ACGME) are patient care, medical and clinical knowledge, practice-based learning and improvement, interpersonal and communication skills, professionalism, and system-based practice. Licensure is not a specifically defined core competency.

32. **C.** Double reading is a prospective method of peer review where two radiologists independently interpret a study and any discrepancy is addressed in consensus. The American College of Radiology's (ACR) RADPEER, consensus-oriented peer review, and practice audits are all retrospective methods of peer review.

33. **B.** The peer-review process should be fair, transparent, consistent, and objective to be effective. A system of arbitration should be in place with the appropriate individual or individuals serving as arbiters. Although a department chair may have the final say regarding underperformance, the department chair may not be the appropriate person to review a specific case. Although some authors have suggested that 3% to 5% of imaging studies should be reviewed, no evidence exists to support this assertion. In order for a peer-review program to be fair, all radiologists within a practice should participate.

34. **C.** Retrospective peer review is easy to perform during daily clinical work because the reviewing radiologist is usually already reviewing images and reports of the comparison study or studies. Because the comparison study may be old, identifying significant errors in a timely manner can be a challenge. Also, anonymity is hard to preserve because it is rather easy to identify the reviewer and reviewee on the basis of who interpreted which examination. Biases, whether conscious or unconscious, can occur with retrospective peer review. For example, junior radiologists may be hesitant to disagree with more senior radiologists.

35. **A.** Practice auditing allows incorporation of objective data, such as lung or thyroid nodule management guidelines, into peer review. Because guidelines or other reference standards are required, the scope of cases that can be reviewed is often narrow. Furthermore, so-called reference standards may not be that accurate. Practice auditing requires reviewing multiple reports or charts and is not easily performed at the point of care.

36. **B.** Although using referring physician feedback in the radiology peer-review process encourages reporting from outside the radiology department, most of the work associated with the peer-review process remains with radiology. Advantages of using referring physician input in peer review include identifying issues with report organization, coherence, and style; improving professional relationships between radiologists and referring physicians; and improving patient care through better communication.

37. **A.** The American Board of Radiology offers subspecialty certification in pediatric radiology, neuroradiology, vascular and interventional radiology, nuclear radiology, and hospice and palliative medicine. These certificates are issued to radiologists who meet additional training requirements and pass required examinations. Many subspecialty areas in radiology such as cardiac, thoracic, and abdominal imaging do not have formal certification.

38. **C.** The four components of the American Board of Radiology's Maintenance of Certification (MOC) program are professional standing, lifelong learning and self-assessment, cognitive expertise, and practice quality improvement (PQI). Peer-review activities can be used to meet the PQI requirements.

39. **D.** Focused professional practice evaluation (FPPE) is used to assess newly credentialed practitioners or practitioners granted new privileges. Ongoing professional practice evaluation (OPPE) aims to monitor professional competency, identify areas for performance improvement, and aid in decisions of continuance of professional privileges. Both FPPE and OPPE are requirements put forth by The Joint Commission (TJC).

40. **C.** Quality dashboards are not described as a primary type of dashboard. Operational, tactical, and strategic dashboards are the three primary described types of dashboards in business intelligence. Quality metrics might be included in an operational, tactical, or strategic dashboard.

41. **B.** Examination volume per location is an operational key performance indicator (KPI) that could go on a dashboard. Other operational KPIs one might encounter in radiology include total examination volume and examination volume per modality. Cost per relative value unit (RVU) and days in accounts receivable are considered financial KPIs, and accuracy of interpretation is considered a quality KPI.

42. **D.** Using a mix of graphics and text to present data on a dashboard can enable dashboard users to easily assess current performance and identify positive and negative trends. A team of major stakeholders, rather than a single individual, typically designs effective dashboards. Having very few key performance indicators (KPIs) can reduce or eliminate utility of a dashboard, whereas having too many KPIs makes a dashboard too cluttered, and also less useful. Data should be archived in standard formats such as structured query language (SQL) databases or comma-separated values (CSV) instead of proprietary formats so as to enable easy data integration, sharing, and manipulation. Nevertheless, appropriate security measures should be taken to protect any sensitive data.

43. **C.** In order for a departmental quality officer to be an effective leader, full support and a mandate of authority from senior departmental leadership is essential. Quality officers must build trusting relationships within and across departments and recognize the value of those relationships. While knowledge of informatics and business may be useful for a quality officer, formal training in these areas is not a requisite for success.

44. **A.** Because quality and safety can affect the entire scope of the practice of radiology, the optimal composition of a radiology quality committee includes radiologists, technologists, managers, nurses, and information technologists. Limiting the committee to just radiologists or senior leadership can greatly reduce the effectiveness of the committee. Radiologists and technologists alone, too, do not fully represent the quality continuum in a radiology practice.

45. **B.** The five key factors related to customer (or patient) satisfaction that apply to any particular service, including radiology, are as follows: reliability, responsiveness, assurance, empathy, and tangibles. Likeability is not identified as a key factor. Structure reports typically do not contribute to patient satisfaction. Whereas cost may be important to patients, cost per relative value unit (RVU) is a financial key performance indicator (KPI) for a radiology department.

46. **A.** Unlike departmental quality committees, members of institutional quality committees are often more removed from operational processes, potentially leading to a disconnect between individuals driving quality improvement and individuals carrying out the activities that lead to quality improvement. Senior leadership from all parts of the institution (administration, legal, nursing, informatics, physician, pharmacy, etc.) is usually heavily involved in institutional quality committees, and these committees usually function best with broad representation given the complexities of large health-care organizations. Institutional quality committees must address both internal and external, publically reported key performance indicators (KPIs).

47. **C.** The Mammography Quality and Standards Act (MQSA) requires that each facility that performs mammography be certified by the Food and Drug Administration (FDA). The Centers for Disease Control and Prevention (CDC) does not regulate medical imaging practices. A state's department of health may regulate the use of X-ray devices and physician and technologist licensure, but mammography is the purview of the U.S. government. The Centers for Medicare and Medicaid Services (CMS) determines payments and requirements for CMS beneficiaries but does not regulate the practice of mammography.

48. **D.** The lead interpreting physician works in close collaboration with lead mammography technologist in oversight of the quality control (QC) process and documentation; in creation of quality assurance policies, procedures, and workflow strategies to fulfil the Mammography Quality and Standards Act (MQSA) regulations; and to identify areas for workflow improvement. The lead technologist or other designee is primarily responsible for performing QC testing and checklists, obtaining training in QC procedures, and maintaining appropriate records of QC activities.

49. **A.** The Mammography Quality and Standards Act (MQSA) requires that an Mammography Equipment Evaluation (MEE) is performed when a new unit is installed, a previously accredited unit is moved from one location to another, or a unit undergoes major repairs or upgrades. A newly hired medical physicist should become familiar with previous MEE reports and any outstanding issues. Issues with radiologist performance should be addressed by the lead interpreting radiologist.

50. **D.** The American College of Radiology (ACR) offers accreditation for mammography, breast ultrasound, breast magnetic resonance imaging (MRI), and image-guided breast procedures. In addition to meeting specific facility-level requirements, the ACR accreditation process also includes evaluation of images of real patients and certain active policies and procedures.

51. **B.** For American College of Radiology (ACR) breast magnetic resonance imaging (MRI) accreditation, the equipment must include a dedicated bilateral breast coil, be capable of simultaneous bilateral breast imaging, and meet all state and federal performance requirements including maximum field strength, maximum rate of change of magnetic field strength, maximum radiofrequency power deposition, and maximum auditory noise levels. A 3.0-T magnet

is not a requirement nor is fellowship training for all interpreting radiologists.

52. **A.** The process of radiologic–pathologic correlation includes confirming that the intended lesion was correctly targeted, confirming that the targeted lesion was adequately sampled, confirming that the pathology results explain the imaging findings (concordance), and providing further management recommendations. Reviewing biopsy slides with the pathologist may be useful for challenging cases and is probably best done in a multidisciplinary review conference. Peer review of biopsy interpretation should be handled within a pathology practice. Although proper specimen handling is essential for the practice of image-guided tissue sampling, it is not a specific component of radiologic–pathologic correlation.

53. **A.** Geiger counters have high sensitivity and are well suited for low-level surveys such as contamination. Cutie-pies are relatively low sensitivity and are well suited for detecting high-flux gamma rays and X-rays. Pocket dosimeters can be used to measure exposure to a person. Photomultipliers are components of imaging equipment and survey meters.

54. **D.** Field uniformity and window setting should be assessed daily on each planar gamma camera. Weekly tests include spatial resolution and linearity check. Periodic tests include collimator performance, energy resolution, count rate performance, count rate linearity, energy resolution, and sensitivity.

55. **C.** In addition to standard gamma camera quality control (QC) measures, SPECT gamma cameras and SPECT-CT gamma cameras require testing of tomographic uni-formity and center of rotation alignment. Blank transmission scan, ambient temperature, and photomultiplier tube gain testing are component of positron emission tomography (PET) QC.

INDEX

Note: Page numbers followed by *f* indicate figures; page numbers followed by *t* indicate tables

A

AAPM. *See* American Association of Physicists in Medicine (AAPM)
ABR. *See* American Board of Radiology (ABR)
Accountable care organizations, 48
Accreditation Council for Graduate Medical Education (ACGME), 94t, 95
ACGME. *See* Accreditation Council for Graduate Medical Education (ACGME)
ACR AC. *See* ACR Appropriateness Criteria (ACR AC)
ACR accreditation
    breast ultrasound accreditation program. *See* Breast ultrasound accreditation program
    mammography
        approval process, 59
        clinical image review process, 59t
        clinical images for, 59
        components, 56
        equipment specifications and quality control, 56
        image identification, 60t
        personnel qualifications, 56
        timing, 56
ACR Appropriateness Criteria (ACR AC), 80
    evidence table, 82f
    ratings table, 81f
ACR phantom image
    four quadrant, 75f
    quality assurance, 56
ACR quality
    accreditation, 1, 1t
    ACR-designated lung cancer screening center, 3
    appropriateness criteria, 7–9
    CT colonography registry, 4–5f
    diagnostic imaging center of excellence, 3
    dose index registry, 2–4f
    improvement database measures, 6t
    national radiology data registry, 1–3, 2f, 2t
    practice guidelines and technical standards, 7
    radiologyinfo.org, 9
    RADPEER, 3–7
Agencies, health care (US)
    Centers for Disease Control and Prevention, 46
    Centers For Medicare And Medicaid Services, 45–46
    Food and Drug Administration, 46
    governmental, health care regulation, 45t
    state medical boards, 46–47
AHRQ. *See* The US Agency for Healthcare Research and Quality (AHRQ)
American Association of Physicists in Medicine (AAPM), 35, 47
American Board of Radiology (ABR), 92–94, 94t
American College of Radiology, 92, 93t
American Society for Radiologic Technologists (ASRT), 47
Appropriate reporting, communication of results, 66
ASRT. *See* American Society for Radiologic Technologists (ASRT)

B

Biologic effects of radiation, medical imaging
    cancer, 15–16, 15f
    cataracts, 16
    pacemakers, 16
    skin burns, 16, 16t
Bi-RADS recommendations, 58
Breast imaging practices, health care
    appropriate utilization, breast imaging
        clinical decision support systems, 50–52
    image acquisition/interpretation, 52
        mammography accreditation programs, 52
Breast MRI accreditation program
    certification for interpreting radiologists, 64t
    components
        clinical images for accreditation, 65–66
        equipment specifications, 64
        personnel qualifications, 64–65
        quality assurance, 65
        quality control, 65
    special considerations
        medicare billing, 63–64
    timing, 64
Breast ultrasound accreditation program
    additional requirements, 62
    clinical images for, 61
    components, 60
    image identification requirements, 60t
    timing, 59–60

C

Center of Rotation (COR), 75
Centers for Disease Control and Prevention (CDC), 46
COGR. *See* Consensus-oriented group review (COGR)
Collimators, 75
Computed tomography (CT), 35
Consensus-oriented group review (COGR), 88, 88f
Credentialing and certification, 92–95
    individual, 92–95
        Accreditation Council for Graduate Medical Education, 94t, 95
        American Board of Radiology (ABR), 92–94, 94t
        credentialing and medical staff appointment, 94–95
        state medical boards, 94
    organizations, 92
        American College of Radiology, 92, 93t
        The Joint Commission, 92
        Leapfrog Group (Leapfrog), 92
CT scanners (quality and safety), 77, 77t

D

Dashboards, 97–103
    designing, 98–103, 98f
    examples, 98–103f
    goals of, 97–98
    key performance indicators, 97t
    types of, 97
DHHS. *See* US Department of Health and Human Services (DHHS)
Diagnostic imaging, professional programs, 46t
Dose calibrator, 70–71
Dose Index Registry, 2–4f
Drug administration, 46

E

EBHC. *See* Evidence-based health care (EBHC)
EBR. *See* Evidence-based radiology (EBR)
Efficacy, 79
EHRS. *See* Electronic health records (EHRS)
Electronic health records (EHRS), 28
Energy resolution, 74–75
Evidence-based health care (EBHC)
    ACR Appropriateness Criteria (ACR AC), 80
    agencies, 79–80
    defined, 79
    practicing, 80
    principles of, 79
    terminology, 79
Evidence-based radiology (EBR), 79–80

F

FDA certification, 52–54, 54t
    components, 52
    equipment specifications and, mammography, 54–56
    key points, 53–54
    personnel qualifications, 54
    timing, 52
Field uniformity, 73–74
Focused practice review (FPR), 89
Focused professional practice evaluation (FPPE), 95
Food and Drug Administration (FDA), 46
FPPE. *See* Focused professional practice evaluation (FPPE)
FPR. *See* Focused practice review (FPR)

120 QUALITY AND SAFETY IN MEDICAL IMAGING

G
Grade B recommendation, 79

H
Hospital Consumer Assessment of Healthcare Providers and Systems (HCAHPS), 28

I
Image gently, 47
Image quality assurance programs
   image quality management, 34–35f, 34–36
      computed tomography, 36
      magnetic resonance imaging, 36–37
      ultrasound, 36
      integration of image QA into radiology workflow, 37, 38f
      image quality rating scale, 39t
      medical imaging chain, 36–37, 36t
      schematic imaging chain, 37f
Image quality management, 34–36
Image wisely, 47
Imaging 3.0, health care programs
   acquisition and interpretation, 47
   coordinating care, 47
   results reporting, 47
Improving quality of reporting, 43
Institute of Medicine (IOM), 50
Intraoperative probes, 73

J
The Joint Commission (TJC), 92

L
Leapfrog Group (Leapfrog), 92

M
Magnetic resonance imaging (MRI), 36
   quality committee and, 107
Mammography accreditation programs
   diagnostic mammography, exam indication, 59t
   MQSA and ACR requirements, 54t
      certification for technologists, 55t
      for interpreting radiologists, certification for, 54t
      medical outcomes audit, 56–57, 57f
   national mammography database, 58–59
   QC tests digital imaging systems, 53t
   screening mammography, 58t
Mammography equipment evaluation (MEE), 54
Mandated by MQSA and complete audit recommended by the ACR, 58
Measuring performance (radiology), 84–85
Medical physicist's survey, the, 54
Monitoring and reporting, complications of
   disclosure of errors, 43
   error reporting systems
      event report components, 42
      mandatory reporting system, 42
      root cause analysis (RCA), 43
      voluntary reporting systems, 42
   errors, causes of, 42, 42t
   error types, medical imaging
      near misses, 41, 41t
      sentinel events, 41, 41t

N
National Mammography Database (NMD), 59–60
National Radiology Data Registry (NRDR), 1–3, 2f, 2t, 59
Near misses, 41t
Nuclear medicine, quality and safety in, 70–77
   CT scanners, 77, 77t
   nonimaging devices, 70
      dose calibrator, 70–71
      intraoperative probes, 72–73
      organ uptake probes, 73
      scintillation detectors, 72
      survey meters, 71–72
   PET scanners, 76–77
      ambient temperature, 76
      blank transmission scan, 76, 77f
      calibration, 77
      normalization, 77
      PMT gain test, 77
   planar gamma camera, 73–75, 75f
      collimator performance, 75
      energy resolution, 74–75
      field uniformity, 73–74, 74f
      spatial resolution and linearity, 74, 75f
   quality control, 70
   SPECT imaging, 75–76
      center of rotation, 75
      collimator hole alignment, 76
      gantry head alignment, 76
      tomographic resolution, 76
      tomographic uniformity, 75–76

O
Ongoing Professional Practice Evaluation (OPPE), 94–95, 95t
OPPE. *See* Ongoing Professional Practice Evaluation (OPPE)
Organ uptake probes, 73

P
PACS. *See* Picture archiving and communication systems (PACS)
Patient safety, medical imaging
   computed tomography, 15f, 17–19
   conventional radiographic examinations, 17, 18f
   fluoroscopy-guided interventions, 20–22, 21f
   screening procedures, 19–20
Patient satisfaction
   assessing, 26–27
   challenges in radiology, 27
Peer review, 84–90
   methods in radiology, 85–89
      advantages and disadvantages, 85t
      comprehensive radiologist performance assessment, 89
      consensus-oriented group review, 88, 88f
      double reading, 87–88
      focused practice review, 89
      practice auditing, 87
      referring physician feedback, 88–89
      retrospective, 85–86, 86t, 87f
   using data, 89–90
Percutaneous image-guided breast interventions, quality assurance for, 63
Personnel safety, medical imaging
   additional considerations for pregnant workers, 23
   justification, 22
   limitation, 23
   optimization, 22–23
PET scanners (quality and safety), 76–77
Pharmacy, quality committee and, 107
Picture archiving and communication systems (PACS), 28
Planar gamma camera (quality and safety), 73–75, 75f
Programs, health care (US)
   accountable care organizations, 48
   choosing wisely, 47, 48t
   image gently, 47
   image wisely, 47
   imaging 3.0, 47

Q
Quality and safety, medical imaging
   biologic effects of radiation
      cancer, 15–16, 15f
      cataracts, 16
      pacemakers, 16
      skin burns, 16, 16t
   history, 13–14
   patient safety, 16–17
      computed tomography, 15f, 17–19
      conventional radiographic examinations, 17, 18f
      fluoroscopy-guided interventions, 20–22, 21f
      screening procedures, 19–20
   personnel safety
      additional considerations for pregnant workers, 23
      justification, 22
      limitation, 23
      optimization, 22–23
   primary goal, 23–24
   radiation quantities and units, 14–15
Quality committees, 105–110
   customer satisfaction, key aspects of, 110t
   department quality officer, 105
   institutional, 108–110
   radiology, 105–110
      makeup, 105, 106f
      responsibilities, 105–110, 106t

R
Radiology
   measuring performance in, 84–85
   peer review methods, 85–89
Radiologyinfo.org, 9
Radiology Information System (RIS), 28
Radiology report turn-around time (TAT), 28, 28t
RADPEER, 3–7
RCA. *See* Root cause analysis (RCA)
Regulating health care
   governmental agencies, 45t
Report turn-around time
   improving, 29–32, 31f
   measuring, 29, 30f
   voice recognition transcription, 28–29, 29t
Resolution, defined, 74
RIS. *See* Radiology Information System (RIS)
Root cause analysis (RCA), 43
Routine preventative maintenance (PM), 54

S

Safety climate survey, 109f
Scintillation detectors, 72
Sentimental events
    mandatory reporting, states having, 107t
    TJC definition, 107
Sentinel events, 41, 41t
Shield method, 71
Spatial resolution, 74
SPECT imaging (quality and safety), 75–76
SPECT phantom, 76
Standard operating policies (SOP), 54t
State medical boards, 94–95
Stereotactic breast biopsy accreditation program
    components, 63
        clinical images for accreditation, 62–63
        equipment specifications, 62
        personnel qualifications, 62
        quality assurance, 62
        quality control, 62
    in independent setting, 63t
    timing, 62
Survey meters, 71–72

T

Thyroid uptake probes, 72f
Timeliness and efficiency, breast imaging
    BI-RADS assessment categories, 67f
    in image interpretation, reporting, and communication of results, 67
    in scheduling, 67
    timeliness in imaging acquisition, 67
Tomographic image reconstruction. *See* SPECT imaging (quality and safety)
Turn-around time (TAT), 28, 28t
    improving, 29–32, 31f
    measuring, 29, 30f

U

Ultrasound-guided breast biopsy accreditation module
    components
        clinical images for accreditation, 62
        equipment specifications and quality control, 62
        personnel qualifications, 61
        quality assurance, 62
    timing, 61

The U.S. Preventive Services Task Force (USPSTF), 79–80
The US Agency for Healthcare Research and Quality (AHRQ), 79
US Department of Health and Human Services (DHHS), 45
USPSTF. *See* The U.S. Preventive Services Task Force (USPSTF)

V

Voice recognition
    transcription, 28–29
    advantages and disadvantages, 29t
Voice recognition (VR), 28